Praise for
How Pakistan Negotiates with

"*This groundbreaking work is an excellent addition to our knowledge of decision making in Pakistan and Pakistan's foreign policy. Drawing from their extensive personal experience and a panel of experts on Pakistan, the authors cover a subject— a diplomatic style—that is relatively untouched in the academic literature. This volume is useful not only as a practical handbook for those negotiating with Pakistanis, but also as a review of the interaction of U.S. and Pakistani foreign policy.*"
—**Walter Andersen,** acting director of South Asia Studies program at the Johns Hopkins University School of Advanced International Studies

"How Pakistan Negotiates with the United States *is an impressive, insightful, and truly important book, especially for Americans who cannot decide whether Pakistan is America's friend or foe. They will learn that the issue is more complex and respective grievances are more reciprocal.*"
—**Zbigniew Brzezinski,** counselor and trustee, Center for Strategic and International Studies

"*A superb analysis of U.S.-Pakistan negotiations, this timely book will be of enormous value to future American negotiators and indeed all U.S. government officials who are involved in the relationship with Pakistan. The authors do an excellent job of explaining how key elements of Pakistani society function, how they think about major issues, and the roles they play (or do not play) in dealings with the United States. All who work with Pakistan will profit from reading this book with care.*"
—**Dennis Kux,** Woodrow Wilson Center and former State Department South Asia specialist

"*Yet again, Ambassadors Howard and Teresita Schaffer have drawn on their vast experience in South Asia to guide U.S. policy toward that crucial region. Their latest book, which decodes Pakistan's methods and motives in dealing with the United States, is both an insightful work of history and a guide for American policymakers and negotiators in the months and years to come.*"
—**Strobe Talbott,** president of the Brookings Institution

"*What better time to have a book that allows us to better understand how Pakistan negotiates. And who but the Ambassadors Schaffer are as well prepared to explore what lies behind the repeated ups and downs in Pakistan's formal and informal*

relations with the United States. The Schaffers offer rich insights into the political culture, authority structures, and personalities that have shaped Pakistan's negotiating style and techniques with friends and adversaries. The authors' highly readable work offers a guide as to how Americans have succeeded and failed with key military and civilian officials at critical historical junctures in U.S.-Pakistan relations. More importantly, the Schaffers locate a major source of the two countries' inability to realize a more reliable basis for cooperation in their failure to recognize their frequently divergent strategic priorities."
—**Marvin Weinbaum,** Middle East Institute

"Howard and Teresita Schaffer have made a very important contribution to USIP's outstanding series about how nations negotiate. Generations of American leaders, diplomats, and military officers have been involved in what the Schaffers describe as a "roller coaster relationship". This exceptional volume will allow a wide audience to benefit from their sharp observations and wise counsel. Here is a special opportunity to learn from two real experts."
—**Marc Grossman,** vice chairman of The Cohen Group and former Under Secretary of State for political affairs.

How Pakistan Negotiates with the United States

How Pakistan Negotiates with the United States

Riding the Roller Coaster

Howard B. Schaffer *and*
Teresita C. Schaffer

UNITED STATES INSTITUTE OF PEACE
WASHINGTON, D.C.

The views expressed in this book are those of the authors alone. They do not necessarily reflect the views of the United States Institute of Peace.

United States Institute of Peace
2301 Constitution Avenue, NW
Washington, DC 20037
www.usip.org

First published 2011.

Printed in the United States of America.

The paper used in this publication meets the minimum requirements of American National Standards for Information Science—Permanence of Paper for Printed Library Materials, ANSI Z39.48-1984.

Library of Congress Cataloging-in-Publication Data

Schaffer, Howard B.
  How Pakistan negotiates with the United States : riding the roller coaster / Howard B. and Teresita C. Schaffer.
     p. cm.
  Includes index.
  ISBN 978-1-60127-075-7 (pbk. : alk. paper) — ISBN 978-1-60127-085-6 (cloth : alk. paper)
  1. United States--Foreign relations—Pakistan. 2. Pakistan—Foreign relations—United States. I. Schaffer, Teresita C. II. Title.
  JZ1480.A57P18 2011
  327.5491073--dc22
                              2010040363

Contents

Foreword

As Howard and Teresita Schaffer note, there are several fine histories of the relationship between the United States and Pakistan, and overviews of Pakistan's state and society. There are also valuable studies of regional relations, covering Afghanistan, India, and Pakistan. America's current military entanglement in Afghanistan has generated a large and angry literature, some of it directed against Pakistan, which has been supporting both sides of the war from the beginning of the United States-International Security Assistance Force (ISAF) struggle against the Taliban.

This book is quite different from anything else: it brilliantly uses the vehicle of negotiating culture to probe deeply into Pakistan's politics, society, and bureaucracy. It is thus far more than the story of how the United States and Pakistan negotiate with each other; it joins the select list of "must read" books on Pakistan. It is also revealing of American diplomacy and negotiating style, notably how Washington has repeatedly succumbed to persuasive Pakistani negotiators (military and civilian), who used to argue that Pakistan was a reliable, staunch ally that had been repeatedly let down by the United States but who now say that Pakistan's weaknesses make it even more important given its shared border with Afghanistan and reignited tensions in Kashmir. In other words, a failing Pakistan is no less a threat to U.S. interests than a successful Pakistan was an asset to American diplomacy. They may well be correct.

The authors describe the trajectory of U.S.-Pakistan relations, both through analysis and numerous mini case studies, and the narrative shows how the two states have found themselves (sometimes unwillingly) engaged across a broad range of issues. These include the spread of nuclear weapons, Pakistan's support for the U.S.-ISAF effort in Afghanistan, and conflict avoidance with India. Pakistan would like to see the United States more active on Kashmir. Americans have resisted this request, although the uprising that began in Kashmir in June 2010—almost another *intifada*—means that Kashmir can no longer be totally ignored by American diplomats in Washington's regional diplomacy.

The two states are also engaged in discussions over Pakistan's social and economic development, now for the first time a high priority concern for American policymakers thanks to the initiative of then senator (now Vice President) Joe Biden and Senator Dick Lugar that now takes the form of the Kerry-Lugar bill which provides $1.5 billion in nonmilitary assistance to Pakistan. Americans are concerned not only about Pakistan's nuclear program, and its relationship to terrorist groups such as al-Qaeda, the Afghan Taliban, and Lashkar-e-Taiba (and its victimization by these groups), but ultimately the very identity and existence of Pakistan. It is not just a question of "whither" Pakistan but fundamentally of "whether" Pakistan.

Discussions of the country's future are part of public conversations in Pakistan (in the press, on its vibrant television channels, in drawing rooms and coffee houses) but also in the army's officer messes. The Pakistan army, no hotbed of radicalism, but certainly willing to use radical Islamists for strategic purposes, remains close to Pakistan's political center of gravity, despite its inability to actually govern and administer the state. It is now led by the taciturn General Ashfaq Parvez Kayani, whose term was extended for three years on July 24, 2010. This was the first time a Pakistani army chief received a term extension from a democratically elected government. The extension was a vote of confidence in Kayani, a tribute to his central role in relations with the United States (he had developed close personal ties to numerous American political and military leaders, who saw in him a channel by which Pakistani policy could be influenced) and proof of the weakness of Pakistan's political order. The game, in short, continues: Pakistan's civilian governments need the military, but this only leads to greater distortions in Pakistan's politics and encourages other countries to listen more to the armed forces as they deal with Islamabad (or Rawalpindi, as is more often the case). Other democracies, including India, also debate the wisdom of negotiating with the generals, while the Chinese have no problem in anchoring their diplomacy in the army—China is by far Pakistan's biggest arms supplier.

The recent catastrophic floods reveal additional information about how Pakistan negotiates with the United States and other countries. The floods, which affected Pakistan from July 2010 onward, constituted the country's third major natural disaster (the first being the 1970 East Pakistan cyclone, the second the 2005 earthquake, both of which caused far more loss of life). Some have characterized the floods as a "black swan" event that might tip Pakistan into chaos, as the economic consequences are likely to be felt for years.

Pakistan tried to negotiate with the international community for disaster assistance, but its reputation as a corrupt state has hurt these efforts—as did the ill-timed European tour of Pakistan's president, Asif Ali Zardari, who wanted to show off his son, Bilawal Bhutto, while also visiting family properties in Great Britain and France. The flood seemed to offer an opportunity for the United States and others to demonstrate their support for the people and state of Pakistan. American officials were in the vanguard of the money-raising effort, eagerly expecting a public relations payoff.

This has not materialized, and the widespread hatred of the United States in Pakistan (India is more popular than America) perversely strengthens the hands of Pakistani negotiators, who are, in effect, pointing a pistol at their own heads and saying, "Help me, or else." Six months after the initial floods, the American aid effort was a case of too much too late, as the damage to Pakistan was in large part the cumulative consequence of years of neglect of the country's irrigation and flood control infrastructure. The army, which performed well in relief efforts, is faced with the problem of a too-weak civilian government, yet it knows that another round of military intervention will do nothing to improve the situation and might further weaken the army itself.

Revelations in Bob Woodward's *Obama's Wars* (2010) also shed light on Pakistan's negotiating style. Woodward's revelations of policy debates at the senior levels of the Obama administration—unchallenged publicly and privately verified—point to the difficulty that the Obama administration has had in negotiating with Pakistan. The term "liars" is frequently deployed by American officials to describe Pakistani negotiators, but then American dealings with Pakistan remain less than credible given the American record vis-à-vis that country over the years. Pakistanis believe that they must be flexible with the truth when vital interests are involved. As one Pakistan told me in 1987, they were lying publicly about America's covert anti-Soviet operations in Afghanistan, so why should Americans cavil at their denial of a quest for a nuclear bomb, which would protect Pakistan from an Indian attack? To bring the story up to date, why should Americans object to Pakistan's support of the Taliban in Afghanistan when it is the Taliban that can serve Pakistan's interests there against Indian encroachment?

As the Schaffers hint, these are positions that cannot be sustained much longer—it may well be that the United States and Pakistan are headed for another break sustaining the up and down that has been the pattern of the relationship for five decades. If this is the case, there is no better explanation to be found than in this extraordinary book of how things went wrong most of the time, even as they went right some of the time.

—STEPHEN P. COHEN
SENIOR FELLOW, BROOKINGS INSTITUTION,
AUTHOR OF *THE IDEA OF PAKISTAN*

Preface

How do nations negotiate? This is a somewhat misleading way to characterize the growing series of studies of national negotiating practices of which this volume on Pakistani negotiating behavior is the most recent. "Nations," as abstractions, do not negotiate. But their officials do, and they bring to negotiating encounters more than personality styles and understandings of issues at play. Their behavior is structured by the institutional context in which decisions are made and implemented, by an understanding of their country's history and its place in the world, and by distinctive cultural negotiating patterns—such as the uses of language, approaches to pressuring or enticing adversaries and friends, and attitudes toward compromise and assertions of authority.

Why study such institutional and cultural influences on negotiating practice? Our research has disclosed that most governments, indeed societies, devote little effort to systematic assessments of negotiating counterparts, be they governments, business enterprises, or organizations of civil society. Most negotiators bring to their task techniques learned by doing, or by having observed seniors whom they have supported in junior roles. With little formal training but perhaps considerable professional practice, such officials are all the more likely to reflect the norms and practices of their society. In the world of the seventeenth and eighteenth centuries, there was in Europe something of a distinctive class of diplomats with a shared language (French) and common negotiating practice. But in the globalized environment of the twenty-first century, diverse societies from all the continents and cultures of the world interact with an intensity reinforced by rapid transport and telecommunications. And they confront each other on a growing range of issues of significant import to the security and economic well-being of their nations and societies.

It is the mission of the United States Institute of Peace to develop and train in techniques of conflict management likely to prevent or resolve disputes without resort to violence. And negotiating—both formal and informal—is in most societies a familiar approach to resolving differences or attaining preferred outcomes. Thus this study—and the more than a dozen in the Institute's cross-cultural negotiating series (see listing in the back of this volume)—are intended to make negotiating practices more productive and preferred as an approach to conflict management through mutual awareness and training in negotiating skills.

—RICHARD H. SOLOMON
PRESIDENT, U.S. INSTITUTE OF PEACE

Acknowledgments

We owe an enormous debt of gratitude to the many people whose support, insights, and research helped us write this book. Many of them are American colleagues and friends who have shared our experience of living and working in Pakistan and our fondness for its people. Bob and Phyllis Oakley, Wendy Chamberlin, David Smith, Robin Raphel, Marvin Weinbaum, and many others among them spent time sifting through their memories with us. Other incisive American Pakistan watchers, such as Steve Cohen, Polly Nayak, and Woolf Gross, also provided enormous support. Many patient Pakistani friends from government, the military, and the academic world reviewed for us the roller coaster–like history of U.S.-Pakistan relations and provided us their understanding of the way bilateral negotiations unfolded. Many others not directly involved in the negotiating process helped shape our understanding of their country.

We relied on the research help of people who worked with us, both at Georgetown University and at the Center for Strategic and International Studies (CSIS). Vibhuti Haté, research associate in the CSIS South Asia Program, kept the program humming while this book was in preparation. Her successor, Uttara Dukkipati, was both a dynamic manager of the program and a stellar researcher. Our work builds on the research help we received from John Dougherty, Sabala Baskar, Caroline Friedman, Elizabeth Laferriere, Alex Matthews, Ashley Pandya, Taylor Salisbury, and Lily Shapiro.

This project was undertaken through the United States Institute of Peace. The Institute's president, Richard Solomon, inspired this negotiating-styles series and gave us the example of his own work on China, a tough act to follow. Steve Riskin provided the support and counsel we needed during the project.

This book has been a family affair, like much else in our closely linked foreign service careers. In closing, we must also thank our sons, Michael and Christopher. Mike was the first fluent Urdu speaker in the family, and Chris was born in Pakistan. Seeing the country through their eyes shaped our perceptions as nothing else could have done. Growing up and moving away spared them the trials of living in a house with two struggling authors, but they were truly present at the creation.

We are grateful for the help these and other friends have provided. Whatever mistakes we have made are ours alone.

1

The Burden of History and Geography

In September 2009, the United States Congress passed legislation tripling economic assistance to Pakistan, an act intended to symbolize and energize the long-term relationship the two countries had been intermittently trying to establish for half a century.[1] Almost immediately, the legislation became not an occasion for celebration but the focus of bitter protests. The conditions and reporting requirements attached to the new assistance—a phenomenon familiar for decades in Washington-watching circles in the Pakistan government—were billed as an insult to Pakistan's sovereignty and an effort to deflect Pakistan from pursuing its national security goals.

This episode is a good thumbnail sketch of the roller coaster these two countries have ridden together. The highs were characterized by close U.S.-Pakistani cooperation, and the lows marked by deep bilateral estrangement. At the high points, Pakistani and American leaders worked closely together, military and economic assistance to Pakistan were among the highest the United States provided to any nation in the world, and the country participated in some of the most important elements of U.S. foreign policy. The roller coaster's downturns, on the other hand, led Pakistanis to see the United States as an unreliable friend that will heedlessly betray a loyal ally when changing global interests and policy priorities prompt it to do so. General K. M. Arif, a leading adviser to General Zia ul-Haq during Zia's long stint as army chief and president of Pakistan in the 1980s, expressed this sentiment well: "[The United States] showed no hesitation in promoting her own self-interest at critical moments even when such actions went

---

1. All of the interviews and conversations with the authors cited in this study—unless otherwise noted—were conducted either in Lahore or Islamabad, Pakistan, in February 2009, or in Washington, D.C., between July 2007 and November 2009.

to the gross disadvantage of Pakistan."[2] Memories of prior fallings-out left Pakistanis with the fear and even the expectation that strong ties would be followed by a steep downward plunge.

The purpose of this book is not to provide an exhaustive historical account of these ups and downs. Excellent studies can be found elsewhere.[3] This book tries instead to analyze the themes, techniques, and styles that have characterized Pakistani negotiations with American civilian and military officials in recent years and to reach some conclusions about what these are likely to be in the future. It focuses specifically on Pakistan's negotiations with the United States because the critical importance of the United States to Pakistan's security has lent a unique character to the way the two countries negotiate with one another.

The book interprets "negotiations" in the broadest sense. They include not only the process by which the two governments reached formal agreements but also the overall conduct of official U.S.-Pakistani dialogue, the formal and informal processes by which they gave shape to this extraordinarily volatile relationship at key points, and the periodic involvement of the United States in Pakistani domestic politics.

Pakistan's approach to negotiations with the United States is shaped chiefly by three factors. The first and most important is Pakistanis' concept of their country's place in the world, including their perception of the United States and the volatile history of U.S.-Pakistan relations. This is especially important because so many of Pakistan's key negotiations with the United States are intended to set the broad terms of the bilateral relationship, and in that context to define what kind of support the United States will provide. Although their styles may differ and the degree of authority they bring to the table will vary, Pakistanis who negotiate with the United States start from a common geopolitical framework. At the core of this framework is Pakistan's need to escape from the shadow of its large neighbor, India, historically perceived as an existential threat. This chronic sense of insecurity has led Pakistan to seek large outside "balancers." This was the original reason for Pakistan's seeking close relations with the United States, and has remained so. Integral to this commonly held Pakistani worldview is ambivalence and mistrust about the United States, whose power makes it important but whose perceived unreliability is uppermost in Pakistanis' minds. Pakistan-

---

2. General K. M. Arif, *Khaki Shadows: Pakistan 1947–1997* (Karachi: Oxford University Press, 2001), 305–06.

3. See, for example, Dennis Kux, *Disenchanted Allies: The United States and Pakistan 1947–2000* (Washington, DC: Woodrow Wilson Center Press, 2001).

U.S. negotiations are an exercise in asymmetrical diplomacy, in which the Pakistanis, acutely conscious of the disparity in national power, try to turn it to their advantage.

The second major factor in Pakistan's negotiating style with the United States is Pakistan's culture. Most of the Pakistani officials who deal with Americans are culturally at home among global and Western elites. Nonetheless, their operating style and expectations are shaped by a society in which the most important bonds are personal, relationships both inside and outside government are hierarchical, and the less powerful often try to turn their weakness into strength.

Finally, the third major factor in Pakistan's negotiations with the United States is the structure of the country's government and political system, notably its divided authority and the outsized role that the military has historically played. Taken together, these elements produce an approach in which negotiators who know their brief well cultivate what one might call "the art of the guilt trip." In important negotiations, Pakistan usually tries to create a sense of obligation on the part of the United States, or to nurture and intensify the fear that failure to honor Pakistan's requests will lead to disastrous consequences for U.S. interests. The objective is to keep the United States firmly in Pakistan's corner and minimize the power disparity between Pakistan and India.

In describing this approach, the book looks first at the ideological core, the prevailing Pakistani view of where Pakistan and the United States fit into each other's worlds. Next, it examines the cultural setting. It then looks in turn at the principal negotiators: the military, civil servants, and civilian politicians. A closer look at the negotiations that launched two of Pakistan's periods of closest cooperation with the United States will illustrate how the traits and institutions that the book surveys come together when Pakistan's national leaders are directly engaged in critical negotiations with the United States. The book then examines briefly how Pakistan deals with the United States when the negotiations directly involve India and concludes with some observations on what this means for U.S. negotiating practices.

To set the stage, one needs to look briefly at Pakistan's relations with the United States over the sixty years of Pakistan's independence. The most significant leitmotif in bilateral ties has been the gap between the strategic objectives of the two sides. Countries' goals in their dealings with one another often differ, but the contrast between the aims of these two allies has been especially marked. This disconnect has often been obscured by a willing suspension of disbelief by each side about the other's objectives, especially in the earlier period of the relationship but persisting to this day.

American interest in Pakistan has been powerfully influenced by geography. Pakistan's location close to the southern reaches of the Soviet Union led Washington in the 1950s and early 1960s to enlist it in U.S.-led Cold War alliances designed to contain potential Communist aggression. Proximity to Afghanistan made Pakistan a vital player in the 1980s when the United States sought to frustrate Soviet efforts to consolidate its military occupation of that Islamic neighbor. And after 9/11, Pakistan's common border with Afghanistan again prompted Washington to revive security ties, this time to combat al-Qaeda and the Taliban on the "central front" of the U.S.-led "global war against terrorism."

Other factors have also helped shape American interest in Pakistan, of course. Over time these have included America's regard for Pakistan's military, its concern for the economic and social development of a large and impoverished Third World country, its fears about Pakistani nuclear weapons, and its desire to be on good terms with a major, diplomatically active Muslim nation. But it is fair to say that if Pakistan had been located somewhere else during the Cold War and the battle against Islamic terrorism, it would not have been as great a focus for American attention as it periodically became.

Before it attracted the attention of the Eisenhower administration as a useful partner in the pursuit of the West's Cold War objectives, Pakistan was marginal to American strategic thinking. Washington's focus was on Europe and East Asia. South Asia was secondary if not inconsequential on its list of priorities. American policymakers rebuffed Pakistani interest in stronger relations, which the Pakistanis were never shy in advancing. This indifference ended in 1954, when Washington brought a very willing Pakistan into the Western security camp. As a member of the U.S.-sponsored Baghdad Pact, later the Central Treaty Organization (CENTO), it became the eastern anchor of a string of countries that stretched across the "soft underbelly" of the Soviet Union. The Eisenhower administration believed that with American and British support, these Muslim nations could help prevent Moscow from advancing its interests in the Middle East. Pakistan's membership in the Southeast Asia Treaty Organization (SEATO), while less significant in Washington's containment strategy, helped give that U.S.-inspired anti-Communist alliance more of a regional, noncolonial character than its American leadership and mostly Western membership would otherwise have suggested. Pakistan was soon unabashedly terming itself America's most allied ally in Asia.

But in entering the Western security system, Pakistan was moved less by its professed, and, in the view of many analysts, dubious anti-Communist credentials than by its interest in obtaining American military, political, diplomatic, and economic support in its long standing confrontation with India. The two countries, in short, decided to pursue common tactical goals, but were moved by quite different strategic objectives. Oral histories and other available documents indicate that U.S. diplomats serving in Pakistan, India, and Washington during the heyday of CENTO and SEATO in the mid- and late-1950s recognized this.[4] But like their successors in American policymaking positions during later periods of close U.S.-Pakistan political and security relations, they were prepared to disregard or at least minimize this key Pakistani motive.

The primacy that successive Pakistani governments gave and continue to give to defending their country against a perceived threat from its much larger and more powerful neighbor began with the bloody, traumatic partition of the British Indian Empire into Muslim Pakistan and largely Hindu India in 1947. Any slim hope that the two countries could soon overcome the bitterness of partition was quickly dashed by the outbreak of fighting between them over Kashmir, an issue both sides regarded as crucial to their basic national interest and ideology. Many Pakistanis believed that India remained unreconciled to partition and was determined to undo it, or at least to force Pakistan to recognize Indian hegemony in South Asia. A good number are still convinced that this is India's ultimate goal.

Consistent with its view of the alliance's purpose, Pakistan sought arms from the United States that it could use against India (while undertaking not to do so). Many of the most important negotiations the two countries undertook focused on the level and type of U.S. military support. On the diplomatic side, the Pakistanis looked to Washington for support at the United Nations and elsewhere on the Kashmir dispute. They argued that the United States owed them this backing because of the alliance relationship. This too

---

4. See, for example, the oral history statements of Ridgway B. Knight, deputy chief of mission at the U.S. embassy in Pakistan from 1957 to 1959, and Christopher Van Hollen, who served there from 1958 to 1961. Knight recalled: "I happened to feel that the Pakistanis were taking us to the cleaners. The entire [military] aid which we were giving them was being used for developing NATO-type military formations—which could only be used against India" (oral history statement, Association for Diplomatic Studies and Training, October 23, 1993, http://memory.loc.gov/cgi-bin/query/r?ammem/mfdip:@field(DOCID+mfdip2004kni02). Van Hollen remembers: "Even though aid was going to Pakistan to [meet the Communist threat], some Pakistanis, at least privately, admitted that they helped Pakistan vis-à-vis India. Nonetheless, we went through the charade of highlighting the Soviet threat, even though people [at the embassy] knew in their heart of hearts that the Pakistanis were receiving their military aid against the larger threat [of India]" (oral history statement, Association of Diplomatic Studies and Training, January 23, 1990, http://memory.loc.gov/cgi-bin/query/S?ammem/mfdipbib:@field(AUTHOR+@od1(Van+Hollen,+Christopher)).

was the subject of much negotiation. Pakistani frustration with the inability of the United States to help resolve the dispute in their favor was heightened by dismay when the Eisenhower and Kennedy administrations sought to repair Washington's frayed ties with nonaligned India, most provocatively, in Pakistan's view, when President John F. Kennedy came to India's rescue after its military had been routed by the Chinese in a border war in the Himalayas. This led many Pakistanis to question the value of the alliance.

Dissatisfied with America's increasingly evenhanded South Asia policy, Pakistan sought to reduce its dependence on Washington by reaching out to the Soviet Union and Communist China. This exposed more than before the fundamentally different purposes Americans and Pakistanis had in maintaining the alliance. The incongruity was revealed even more starkly when in 1965 the Pakistanis launched an unsuccessful war to wrest Kashmir from Indian control, using against India weapons the United States had supplied them to contain Communism. Washington promptly cut off arms shipments and suspended new economic assistance to Pakistan. It took the same action toward India, but with much less effect, given Pakistan's far greater dependence on U.S. arms.

The India-Pakistan war of 1965 effectively ended the already badly disheveled U.S.-Pakistan alliance. It was a messy divorce. Each side accused the other of bad faith. The Pakistanis claimed that the United States had been bound by treaty to come to their assistance and had reneged on its commitment by not supporting them against Indian aggression. The Americans were furious at Pakistan for its misuse of U.S.-supplied weapons. More broadly, the conflict solidified the conclusion in Washington that Pakistani and Indian preoccupation with their seemingly insoluble internecine disputes ruled out either one playing a useful role in helping the United States achieve its global Cold War objectives. For many American policymakers, it was "a plague on both their houses."

The pattern of differing U.S. and Pakistani motives in a period of prolonged and intense collaboration repeated itself to a lesser degree in the 1980s, when Washington enlisted Islamabad as a vital "frontline state" in its effort to force the Soviets out of Afghanistan. This restoration of security and political ties gave Pakistan a greater prominence in American Cold War strategy than it had held before, even in the heady days of the 1950s. In the intervening years, Pakistan had reached center stage in Washington only briefly, in 1971, when it facilitated the Nixon-Kissinger opening to China (another example of the importance of geography). Pakistan was also the beneficiary of the famous U.S. "tilt" in the Bangladesh War of 1971. But despite this pro-Pakistan stance the United States did not intervene to save the country from defeat and dismemberment, and Pakistanis became even more convinced that the United States could not be counted on to provide meaningful assistance when the chips were down.

Following the war U.S.-Pakistan relations took on an increasingly negative character. Pakistan's nuclear ambitions, its 1977 return to martial law under General Zia, the military regime's promotion of Islamic fundamentalism, its widespread violations of human rights, its failure to prevent the destruction of the American embassy by an excited mob, and other disturbing developments figured prominently in Washington's assessment. When the Soviets marched into Afghanistan at Christmas 1979 there were few redeeming features in the relationship, and few American and Pakistani policymakers had much hope that things would get better.

That invasion dramatically changed American priorities in Pakistan. Major preinvasion concerns, such as Pakistan's nuclear weapons program, which had only recently led to a suspension of economic and military assistance, were downplayed as Washington scurried to counter the Soviet move. But the Pakistanis did not react to America's call for a restoration of security relations with the enthusiasm that had accompanied their joining the Western camp in the 1950s. Their experience in 1965 and 1971 had made them skeptical of American steadfastness, and they demanded a high price for their cooperation.

If the U.S. purpose in reactivating the security relationship was to force the Soviets out of Afghanistan and, for some policymakers, to bleed them severely in the process, Pakistan's motives were less single-minded. It was more concerned than the United States about post-Communist arrangements in Afghanistan. It sought to ensure that Afghanistan would be ruled by a friendly government that would not conspire with India against Pakistan's interests.

Like the rulers of Pakistan in the 1950s, Zia also saw strong relations with the United States as an "equalizer" in Pakistan's continuing confrontation with India. He successfully sought from Washington a menu of arms, including sophisticated fighter aircraft, heavy armor, and antisubmarine weapons that were much more suitable in countering India than in warding off Soviet threats. The favor he won in Washington for his firm stand on Afghanistan and his willingness to rally other Muslim countries against the Soviet occupation contrasted with American dismay at India's pro-Soviet position. The invidious comparison led the United States to show no sympathy for the Indians' accurate accusation that Pakistan wanted U.S. arms to use against them.

This second U.S.-Pakistan entente started to unravel when the Soviets left Afghanistan in early 1989. As U.S. interest in Afghanistan's future faded and Pakistan lost its frontline status, old problems in U.S.-Pakistan bilateral relations resurfaced. The nuclear issue did so with a vengeance. Washington had been disinclined to probe too carefully into the status of Islamabad's nuclear weapons program while the Soviets were still in Afghanistan. But in 1990, after their withdrawal, the George H. W. Bush administration concluded that it could no longer certify that Pakistan did not possess a nuclear device. As stipulated in 1986 legislation (the Pressler Amendment), this meant that Pakistan could not receive U.S. military assistance or most forms of economic aid, an enormous setback in the relationship. Even the training of Pakistani military officers in the United States was ruled out. Military-to-military relations had always been an important element in shaping attitudes on both sides. Ending them cut off American contact with rising stars in the Pakistan armed forces who might well come to play a major role in the governing of the country.

As in the 1960s following the first breakdown of their alliance, U.S.-Pakistan relations entered a negative phase. The Pakistanis, who had been confident that their role in Afghanistan would somehow prevent the United States from imposing Pressler Amendment strictures, were surprised and embittered when it took the drastic action the legislation called for. American policymakers, for their part, came to regard Pakistan mainly as a set of problems. Dealing with these difficult and unrewarding issues became the focus of American diplomacy in the 1990s, a decade when Washington's inability to offer most forms of support weakened its bargaining power.

Interestingly, despite the sense of betrayal Pakistanis felt about the aid cutoff, Pakistan continued to look for other ways of reconnecting with the United States. It joined the coalition that the United States organized following Iraq's seizure of Kuwait in 1991, sending troops to Saudi Arabia. The United States appreciated this decision, which was not without controversy in Pakistan; indeed, Pakistan's army chief publicly took issue with Prime Minister Nawaz Sharif's decision to join the coalition.

In the next decade, the United States and Pakistan wrestled with a number of painful issues, starting with Pakistan's continuing nuclear ambitions. Islamabad's nuclear weapons tests in May 1998 following India's tests earlier that month spelled the definitive failure of U.S. efforts to dissuade it from joining the nuclear club. Pakistan's covert support for an insurgency in Indian-administered Kashmir and its role in the acts of terrorism that accompanied the uprising were another problem area. So was the Pakistan army's 1999 foray into Indian-held territory in the Kargil area of the disputed state. This led to a limited, undeclared war between the two claimants that required the personal intervention of President William Clinton to resolve in White House negotiations with Prime Minister Sharif. Other troubling developments for American policymakers included Pakistan's support for the Islamic fundamentalist Taliban government in Afghanistan, which Pakistan had helped bring to power, and the overthrow of the elected constitutional government of Sharif in a military coup. As the century ended, Washington's newfound favor for India further complicated U.S.-Pakistan ties, as it had forty years before.

By September 2001 Pakistan seemed to many American policymakers and observers a close-to-failing state beset by a host of intractable political, economic, social, and ethnic problems. In their view, it pursued many policies at home and abroad that conflicted with U.S. interests. It was under more congressionally mandated sanctions than any other country with which Washington enjoyed regular diplomatic relations.

The events of 9/11 changed U.S.-Pakistan relations even more suddenly and dramatically than had the 1979 Soviet invasion of Afghanistan. Under intense pressure from Washington, the government headed by General Pervez Musharraf was compelled to make a 180-degree turn in Pakistan's Afghanistan policy. Musharraf abandoned his Taliban protégés and made available to the United States an array of overflight, basing, and intelligence facilities it could use as it prepared to invade Afghanistan. For these, Pakistan was generously rewarded with long-term military and economic assistance as well as substantial funding to compensate its armed forces for their cooperation. Washington also made Pakistan eligible to receive advanced American arms ordinarily available only to its NATO allies. As America's new and seemingly indispensable partner, Musharraf became a favored figure in the George W. Bush White House. Concern about the authoritarian nature of his rule and other pre-9/11 misgivings were brushed aside.

Less than a week after 9/11, when Musharraf explained to his skeptical countrymen his decision to join the American effort, he stressed that India would have benefited at Pakistan's expense if he had not complied.[5] New Delhi had welcomed Washington's joining the antiterrorist battle it had been pursing for decades, most notably against Pakistani-supported insurgents in Kashmir. Musharraf feared that if he did not accept American demands Washington would turn to India as its regional partner in the war against terrorism.

---

5. President General Pervez Musharraf, "Address to the People of Pakistan" (televised speech, Islamabad, September 19, 2001), www.americanrhetoric.com/speeches/pakistanpresident.htm.

The anti-Indian card figured once again in Pakistanis' choice of equipment from the American arsenal that opened to them once more after 9/11. This included F-16 fighter aircraft, much more useful in a conventional war against India than in counterinsurgency operations against the Afghan Taliban and their Pakistani Islamic extremist supporters. When India-Pakistan tensions spiked, as they did following a December 2001 attack on the Indian parliament by extremists with links to Pakistan, the Pakistanis found themselves on the receiving end of strong U.S. pressure to put an end to terrorism originating from their territory. From the U.S. perspective, the activities of the extremists who had attacked India were outside the implicit rules of the game of U.S.-Pakistan relations; from Pakistan's perspective, the United States was seen as falling short of the duty of an ally.

As in the other heydays of U.S.-Pakistan cooperation, Islamabad's objectives in Afghanistan differed from Washington's, even after the drastic policy changes the Bush administration pressed it to make. Pakistan's earlier ties with the Taliban limited the role it played in international efforts led by the United States and the United Nations to launch and carry out the so-called Bonn Process to stabilize and rehabilitate Afghanistan. As always, it preferred that the government in Kabul be led by Pashtuns, whose tribal brethren also lived across the border in Pakistan. It detested the Northern Alliance and had scant regard for Hamid Karzai, who emerged from the Bonn Process to become, with American sponsorship, Afghan president. Karzai's cooperation with India resurrected old Pakistani fears of being caught in a pincer formed by two hostile neighbors.

At least some Pakistani intelligence officers who had worked with the Taliban when they were in power maintained contact with Taliban remnants after the regime was overthrown. Meanwhile, the Musharraf government showed much greater determination in rounding up al-Qaeda elements operating in Pakistan territory than it did in combating the Taliban and their Pakistani collaborators as the Taliban reorganized in the rugged areas along the Pakistan-Afghanistan border and crossed it to resume the fight in Afghanistan. As the situation in the frontier area and in Afghanistan worsened, Washington increasingly demanded that Pakistan "do more" and feared that Pakistanis considered the war in Afghanistan "America's war," not theirs.

By mid-decade, Pakistan was still described by the U.S. leadership as a critical ally against terrorism, but increasingly it was also described as part of the problem. When the Obama administration took office, it appointed a high-level special envoy, Richard Holbrooke, to develop and implement a strategy toward both countries. Pakistanis' hopes that he would devote significant attention to their primary concern, India, were quickly dashed. At the same time, Pakistan itself faced a domestic insurgency spearheaded by the local equivalent of the Taliban. Pakistan's role in Afghanistan and the movement of insurgents back and forth between the two countries had become the major source of tension between Pakistan and the United States. The fundamental problem that had plagued earlier periods of close U.S.-Pakistan collaboration was still in place: differing anxieties and objectives in both countries.

Pakistan and the United States agree on the facts and chronology of their shared history, but they tell very different stories with those facts. For Americans, the narrative is one of willful disregard by Pakistanis for U.S. concerns about which they have been amply warned. In 1965, Pakistan ignored U.S. strictures against using in combat against India the arms Washington had supplied to confront potential Communist aggression. In 1990, the relationship came apart when Pakistan ignored U.S. warnings that developing a nuclear explosive device would lead to an aid cutoff.

Pakistanis interpret both these events as betrayals of explicit or implicit U.S. commitments. For them, the dominant themes are disappointment and unreliability. Pakistan's negotiators look on the United States as a country critical to Pakistan's security, but one that Pakistan cannot count on in times of trouble. A major theme of Pakistan's history is insecurity, and this makes Pakistanis acutely conscious of the disparity of size and power between themselves and the United States. This accentuates their view that the United States routinely threatens Pakistan, that what the Americans see as forcefulness is really arrogance, and that the negotiating process as conceived by the United States is really a series of U.S. demands that Pakistan is forced to accept. The United States has always been a key element in Pakistan's strategy of balancing India's size and power. Despite concerns about U.S. faithlessness, Pakistan governments have looked for ways of getting and keeping a U.S. connection.

At the same time, during the times of closest Pakistan-U.S. cooperation, Pakistani leaders have been convinced that, however useful they found the relationship with Washington, the United States needed Pakistan more. They drove a correspondingly hard bargain on the major issues in the relationship. The case studies in chapter 7 examine this dynamic more deeply.[6]

---

6. This section draws on authors' interviews with Lt. Gen. (ret.) Javed Hassan, former Pakistani defense attaché in Washington; former foreign secretaries Tanvir Ahmed Khan and Shahryar Khan; former diplomats Touqir Hussain and Tariq Fatemi; Prof. Riffaat Hussein, Qaid-e-Azam University; former information minister Mushahid Hussein; and Maj. Gen. (ret.) Mahmud Durrani, former ambassador to the United States.

Throughout the ups and downs of U.S.-Pakistani relations—what one might call three marriages and two divorces—Pakistanis have felt that the United States used Pakistan when it was convenient, and abandoned it when Pakistan was no longer needed. One former Pakistani official commented that his country could not even count on its American lobbyists, recalling a time in the early 1990s when a lobbyist hired by the Pakistan embassy presented the Pakistanis with a paper on how they might dismantle the nuclear devices they had assembled but still not tested.[7] Pakistanis recognize that the United States acts to protect its own interests, but many believe that U.S. negotiators expect Pakistan to subordinate its interests to those of the United States. Not surprisingly, this causes resentment. Pakistani victimhood is a recurring theme. The material circulated by the Council on Pakistan Relations, an advocacy group run by Pakistani-Americans, asserts that "no country has suffered as much as Pakistan for being an ally to the United States."[8]

Especially in the period since 2001, these sentiments have become part of the political lingua franca of Pakistan, and anti-Americanism has been on everyone's lips—even as the country's leaders, both civil and military, recognized that they needed the United States. This has occasionally made the United States a kind of domestic political lightning rod in Pakistan. Unpopular decisions were blamed on U.S. pressure, while at the same time leaders, including both Musharraf and Asif Zardari, strove to remain close to Washington even as they tried to demonstrate politically that they were not overly influenced by the United States.

These perceptions of the United States include more than their share of paradoxes. One constant, however, is the enormous influence that Pakistanis attribute to the United States. More than almost anywhere in the world, the U.S. ambassador and the U.S. government are looked upon as all-powerful, for good or ill. Pakistanis emphasize this view of an all-powerful America, using it as an additional argument why the United States must surely be able to honor Pakistan's needs. U.S. officials, by contrast, are acutely conscious of the limitations on their influence. They have little expectation of being able to achieve results by pulling strings, in a country of 170 million people with a complex, messy political culture, an army accustomed to being the country's main political force, and widespread anti-American sentiment. Given the burden of history both sides carry and the magnitude of the forces both sides believe are in play, negotiations often appear to reflect more than the specific issues on the table: they are intended to validate or invalidate a larger

7. Mushahid Hussein, interview.
8. Council on Pakistan Relations, www.pakistanrelations.org (accessed July 24, 2009).

concept of rights and duties, or an overarching view of the capabilities of the United States and Pakistan.

2

The Starting Point:
Pakistan's Place in the World

When Strobe Talbott, President Clinton's deputy secretary of state, arrived in Islamabad in May 1998 on a "mission impossible" to dissuade Pakistan from matching the Indian nuclear test that had just shocked the world, his first official meeting was a "bracing experience." Foreign Minister Gohar Ayub started his remarks, Talbott recalled, with "a history lesson featuring the perfidy of India dating back to 1947 ('a habitual aggressor and hegemon') and the inconstancy of the United States ('a fair-weather friend'), whose various cutoffs of military aid had deprived Pakistan of its 'qualitative military edge.'"[1]

This moment captures the most important influence on the perspective of Pakistani negotiators approaching serious discussions with the United States: their view of Pakistan's place in a dangerous world in which the country's very existence is threatened. This is the starting point for Pakistan's negotiators. Their cultural background, their experience dealing with Westerners, and the patterns of interaction between the stronger and weaker members of Pakistan's society and civil and military bureaucracy shape the ways that they use this view of Pakistan's identity and its place in the world in dealings with the United States. The previous chapter examined Pakistan's view of the United States. This chapter explores the other key elements of this national geopolitical identity: the rivalry with India, the overlapping layers of loyalty that influence Pakistan's ties with Afghanistan, the "all-weather" friendship with China, and Pakistan's place in the *ummah* (global Muslim community).

---

1. Strobe Talbott, *Engaging India: Diplomacy, Democracy and the Bomb* (Washington, DC: Brookings Institution Press, 2004), 60.

Escaping India's Shadow

Pakistan's view of the world begins with the trauma of the 1947 partition of India, and the chronic insecurity that it engendered. This is the starting point not only for Pakistan's foreign policy but also for its approach to negotiating with its principal international friends.[2] Not every high-level encounter with Americans starts with the recitation of history that Strobe Talbott described, but many do. Pakistan's position as a country one-seventh the size of its giant and, to Pakistanis, hostile neighbor is always at least in the background. The most painful part of this history—the "core issue," in the term preferred by Pakistani officials and commentators—is Kashmir. Pakistanis believe they have been cheated and betrayed by both India and the international community. They feel that the very structure of their history and geography makes them dependent, vulnerable, and discounted. At the same time, national pride and the need to play up the ways in which they believe Pakistan is superior to India are important themes in their dealings with foreigners.

Pakistani negotiators often try to impress on their U.S. counterparts that Americans and others who have not had to deal with India from a position of weakness do not understand Indian ambitions and guile. As they argue it, Americans are taken in by the Indians and fail to recognize the overbearing, bullying policies and practices India inflicts on Pakistan and the other smaller countries of South Asia. Most Pakistanis believe that Americans are not aware of India's longstanding hegemonic goals and the dangers to Pakistani and U.S. interests that they entail.

Pakistani tactics to correct these impressions and instill their own understanding of what the Indians are up to will vary, of course, with individual Pakistanis, their American interlocutors, the nature of the negotiations under way, and current circumstances. Americans familiar with subcontinental history and politics may receive a more nuanced presentation than newcomers to South Asia. The highly one-sided interpretations Pakistanis provide stress India's unwillingness to accept Pakistan and its other regional neighbors as fully independent states entitled to pursue their own policies and go their own ways. In its crudest form, this approach focuses on dire Indian plots to undo Pakistan by breaking it up into smaller units or making it a vassal state, or both. This fear is fed by one of the most traumatic events in Pakistan's history, India's support for the breaking away of East Pakistan in 1971. For many Pakistanis, the memory of this time is still vivid.

---

2. See, for example, Abdul Sattar, *Pakistan's Foreign Policy 1947–2005: A Concise History* (Oxford: Oxford University Press, 2007), which starts the first substantive chapter (p. 8) with the line, "The foreign policy of Pakistan was to be molded in the crucible of interaction with its neighbor India."

Aware that Americans are impressed by Indian democracy and contrast it favorably with the congenital weakness of Pakistani civilian political institutions, Pakistanis will at times point to defects in the way India is governed, especially the way its Muslim minority is treated. Pakistanis are well-versed in their version of the truth and will have facts and figures ready to support their accounts. They contrast the hierarchical character of the Hindu caste system with the more egalitarian ethos of Islam.[3] Stereotypes frequently found among Pakistanis hold that Indians are more duplicitous, less honest, and less courageous than Pakistanis. Some military officers in years past were fond of saying that vegetarian Indian troops could never hold their own against their carnivorous Pakistani counterparts. Pakistani negotiators and briefers will call attention to India's overwhelming strength, especially its military capabilities, and argue that the bellicose way India has used this superiority in the past indicates that it would be prepared to do so again if the opportunity arose.

The approach Pakistanis use with Americans knowledgeable about South Asia includes these and other points critical of India in a more nuanced form. But even those Pakistanis who do not accept the cruder versions of these stereotypes are eager to persuade the American side that Indians (unlike Pakistanis) are not to be trusted, and that India's claims that they prefer a stable and secure Pakistan as their neighbor are false.

Pakistanis' discussion of the rights and wrongs of the Kashmir issue is of course a long standing element of their foreign policy, but it is also part of this effort to denigrate India and Indians. Pakistani diplomats and senior defense staff have at their fingertips a well-rehearsed history that begins with New Delhi's deceit in bringing about the "fraudulent" accession of the disputed state to India in 1947, goes on to discuss the Indians' stubborn refusal to accept United Nations resolutions calling for a free and fair plebiscite despite their early undertaking to promote one, and ends with a vivid description of the lamentable condition of Kashmiri Muslims under the heel of an Indian "army of occupation" whose numbers Pakistanis routinely exaggerate. (The Indians, of course, have their own interpretation of events, including some different distortions, which they too are ready to provide.) Americans who have discussed the Kashmir issue with Pakistanis usually find that little pur-

---

3. A detailed exposition of the argument that the social structure at the base of Hinduism coupled with its lack of a clear credo makes Indian society and the Indian military in some fundamental sense weaker than Pakistan's can be found in Javed Hassan, *India: A Study in Profile* (Rawalpindi: Army Education Press GHQ, 1990). Hassan, who retired from the army as a lieutenant general, wrote the book when he was a lieutenant colonel, and it was part of the curriculum for Pakistani officers in training for many years.

pose is served in trying to argue about the narrative their interlocutors serve up. It is better, instead, to focus on what can be done to bring the problem closer to settlement.

Undercutting Indians in American eyes reflects Pakistani concern that Washington regards India as the more important of the two in ways that disadvantage Pakistan. These apprehensions have always been present, even in the heyday of the U.S.-Pakistan security alliance in the 1950s and early 1960s. In those halcyon years of the bilateral relationship Pakistanis were sensitive to any American policies that seemed to them to reflect an interest on Washington's part in developing better ties with New Delhi. A good example was Pakistan's annoyance with the Eisenhower and Kennedy administrations for stepping up economic assistance to nonaligned India (though the level of this aid on a per capita basis was always well below what Washington provided Pakistan). The Pakistanis were even more resentful when the Kennedy administration came to India's rescue following the rout of the Indian army in the Sino-Indian border war. They asked at that time what the purpose of their alliance with the United States was if nonaligned India got equal treatment with Pakistan, America's "most allied ally in Asia." More broadly, Pakistani diplomacy during most of the long East-West confrontation was designed to reinforce the sour perceptions U.S. policymakers and informed American public opinion had toward India as a moralizing, pretentious, and hypocritical country that leaned toward the Communist bloc abroad, pursued socialist economic policies at home, and was almost always unhelpful to Washington's efforts to promote U.S. global and regional interests.

Pakistani fears that the United States would "tilt" toward India were heightened by developments after the Cold War ended. U.S.-Indian relations became substantially stronger, especially during the George W. Bush administration. As the Pakistanis are painfully aware, Washington has come to see India as a rising global power and an incipient economic powerhouse, an attractive partner for American strategists and business people. Some influential Americans view it as a useful Asian counterforce to an aggressive China, with which Pakistan has historically enjoyed a warm relationship. And the demise of the Soviet Union meant that Americans no longer worry about New Delhi's ties to Moscow. The United States and India now sometimes even describe each other as "natural allies," an enormous reinterpretation of the relationship from the norm of Cold War days.

At the same time, the United States has also drawn closer to Pakistan, for different reasons. These relate almost exclusively to Pakistan's role in the

U.S.-led effort to combat al-Qaeda and the Taliban, a part it reluctantly accepted under American pressure following 9/11. For much of the last decade, Washington could rightly claim that it enjoyed the best relations it ever simultaneously had with New Delhi and Islamabad. It also could assert more justifiably than it had in the past that U.S. policy in South Asia was not a "zero-sum game" in which improved American relations with India entail weakened ties with Pakistan (and vice versa). Washington plausibly insists that the United States has "de-hyphenated" India and Pakistan in its approach to South Asia. (Ironically, the term "Indo-Pak" once used in describing American policy in the region has now been succeeded by a fresh hyphenation, "Af-Pak," which the Pakistanis find demeaning and distasteful.)

These assurances have not stilled Pakistani concerns that America will favor India on matters important to Pakistan. Islamabad wants the United States to deal with it as New Delhi's equal, and reacts sharply to any deviation from this norm. For example, the refusal of the U.S. government to consider a civil nuclear deal with Pakistan similar to the one it negotiated with India is seen as clear evidence that the United States has downgraded its ties with Pakistan, and is often referred to as discrimination against Pakistan.

Pakistan's call for equal treatment and its worry that it will not get it are closely related, of course, to its efforts to counterbalance the Indian threat that is still the central element in the country's chronic sense of insecurity. This effort is not limited to Pakistan's dealings with the United States, though Washington has usually been its prime target. Pakistan governments of various political persuasions have looked to China, the oil-rich Arab nations, other Muslim countries, and occasionally even the Soviet Union for diplomatic, political, and economic backing. Pakistan recognizes that it is no longer in India's league in terms of overall power, if it ever was. It will continue to look for support from the United States and other outsiders to keep it strong enough to deter the aggressive Indian designs that it considers its primary challenge. Only a marked improvement in its relations with India, including significant steps toward a settlement of their Kashmir dispute, will lead Pakistan to change this policy. Until that unlikely development takes place—and it has eluded the two countries for six decades—Pakistan will continue to see India as a basically hostile neighbor, and its negotiators will probably continue to believe that making India look bad is an important part of their task.

Afghanistan: India's Cat's Paw

Two of the periods of closest U.S.-Pakistan relations, the 1980s and the years since 9/11, involved intense collaboration on Afghanistan. In both cases, the United States and Pakistan had identified a common security threat—in the first case, the Soviet army, and in the second, the toxic blend of chaos and a Taliban-led insurgency in Afghanistan—and worked together to counter it. But both Pakistan's strategic objectives and its officials' negotiating tactics are significantly influenced by the conviction that the biggest threat to Pakistan from Afghanistan lies in the historically friendly ties between New Delhi and Kabul. These issues are central to any U.S.-Pakistan negotiation involving Afghanistan. As with Pakistan's view of India, they also form part of the narrative of danger that is the foundation for the negotiator's approach.

Pakistan has had difficult relations with Afghanistan for most of its life. Afghanistan voted against Pakistan's admission to the United Nations. Over the years, separatist movements in northwestern Pakistan received support from the Afghan government, and the two countries have an unresolved border dispute. The key point that shapes the Pakistani negotiators' framework, however, is India's role. Pakistanis are convinced that India is working with Afghanistan to cause problems for the Pakistanis in the areas along the Afghan-Pakistani border, especially Balochistan and the Federally Administered Tribal Areas (FATA). If there is a foreign policy red flag for Pakistan, this is it, and officials painting a picture of the dangers surrounding Pakistan will emphasize it. Many Pakistanis are convinced that India is using its consulates in cities close to the border, such as Jalalabad and Kandahar, to fund and otherwise promote anti-Pakistan sentiment among Baloch and Pashtuns unhappy with what these ethnic groups consider the dominant—and domineering—power of the country's Punjabi majority. Pakistanis similarly see an Indian hand behind the nationalist movement in Sindh Province. Although Indians and Pakistanis habitually exaggerate the other side's activities, the charges may well have some basis.

In the negotiating setting, Pakistani officials will cite Afghanistan as another instance of the familiar theme of the danger their country faces and the central role India plays in that danger. In making this argument, they routinely play up a worst-case version of both the facts and the analysis involved. One often hears, especially from military officers, that India has established not the officially acknowledged four consulates but twenty-one, and that all are basically stations for espionage and subversion. Americans who question this version of the facts are accused of being hopelessly naive.

More generally, the United States takes a far more benign view of India's intentions in Afghanistan than Pakistan does. This view is likewise regarded as naive, if not duplicitous, by Pakistani officials.

Pakistani officials are well aware that Islamabad's major strategic objective in Afghanistan is not shared by Washington. This is the concept of "strategic depth." Coined during the government of Zia ul-Haq in the 1980s, when it had particular salience, it has been defined in different ways. For some, it has meant the availability of Afghanistan as a safe rear area for Pakistani forces fighting India on their eastern front. More recently, General Ashfaq Kayani, Pakistan's chief of army staff, said in a February 2010 press conference: "We want strategic depth in Afghanistan but do not want to control it. . . . A peaceful and friendly Afghanistan can provide Pakistan a strategic depth." (The concerns Kayani expressed in the same press conference over India's offer to help train the Afghan army throws light on what he considered to be "friendly.")[4]

But however it is defined, the concept reflects Pakistan's interest in a pliant government in Kabul—some would say a client state—that will not cause trouble in its Pashtun or Baloch areas or develop close ties with India. In its view, Afghanistan must not be allowed to become a hostile staging ground next to Pakistan's most volatile provinces in the event of another India-Pakistan war. For its part, Washington would like to see friendly relations between Islamabad and Kabul, but it had serious problems with the Afghan government that came closest to being a Pakistani client, the Taliban regime that was driven from power after 9/11.

Pakistan has tried to establish decent if not warm relations with the post-9/11 Afghan government headed by Hamid Karzai. Although the Musharraf government renounced the Afghan Taliban at the insistence of the Bush administration, Pakistani officials, especially operatives presently or previously connected with the Inter-Services Intelligence Directorate (ISI), continue to maintain ties with their former Taliban clients. Some commentators have called these continuing contacts Pakistan's "rainy day policy," an effort on its part to hedge against the failure of the Karzai government or the premature exit of the United States and its NATO partners.[5] Such an approach is understandable given Pakistan's view of America's unfaithfulness to its commitments.

---

4. Zahid Hussain, "Kayani Spells Out Terms for Regional Stability," *Dawn*, February 2, 2010, www.dawn.com/wps/wcm/connect/dawn-content-library/dawn/the-newspaper/front-page/kayani-spells-out-terms-for-regional-stability-220.

5. The "Wikileaks" publication in July 2010 of secret U.S. documents that provided details of these ISI activities has given greater credibility to this interpretation.

In the period since 9/11, and especially after 2005, problems along the Pakistan-Afghanistan border have come to dominate U.S.-Pakistan relations. This difference in perspectives on Afghanistan has added an undercurrent of deep suspicion to the most important U.S.-Pakistan discussions. Overtly, the U.S.-Pakistan dialogue rested firmly on the assumption that the two countries were pursuing a common objective, the establishment of a stable, well-governed Afghanistan that maintains peaceful relations with its neighbors. But beneath the surface, the Pakistan government was deeply anxious about the character of the Afghan government and especially about its relations with India. Especially in light of Pakistan's doubts about U.S. staying power, this concern can trump Pakistan's efforts to keep the United States happy. It often leads Pakistani officials to dissemble or to offer oral reassurances about Islamabad's policies and practices not matched by reality. It can also lead to a rash of accomplishments related to Afghanistan—arrests of senior al-Qaeda figures, for example—timed to occur just before contacts between top U.S. and Pakistani leaders. Discussions of Afghanistan and the border problems that appear to be about specific operational details—the staffing of the Pakistan army's border posts, for example, or military coordination among Afghanistan, the United States, and Pakistan—are really, in the minds of the Pakistani participants, about neutralizing the perceived threat from India through Afghanistan. Because the structure of U.S.-Pakistan relations since 9/11 has been based on the premise that the two countries are working in sync on Afghanistan, the issue that most worries the Pakistanis—the Indian role and presence—is "the elephant in the room," a looming presence over important U.S.-Pakistan negotiations that cannot be entirely resolved. These Pakistani concerns preclude Washington from looking to India for any significant role in Afghanistan other than assisting in economic and social reconstruction.

Pakistani negotiators generally try to keep the United States away from the details of their political and intelligence relationships in Afghanistan. This reflects both Pakistan's focus on the Indian role and the fact that Pakistan's relations with Afghanistan have been run primarily through intelligence channels. In the 1980s, Pakistan was quite successful in this effort: the United States agreed to conduct its policy of support for the mujahideen resisting the Soviet army almost entirely through the Pakistan government, with the ISI as the primary conduit. The complexity of the tribal societies involved and the fact that the United States knew relatively little about them gave Pakistan a plausible reason to insist on a free hand. By keeping the United States at arm's length, Pakistani negotiators were able to protect their priorities in Afghanistan from prying eyes and to avoid awkward discussions with the United States about conflicting goals.

During the post-9/11 period, the United States has been in the middle of things, with troops on the ground in Afghanistan, making it harder to conceal Pakistani operations. U.S.-Pakistan tensions over Afghan policy have been correspondingly greater. During this more recent period, the two countries' different concerns and priorities have come up in different form. The United States insisted that Pakistan make a more robust and effective effort to prevent Taliban and al-Qaeda operatives from using Pakistani territory to launch attacks into Afghanistan. Pakistan, for its part, has claimed it was doing all it could, given the difficult terrain and complex political situation—and has blamed the problems along the border on the disruptions caused by the U.S. military presence in Afghanistan.

China, the "All-Weather Friend"

Pakistani views of other international players and issues also influence how Islamabad approaches negotiations with Washington. China heads the list of reliable friends, as Pakistani leaders and officials see it, and plays several roles in Pakistan's approach to negotiating with the United States. It provides a contrast to some of the U.S. characteristics that Pakistanis find troublesome and represents an alternative source of aid and support in case of a fresh downturn in relations with the United States.

Pakistan originally was attracted to China as a reliable opponent of India, not least on the issue of Kashmir. Beijing's policies on the disputed state have shifted subtly back and forth between a pro-Pakistan and a more neutral stance after the late 1990s. China has never been willing to intervene meaningfully on Pakistan's behalf in India-Pakistan confrontations. Nonetheless, Pakistanis see China as their one true friend among the major powers. They value, perhaps overvalue, their longstanding ties and are reluctant to criticize Beijing when it adopts policies that are contrary to Pakistan's interest. In this context, Islamabad has been consistently circumspect in its reaction to Chinese clashes with Muslims within China, such as the Uighurs. This contrasts sharply with the widespread attention it gives to anti-Muslim activities in India. The Sino-Pakistan relationship is for the Pakistanis an "enduring entente" and "all-weather highway."

Pakistanis contrast this seeming Chinese fidelity with America's mercurial, untrustworthy approach. They also favorably contrast China's practice of conducting diplomatic exchanges quietly and behind the scenes with what they regard as an incessant drumbeat of public demands and noisy critical comments aimed at them by multiple power sources in Washington. This customary Chinese discretion leads Pakistanis to pay greater heed when Beijing *does* weigh in. This happened, for example, in 2007: a phone call from the Chinese leadership galvanized the Musharraf government into action against Islamic extremists based in Islamabad's Red Mosque, who had been taking the law into their own hands for at least six months. It was the radical students' freelance action against Chinese residents of the city that tipped the balance.

Pakistanis see their friendship with China as a hedge against a new rupture with the United States and a protection against U.S. unwillingness to provide both symbolic and material support on the international scene. Thus, when the United States signed a civilian nuclear agreement with India, Pakistan was quick to engage in discussions with China about civilian nuclear trade. The argument that "we'll get it from China" has had little impact in U.S.-Pakistan negotiations, especially since the United States and China developed relatively friendly relations, but China is seen as a useful reminder to Americans not to take Pakistan's dependence for granted. Pakistanis would strongly resent any serious American effort to develop an understanding with India to confront an aggressive China. They would see it as further dangerous evidence of the United States' tilt to India that they so much fear. Such a U.S.-Indian entente would further complicate Islamabad-Washington relations and would strongly influence the outlook that Pakistani negotiators brought to the bargaining table.

Competing Visions of Islamic Identity

Pakistan was founded as the homeland for Muslims of the subcontinent. This gives its membership in the larger global *ummah* particular emotional resonance. Pakistan's identity as a Muslim state stands in contrast to India's self-proclaimed identity as a multireligious, multicultural state. Pakistanis will sometimes tell foreigners that their Muslim culture is "completely different" from Indian culture, glossing over the many traditions, family practices, languages, and habits of mind that Pakistan shares with adjoining areas in India.

Since its birth, however, Pakistan has been torn between different interpretations of its Islamic identity. The country's founder, Muhammad Ali Jinnah, had a nationalist concept. He spoke of Muslims in effect as an ethnic group within the subcontinental mosaic. His famous statement made on the eve of Pakistan's independence in 1947 embodies this vision: "You are free to go to your temples, you are free to go to your mosques or to any other place of worship. . . . You may belong to any religion or caste or creed—that has nothing to do with the business of the State."[6] This vision is still close to the hearts of Pakistan's bureaucratic elites, some of its leading politicians, and other influential people—those whom Americans refer to as "secular." Most of the civilians and many of the military negotiators the United States deals with are in this group.

A competing concept is favored by the Islamic religious parties, which have long pushed for Pakistan to adopt an explicitly Islamic religious and legal framework. But Pakistan's Sunni majority includes followers of several different schools of Islamic jurisprudence, as well as several different Islamic religious movements that frequently disagree over important elements of religious practice and the role of Islam in the state. In addition, there is a Shia population of about 20 percent.[7] Pakistani governments under political pressure have on several occasions introduced proposals for extending sharia law. Zulfiqar Ali Bhutto introduced prohibition when he was on the ropes in 1977, and Nawaz Sharif introduced an Islamic law bill in 1991. Such proposals tend to divide the religious political constituencies rather than unite them behind the new legislation, because of uncertainty about how the legislation would treat the different Islamic constituencies. However, it is politically risky to oppose such proposals, or indeed to do or say anything that criticizes Islamic way of life.[8] The Urdu language makes it hard to argue for a religiously neutral view of the state. The usual Urdu rendering of "secular" is a term that literally translates as "unreligious," with highly negative connotations of "un-Islamic."

This helps to explain the political paralysis that initially greeted the attempted takeover in Swat and other areas by the Pakistani Taliban movement in 2007–09. It also helps to explain the acute anxiety that occurs whenever Washington tries to persuade Islamabad to take vigorous action against extremist Islamic groups in Pakistan. Quite apart from the fear induced by the murderous tactics of the Pakistani Taliban, political leaders, officials, and military leaders alike shrink from publicly criticizing devout Muslims who

---

6. Muhammad Ali Jinnah, presidential address to the Constituent Assembly, Karachi, August 11, 1947, www.insaf.pk/Media/InsafBlog/tabid/168/articleType/ArticleView/articleId/1553/Mr-Jinnahs-presidential-address-to-the-Constituent-Assembly-of-Pakistan-August-1947.aspx#.

7. CIA, "Pakistan," *The World Factbook*, June 1, 2009, June 19, 2009, https://www.cia.gov/library/publications/the-world-factbook/geos/pk.html.

8. Farzana Shaikh, *Making Sense of Pakistan* (London: Hurst, 2009), is a particularly good discussion of the historical roots and current ramifications of the problem of Pakistan's multiple identities.

claim only to want Islamic law. This reluctance has been heightened in recent years by concern on the part of those who oppose the Taliban and other Islamic extremists about being branded pro-American.

In foreign policy, Pakistan has looked for political support from Arab countries and economic support from the wealthier of them in its efforts to counterbalance Indian superiority. Not all its relations with Muslim countries are harmonious: besides its "neighbor problems" with Afghanistan, Pakistan has had serious differences over the years with Iraq, which it regarded as pro-Indian, and with Iran, which it accuses of fomenting sectarian violence by patronizing Shia activists inside Pakistan. It seeks to play a leading role in international Muslim organizations. An important example is the Organization of the Islamic Conference, which Pakistan periodically tries to use to provide international endorsement for its grievances against India, especially over Kashmir. Muslim countries that have opposed such moves, as Iran did some years ago, have seriously complicated their relations with Pakistan. After the dissolution of the Soviet Union, Pakistan sought to develop close economic and political relations with the newly independent Muslim states of Central Asia, with mixed results.

Pakistanis almost viscerally support Muslims in their struggle against Christians and Jews in contested areas such as Palestine, Bosnia, and the Caucasus. After India established warm relations with Israel in the early 1990s, some Pakistanis charged that a sinister Washington–New Delhi–Jerusalem axis (a "Christian-Hindu-Jewish cabal") threatens Pakistan and Islam. Musharraf drew raised eyebrows at home when his foreign minister had what was described as a spontaneous, chance encounter at the United Nations with his Israeli counterpart in September 2005. Many Pakistanis believed that this was a blatant effort to curry favor with Washington; in any case, it sank without a trace.

More broadly, most Pakistanis are convinced that Westerners, and especially the United States, are hostile to Islam and Muslim aspirations. In surveys taken in 2007 and 2009, 73 and 74 percent respectively of respondents in Pakistan said they believed that it was a U.S. goal to "weaken and divide" the Muslim world.[9] Both polling and anecdotal evidence suggests that these views are widely shared across the political and economic spectrum.

---

9. Stephen Kull, "Muslim Public Opinion on US Policy, Attacks on Civilians and al Qaeda," *World Public Opinion*, April 24, 2007, www.worldpublicopinion.org/pipa/pdf/apr07/START_Apr07_rpt.pdf; Steven Kull, Clay Ramsay, Stephen Weber, Evan Lewis, and Ebrahim Mohseni, "Public Opinion in the Islamic World on Terrorism, al Qaeda, and US Policies," *World Public Opinion*, February 25, 2009, www.worldpublicopinion.org/pipa/pdf/feb09/STARTII_Feb09_rpt.pdf.

Close U.S. relations with Israel and the perception that U.S. policy is anti-Palestinian is probably the single most powerful factor behind this perception. Pakistan governments friendly to the United States are acutely aware of this and have urged American leaders to adopt a more neutral position on the Arab-Israel dispute. Americans who lived in Pakistan in the 1970s found consciousness of the Islamic factor, and of the Palestinians as the symbol of a perceived U.S. anti-Muslim stance, much less powerful then than it is today. The "hot button" issues that have raised anti-Western outrage in the Muslim world in recent years, such as the issue of cartoons that satirized the Prophet Muhammad, have had huge emotional resonance in Pakistan. The same is true, with far greater impact on the United States, of reports of prisoner abuse at Abu Ghraib and Guantánamo. As will be shown in the next chapter, these beliefs feed into a Pakistani predisposition to believe that the world is conspiring against them, individually and nationally.

Even if Pakistanis do not agree on exactly what their Islamic identity means and which of their identities should take priority, their perceptions of U.S. attitudes toward Islam reinforce the sense of "us and them" in the U.S.-Pakistan negotiating setting. This attitude also heightens the suspicion that is always an undercurrent in U.S.-Pakistan negotiations, even when both countries are trying to build an enduring relationship on the premise of important shared strategic interests. In a nutshell, Pakistan's Muslim identity, its friendship with China, and its misgivings about Afghanistan all in the end come back to the two main themes that dominate the Pakistani negotiator's view of the world: the danger from India and the unreliability of the United States.

3

Between Pakistani and
Cosmopolitan Cultures

U.S. government officials making their first official call on a senior
Pakistani government official are often struck less by the differences
from the officials they meet at home than by the similarities. Senior
officials usually speak excellent English, are quite familiar with American
idiom, may have studied in the United States, and often have relatives living
there. They move easily in the international diplomatic cultural environment,
and specifically in the English-speaking West. This sense of common membership in a global elite is even stronger when U.S. and Pakistani officials
meet outside Pakistan. This cultural comfort with Americans coexists with
considerable political distrust.

Despite this shared professional idiom, Pakistani officials' dealings with
their American counterparts are shaped by the culture in which they are
rooted. This chapter looks at Pakistan's national cultural characteristics and
how they color interactions with Americans. The view of history, of Pakistan's place in the world, and of the United States described in the preceding
chapters tells us how Pakistani officials see themselves; the cultural prism
colors how they express themselves.

The role of culture in diplomacy in general and negotiations in particular
is the subject of a rich literature, including earlier volumes in this series.
The definition of culture this study uses was succinctly expressed by Tamara
Cofman Wittes in *How Israelis and Palestinians Negotiate*: "the product of
the experiences of individuals within a given social group, including its representations in images, narratives, myths, and patterns of behavior (traditions), and the meanings of those representations as transmitted among the

group's members over time and through experience."[1] Raymond Cohen, in *Negotiating across Cultures,* distinguishes three salient features of culture: it is a quality not of individuals but of society; it is acquired by individuals from their society; and each culture is a unique complex of attributes subsuming every area of social life.[2]

In the terminology used in the literature on cross-cultural negotiations, Pakistan is a high-context society, more attuned to the rights and obligations of the group than to those of the individual. It is a society in which honor is all-important and hospitality a solemn obligation. Many of the classic points of friction with the more individualistic and task-oriented approach of most U.S. officials crop up in U.S.-Pakistani negotiations, sometimes significantly modified by the geostrategic context and government structure within which Pakistan's negotiators operate.[3]

The Social Web

Pakistanis live in a world in which the most important relationships are personal. Who you are starts with your family, its regional and social roots, and its network of relations, friends, and adversaries. The languages of Pakistan have a highly differentiated set of terms for family relationships: "maternal uncle" and "paternal uncle" are different words, and in some cases older and younger relatives are addressed by different terms. Close friends are often referred to by family names. To be allowed to call someone "brother" is a mark of intimacy. (This can be confusing to Americans: despite the complex array of words used to describe family relationships in the languages of Pakistan, "brother" is a highly elastic term. Cousins may be referred to as "cousin brother," or just "brother" for short.)

This is a hierarchical world: the family patriarch is at the top of the pyramid, and an elder brother remains "senior" for life. In the world of politics, for example, former prime minister Nawaz Sharif was always very deferential to his father. Among the sons, it is commonly accepted that the younger brother, Shahbaz Sharif, is cleverer and more decisive than his elder brother, Nawaz. Nonetheless, it is the elder brother who became prime minister twice during the 1990s, and the political turbulence since then has not upset

---

1. Tamara Cofman Wittes, ed., *How Israelis and Palestinians Negotiate* (Washington, DC: United States Institute of Peace Press, 2005), 4.

2. Raymond Cohen, *Negotiating across Cultures: International Communication in an Interdependent World* (Washington, DC: United States Institute of Peace Press, 2004), 11.

3. For an especially lucid discussion of "high-context" and "low-context" negotiating styles, see ibid., 25–43.

this pecking order. The patriarch—the Sharif brothers' father—was said to insist on maintaining the proper order, with the elder son in first place. In traditional households, older siblings marry before their juniors are allowed to. Many Pakistanis will identify someone not as "my brother" but as "my elder brother." ·

This hierarchical structure affects family obligations. Even when circumstances get in the way, as they often do in today's highly mobile middle-class and elite families, growing numbers of whom have come to live in the United States, the old ways represent the standard for culturally approved behavior. As in many other countries, family obligations take precedence over many work obligations, and especially over social events. This is especially true for women, who may be expected to take off on a moment's notice to attend an ailing relative or a daughter who has just had a baby.

Relationships with people up and down the power structure take on some of the qualities of this family hierarchy. As in many countries, rural life in Pakistan rests on a web of obligations, traditional and financial. Most of the senior officials who negotiate with the United States grew up in an urban or semiurban setting, but social patterns that characterize rural life remain at least as theoretical social norms in towns and cities.

In urban as well as rural Pakistan, older relatives and especially close friends may be referred to as "uncle" or "auntie." The "uncles" and "aunties" may reciprocate by calling that person "son" or "daughter," both used as terms of affection and intimacy. During Benazir Bhutto's first stint as prime minister in the early 1990s, it was said that she had surrounded herself with veterans of her father's government—but not with those senior enough to be allowed to call her "daughter."

Foreign countries and officials do not fit directly into this social structure, but it affects their interactions with Pakistanis in two ways. At the national level, Pakistanis dealing with the United States treat their countries' power disparity as very loosely analogous to unequal social relationships in Pakistani society. Pakistani leaders and officials are acutely conscious of being the weaker power. General K. M. Arif, one of President Zia's closest colleagues, has emphasized this point: "Pakistan is a developing country. The United States is a superpower. A measure of inequality and unfulfilled expectations is a built-in element of the unequal relations between them. At times, the undercurrents of this reality have created avoidable acrimony and bitterness in the relationship."[4]

---

4. General K. M. Arif, *Working with Zia: Pakistan's Power Politics 1977–1988* (Karachi: Oxford University Press, 1995), 343.

As may happen in social relationships among unequals in Pakistan, Pakistani negotiators sometimes try to emphasize their dependence. In parts of rural Pakistan, a supplicant will touch the feet of someone from whom he needs a favor, reinforcing the relationship of dependency within the traditional system of power and patronage. In less dramatic fashion, a Pakistani from a small town or the rural areas may approach a negotiation in a shop by emphasizing his modest means. International negotiations do not begin to approach this degree of self-abasement, but the oft-heard reminders to Americans of how much Pakistan depends on the United States recall this pattern.[5]

Weakness, Strength, Respect, and Honor

Pakistani negotiators' consciousness of weakness coexists with a well-developed national pride and honor. This expresses itself in different ways, as the discussion of the different styles of military and civilian officials in the following chapters will show. As the weaker party in an asymmetrical negotiation, Pakistanis also try to turn their weakness into strength. The classic example was the argument, often heard during the Musharraf years when the United States and Pakistan were arguing and collaborating over control of the border with Afghanistan, that too much U.S. pressure would push Pakistan over a cliff, with devastating results for the United States.

Insisting on the respect due Pakistan as a nation, and its representatives personally, is a constant. Perhaps the clearest example is the bitter criticism national leaders and government officials face when they are believed to have given away the country's respect or honor too easily. Musharraf's speech explaining his decision to join the U.S.-led "war on terror" after 9/11 drew particularly bitter fire from columnist Ayaz Amir, who repeatedly attacked him for simply rolling over and giving in to U.S. demands without asking enough in return.[6]

While officials and commentators alike are uniformly sensitive to questions of respect, there is less agreement on how best to preserve respect for Pakistan. Pakistanis are far less protocol conscious than some other honor-oriented societies. Pakistani national leaders give U.S. visitors remarkable

---

5. This section draws on the authors' own experience and their interviews with Lt. Gen. (ret.) Javed Hassan, Prof. Riffaat Hussein, Mushahid Hussein, Prof. Anita Weiss, Prof. Paula Newberg, and Wendy Chamberlin.

6. A particularly good example is Ayaz Amir, "Friends with America," *Dawn*, March 18, 2005, www.dawn.com/weekly/ayaz/20050318.htm. See also Ejaz Haider, "Holbrooke's Courtiers," *Daily Times*, June 7, 2009, www.dailytimes.com.pk/default.asp?page+2009\06\07\story_7--6-2009_pg3_3.

access and make themselves available to a parade of visitors from the U.S. executive branch, military, and Congress.

By the same token, Pakistanis working in Washington or visiting there are stung by the relative inaccessibility of members of Congress and other senior Americans. They find it personally and nationally insulting when visiting parliamentarians, Supreme Court justices, and other senior personalities are unable to get "face time" with their American counterparts. Most galling of all is the difficulty of getting top U.S. officials to attend social functions on behalf of their visiting Pakistani opposite numbers.

The relatively open style of communication that is prized in the United States can come across as disrespectful. The kinds of criticism, implicit or explicit, that are standard fare in congressional hearings leave Pakistanis feeling bruised. Often, it comes back to the comparison with India: any action in which the United States appears to take India more seriously than Pakistan will appear in Pakistan as a lack of respect for Pakistan.[7]

Friendship—Personal and National

The personal relationships, primarily family ties, and secondarily connections of friendship on which Pakistani society runs, go back into childhood or into the formative years of a person's professional life. The bond between high school classmates, class fellows at military academy, or "batchmates" in the foreign service and civil service—people who were members of the same basic training class—is powerful and enduring. The extent and intensity of personal relationships between Pakistani officials and their American counterparts differ widely. The substance of negotiations will still be driven by national positions, but when U.S. negotiators are able to build personal ties with their Pakistani counterparts, this can greatly facilitate the negotiating process.

Exchanging chitchat about families, education, social background, and the like is a valuable step an American official can take to give Pakistani counterparts a sense of who he or she is. The stereotype that Americans are rootless and not especially attached to their families is widely believed. Americans who are comfortable talking about their family ties and their attachment to U.S. traditions and hometowns may find their counterparts more willing to listen to them on other issues as well. Pakistanis appreciate it when Americans have traveled in the less well-known parts of Pakistan and can relate to their hometowns. For officials stationed in Pakistan, learning

---

7. This section draws on the authors' personal experience and on interviews with Richard Armitage, Riaz Khokhar, Abida Hussein, and Robin Raphel.

some Urdu is a good way to show that one cares about Pakistan. A common hobby or avocation may provide the informal setting for a personal relationship. Former diplomatic officials on both sides have spoken warmly of their "tennis diplomacy" or hunting trips. At the same time, Pakistani officials like to put their negotiations in the context of their view of Pakistan's complicated relations with India and the United States, a task which they find easier when dealing with officials who are relatively new to the area—especially those who do not have extensive prior experience in India.

Pakistani leaders have generally tried to build a personal equation with key Americans. Absent confidence in the staying power of the United States, a personal relationship may seem a stronger anchor for U.S. support to Pakistan than an institutional or impersonal tie. Pakistan's national leaders usually try to put their relations with the U.S. president on a personal footing, with uneven results. But in many cases, they do achieve at least one key personal bond with an American official. President Zia's closeness to Ambassador Arnold Raphel, for example, went back over ten years to Raphel's service as a political officer in the U.S. embassy in Islamabad.

Often, both Pakistani and American leaders personalize U.S.-Pakistan relations. The connection between Presidents Pervez Musharraf and George W. Bush is a good example of this phenomenon. Even after Musharraf's power ebbed following a series of political missteps in 2007, the appearance of a close personal tie between him and President Bush encouraged others in the Bush administration to treat him as the one essential player in Pakistan's turbulent political mix. Following the election of February 2008, in which Musharraf's party was badly beaten, President Bush telephoned Musharraf (and not the two political leaders whose parties had been more successful), reinforcing the impression that their personal tie would ultimately rescue Musharraf from his political travails. In the end, the political forces in Pakistan took their own path, and Musharraf was forced to leave the presidency six months after the election. President Bush, despite his highly personal approach to relations with Pakistan over the preceding seven years, did not prevent this from happening. Nor could he have.

Personal relationships are tremendously valuable for doing long-term business in Pakistan, but making a relationship personal and not just official also creates expectations on both sides that can lead to disappointment. Pakistanis will expect their friendship to be matched by help for Pakistan (or sometimes for themselves). It is unseemly or worse to question a friend's actions or motives, so criticism from U.S. officials, especially in public, is wounding. One retired Pakistani diplomat commented that in Urdu literature, stories about close friends treat them as something like sweethearts. Against this background, policy differences may be cast as betrayals of personal friendship. The hurt feelings engendered by this kind of difference are real, but they can also be played up in order to intensify the American official's sense of obligation.

Americans do not necessarily expect favors from their personal friends, but they do expect honesty, even on difficult subjects. In relations between Pakistanis and Americans, this can lead to miscommunications on both sides. What Americans regard as bluntness, candor, or honesty may come across to Pakistanis as rudeness, disrespect, or unfriendliness. There are times when "full and frank discussions" are important, but they require careful thought and considerable skill. On the other side, what Pakistanis regard as delicacy or strategically necessary deception may strike their American interlocutors as fundamental dishonesty, calling into question the validity of the rest of their relationship. One retired American official recalled an occasion when President Zia spent several hours in private conversation with Ambassador Raphel, and never mentioned that he was planning to fire the prime minister. When Zia took this action the next day, Raphel was shocked and upset, a reaction that Zia clearly never expected.

The emphasis on personal relationships has led generations of Pakistani officials to continue cultivating American friends who were no longer in power. This has earned them tremendous personal loyalty from Americans whom they received like visiting royalty when other countries treated them like has-beens. The classic example is Richard Nixon, who was given a spectacular welcome in Pakistan in 1967 when he was out of office and seemed to have little prospect of returning to a position of power. At his previous stop, in New Delhi, the Indians had paid him scant attention. When he did return to the White House, Nixon returned the favor. His famous "tilt" toward Pakistan and cutoff of aid to India in 1971, during the war that eventually led to the splitting of Pakistan and the birth of independent Bangladesh, had a strategic purpose. But it almost certainly also reflected Nixon's appreciation for his warm reception when he was in the political wilderness. More to the point, his Pakistani hosts believed that their loyalty to him in times of misfortune was both good behavior by a friend and a good strategic investment.

Pakistani officials' view of national relationships can take on some of the coloration they give to personal ties. Retired officials, both civilian and military, are careful to state that national relations, unlike personal friendships, are driven by basic interests rather than by a web of social obligations. At the same time, a widely heard lament about U.S.-Pakistan relations is that the United States treats them as "transactional," or bound up in a series of quid pro quos (conditions on military supply, for example, or favors given or promised in return for cooperation against the Taliban insurgency). Pakistanis contrast this with a "true friendship," in which no such specific conditions are negotiated, a description that many Pakistani officials would apply to their ties with China. Interestingly, several former American officials described Pakistan's approach as transactional, suggesting that both Pakistanis and Americans may expect an unrealistic level of political selflessness.[8]

Hospitality

Pakistan's is a hospitality culture. The obligation of a host toward a guest is strongest and most famous in Khyber Pakhtunkhwa, formerly known as North-West Frontier Province, and especially in the areas where tribal and clan culture is still strong. In its tribal version, a guest is entitled to *melmastia*, not just a gracious reception but sanctuary and protection against external enemies.

Hospitality does not always place such heavy requirements on the host, but it is a critical element in social relations everywhere in the country. Offering a visitor something to eat and drink is a requirement; not to do so is insulting. The sequence of food and drink follows the pace of the meeting. In a high-level meeting, the visitor may be offered juice first, then sandwiches and savories, then sweets, and finally tea. If all the "courses" arrive quickly, it probably means the host is in a hurry. The guest is expected to nibble but need not sample, or finish, everything. The tradition of *melmastia* means that an affront suffered while one is a guest weighs especially heavily.

The more restricted American practice for entertaining official visitors can be jarring to Pakistanis. The fact that many offices in the United States do not routinely offer coffee or tea to visitors is unsettling even for Pakistanis experienced in the ways of Washington. Pakistanis keep track of the Americans who are assigned to receive major visitors, and whether and by whom they are received for a meal. Musharraf's reception by four U.S. cabinet officers when he dropped into Washington with very little notice on a weekend in late 2004 was taken in Pakistan as an indication of the strength of his ties

---

8. This section draws on the authors' personal experiences and interviews with Richard Armitage, Matthew Daley, Shahryar Khan, Lt. Gen. (ret.) Javed Hassan, Abdul Sattar, Wendy Chamberlin, Christine Fair, Daniel Markey, Col. (ret.) John Gill, William Milam, Col. (ret.) David Smith, Milton Bearden, Col. (ret.) Woolf Gross, and Shuja Nawaz.

to the Bush administration.[9] Keeping book on the social schedule extends to opposition politicians as well. During the 1990s, when Nawaz Sharif and Benazir Bhutto alternated stints as prime minister and as opposition leader, they went to some effort to one-up each other, trying to obtain a higher-ranking reception as opposition leader than their rival had received.[10]

Guests have obligations too. Pakistanis will generally bring a gift when going to someone's house for a meal; arriving *khali haath*—empty-handed—is a source of shame. Pakistani officials understand that American customs are different, but they appreciate it when American visitors show appreciation for their hospitality.

Conspiracies and Truth Telling

Conspiracies abound in the cultural world of Pakistan. Americans are generally attracted to the simplest and most straightforward explanation of events—the straight line connecting two points. Oftentimes, Pakistanis find complex and conspiratorial explanations more convincing. Family and political feuds are not unusual in Pakistan, and this pattern of social relationships lends credence to the broader assumption that life is played out as a series of plots and subplots with complex and sinister twists and turns. It is instructive that the word for "conspiracy" appears in an early lesson in materials that were in use for many years to teach Urdu to foreign students.[11]

This turn of mind affects the way Pakistanis interpret the process of negotiations as well. An American may explain U.S. inability to satisfy some Pakistani request on the basis of bureaucratic procedures or legal obstacles: the U.S. system, for reasons that have nothing to do with Pakistan, is simply not set up to grant the request. Seen from the Pakistani perspective, however, this may "prove" that the U.S. government is carrying out a larger policy of keeping Pakistan down, perhaps as part of a conspiracy in which the country's enemies (or the government's political opponents) are involved.

Reinforcing the tendency to look for conspiracies is a widespread desire to blame others, outside of Pakistan, for Pakistan's difficulties. Pakistan does

---

9. David Sanger, "In Meeting with Musharraf, Bush Praises Pakistani Troops," *New York Times*, December 5, 2004, www.nytimes.com/2004/12/05/international/asia/05pakistan.html?scp=1&sq=dece mber+5+2004+musharraf&st=nyt, and "Bush Tells Musharraf He'll Focus on Palestinian State," *Daily Times* (Lahore), December 5, 2004, www.dailytimes.com.pk/default.asp?page=story_5-12-2004_pg1_1.

10. Teresita Schaffer's experience as deputy assistant secretary of state.

11. One former U.S. official with long experience in Pakistan and the Middle East commented that Pakistanis' propensity to see conspiracies put them roughly in the same league with Egyptians and Jordanians, but slightly below Syrians, and nowhere near the Lebanese or the Iranians.

not have a culture of public repentance or acceptance of responsibility for errors. Setbacks are typically followed by pointing fingers at others. After its military reverses, the army has not engaged in the kind of "lessons-learned" exercise that is sometimes carried out elsewhere. The internal reviews conducted by the army after its devastating defeat in 1971 were never publicly released, nor were military officers disciplined for their role in the defeat.

Accountability efforts following a change in government have focused entirely on the people who just lost power. There has been no "truth and reconciliation commission" or similar mechanism. Because Pakistan has been ruled by the army for over half its independent existence and because the army's major actions have ended badly—the war Pakistan initiated in 1965, for example, ended without the change in the status quo that Pakistan sought, and the war in 1971 ended with Pakistan cut in half—the country's strongest and proudest institution has been a powerful force for avoiding painful introspection in public life. Pakistanis, especially military officers, tend to be very sensitive about foreigners bringing up these events.

This tendency to shift responsibility for Pakistan's mistakes can inhibit policy dialogue outside the military sphere as well. For all the skill and sophistication of Pakistan's financial officials, it is all but impossible to have a candid discussion on the economic consequences of Pakistan's badly skewed revenue system, for example, or on the impact of Pakistan's concentrated patterns of land ownership.

Because the United States is seen as extraordinarily powerful, both in general and in relation to Pakistan's political life, many prevalent theories of who is to blame cast the United States in the role of chief conspirator. Conspiracy theories can achieve wide public resonance, making it more difficult for the government to disregard them. The proposition that the 9/11 attacks must have been carried out by Jews because Jewish employees at the World Trade Center "all escaped death" was retailed by astonishingly senior and sophisticated officials.[12] Later, in the spring of 2009, anecdotal information suggested that large sections of the public believed that the United States was engaged in a conspiracy to break up Pakistan, and was even involved in fomenting the Taliban attacks that convulsed the country. The fact that the Taliban were clearly described as an enemy by one American after another did little to dilute the power of this myth. The myth also persisted in spite of

---

12. Michael Schaffer, who was a correspondent for *U.S. News and World Report* reporting from Pakistan in the fall and winter of 2001, recalled having heard this story seriously advanced in private conversations by Brigadier Rashid Qureshi, then spokesman for the army.

a nearly universal practice of referring to the campaign against the Taliban as "America's war."

Americans dealing with this kind of situation usually repeat their own (nonconspiratorial) description of what the United States is doing and why. This has limited impact. Given Pakistanis' view of the dangerous and unreliable role the United States has played in their country, what sound to Americans like outlandish theories have a level of credibility that resists mere contradiction.

Pakistani analysts note that Islam permits the use of lying and deception when these are essential for the defense of the Muslim people. According to former secretary of state George Shultz, Zia specifically said as much to President Reagan.[13] Pakistanis assume that Americans will follow the same practice. One person who served in the State Department during the 1980s recalled having been told by Pakistani officials he knew well that since Pakistani officials were lying about Pakistan's role in Afghanistan, they expected their American counterparts to lie about the existence of Pakistan's nuclear program.[14]

American officials have observed that in both matters of state and the ordinary transactions of daily life, there is a strong tendency to tell an interlocutor, especially a powerful one, what he or she wants to hear. As Ronald Spiers, who was U.S. ambassador to Pakistan in the early 1980s, argued in an oral history interview, "The culture of the subcontinent makes it impolite to tell someone the truth if it offends them or makes them uncomfortable." He found an example in his dealings with a launderer. "If you send something to the launderer and he knows that you want it back the next day, he will tell you that it will be done although he knows full well that it is impossible. For Pakistanis, that is not a lie, it is politeness."[15]

This blurry line between honesty and providing the desired answer may help account for the fact that Pakistani officials seem to be comfortable with deception and selective information in their dealings with the United

---

13. George Shultz, *Turmoil and Triumph* (New York: Scribner's, 1993), 1091. The occasion was a telephone conversation between the two presidents about the impending Geneva Accord that provided for Soviet withdrawal from Afghanistan. "I heard the president ask Zia how he would handle the fact that they [Pakistanis] would be violating the agreement [by continuing to allow Pakistan to act as a conduit for the flow of arms to the Afghans against the Communists]. Zia replied that they would 'just lie about it. We've been denying our activities there for eight years.' Then, the president recounted, Zia told him that 'Muslims have the right to lie in a good cause.'"

14. Authors' correspondence with Stephen Cohen, September 2009.

15. Ronald Spiers, oral history statement, Association of Diplomatic Studies and Training, November 11, 1991, http://memory.loc.gov/cgi-bin/query/S?ammem/mfdipbib:@field(AUTHOR+@od1(Spiers,+Ronald+I+,+1925-)).

States. For American officials, the lesson is that they should not assume that Pakistani counterparts will provide what Americans would consider to be all the important facts, especially in times of tension.[16]

Time and Continuity

U.S. officials are usually in a hurry. They have deadlines imposed by travel schedules, by their bosses' demands for information, or by Congress. They are usually locked into schedules when they visit Pakistan. This allows little time to get to know their counterparts or to deal with surprises. For Pakistanis, speedy performance seldom has the same urgency as it does for Americans. This is especially true when negotiating complex instruments that require interagency clearance in both governments. Pakistanis do not take well to being rushed, and explanations about the time lines built into the U.S. bureaucratic or congressional process have little impact (or, worse, either feed resentment of overbearing American habits or are regarded as a negotiating ploy). On the other hand, Pakistanis have been known to use deadlines as an argument when dealing with Americans—and they have found Americans more responsive to this treatment than Pakistanis are.

Most Pakistanis working in Washington adapt to the greater expectation of punctuality, and former ambassadors talk about how they made it a point to distill their talking points down to the bare minimum, to ensure that their main concerns would get across. The standard program for state visits to Washington, for example, gives leading U.S. figures little time with their guests. Unless some special arrangements are made—as was done, for example, when President George W. Bush invited Musharraf to his ranch in Crawford, Texas—this can leave visitors feeling hustled rather than graciously received.

Another dimension of punctuality comes up most often when one is dealing with politicians. In Pakistan, the person who arrives last at a social function or appointment is positioning him- or herself as the most important person there. Americans visiting a politician's constituency, for example, are sometimes baffled to observe that their host seems to be delaying their departure for a planned event. Especially for a politician on his home turf, it is important to ensure that other members of the local power structure are in place before one arrives, so as to preserve one's own high standing in the

---

16. This section draws on the authors' personal experiences and on interviews with Col. (ret.) John Gill, Col. (ret.) David Smith, Lt. Gen. (ret.) David Barno, Mushahid Hussein, Milton Bearden, Polly Nayak, and Ryan Crocker.

pecking order. This can cause anxious moments at social events for Americans visiting Pakistan or, more rarely, for Pakistanis visiting Washington.

Pakistan's basic foreign policy priorities have remained remarkably stable since the country became independent. This contributes to a longer-term perspective about their dealings with the United States than is typical of the way U.S. officials think about Pakistan. Pakistani officials have been trying for six decades to line up reliable outside supporters to balance India. Any given negotiation with the United States fits into this long-term goal.

Memories are long, too. The roller coaster pattern of U.S.-Pakistan relations leads Pakistani officials to be skeptical of the lasting value of what they are negotiating. As one observer put it, Pakistanis have the sense that "the United States is looking for a flirtation rather than a *nikah* [a marriage contract]."[17] This paradoxically reinforces Pakistan's tendency to look for short-term gains. Officials convinced that there will be a third "divorce" want to ensure that Pakistan reaps whatever benefits it can before then.

In a society that runs on personal relations, Pakistanis remember who their friends are—and who has been unsympathetic. The U.S. pattern of rotating officials every few years carries a cost. This has been especially true in the post-9/11 period, when officials serving in the U.S. embassy and consulates in Pakistan often stay only for one year. It is these officials who under normal circumstances would have the primary personal relationships with their Pakistani counterparts. When officials assigned in Pakistan do not have the opportunity to develop real relationships, or to learn much about the country and its ways, U.S.-Pakistani negotiations are more vulnerable to misunderstandings and stereotyping.[18] The U.S. government needs to find a way to keep its key officials in Pakistan for longer tours of duty.

The Press and Sources of Information

Pakistan's English-language press is widely accessible to Americans. The Internet versions of major newspapers are well edited and attractively displayed. At least since the 1990s, the English-language press has been remarkably free to publish opinions critical of the political leadership (although less free to criticize the military). This openness reflects the kind of cosmopolitanism that is current among Pakistan's English-speaking elites. This does not make

17. Mushahid Hussein, conversation with authors.

18. This section draws on interviews with Patricia Haslach and Andrew Haviland, Wendy Chamberlin, Col. (ret.) David Smith, Walter Andersen, Mushahid Hussein, Maleeha Lodhi, Riaz Khokhar, and Shuja Nawaz.

it pro-American—indeed, the United States is a favorite whipping boy—but it means that some of the more colorful preconceptions about the world and the United States that many Pakistanis hold are not often expressed there.

The vernacular press and electronic media, which have a much wider audience, offer a different narrative of Pakistani political life and the United States' role in it. Criticism of the army in the vernacular media is dealt with more harshly than in their English counterparts. More important, the vernacular media give full cry to flamboyant conspiracy theories about what the United States represents and what it is trying to do in Pakistan. Similarly, vernacular news outlets are typically far more emotively hard-line against India. Because these sources are not readily available in translation or on the Internet and are rarely cited by American journalists covering Pakistan, Americans may find it difficult to relate to the emotional climate they are dealing with in Pakistan. This probably contributes to a tendency by Pakistani officials to assume that their American counterparts are uninformed about Pakistani public opinion. They may also assume that American officials will not notice some of the more offensive statements figures like Abdul Qadeer Khan, the scientist responsible for making Pakistani nuclear technology available to North Korea and Libya, have made in the vernacular press.

At the same time, Pakistani officials will cite stories in the vernacular press to argue why Islamabad cannot do something that Washington wants. It is hard for their American counterparts to contest these arguments unless they have read these Urdu accounts themselves or been provided them in English translation, both unlikely.

Whose Rules Apply?

Pakistani negotiators are often willing to structure negotiations in the way that their interlocutors suggest, in contrast to officials of some other countries who have a strong predisposition to insist on their own practices and venues.[19] A number of current and former Pakistani officials commented that they did not have strong views about whether negotiations should take place in the United States or in Pakistan. If Pakistan was expected to make important decisions, some officials felt it was more effective to hold meetings in Islamabad. But for most negotiations, Pakistani officials justifiably pride themselves on being able to operate in the U.S. cultural milieu, and

---

19. China is a particularly telling example. See Richard H. Solomon, *Chinese Negotiating Behavior: Pursuing Interests through Old Friends* (Washington, DC: United States Institute of Peace Press, 1999). The theme of the importance of "Chineseness" in China's negotiating style runs through the whole argument of the book.

indeed, many welcome the chance to travel, visit with U.S.-based relatives, and spend time in the United States.

In one respect, foreign interlocutors' "rules" almost always apply: Pakistani central government officials conduct all their business with Americans in English. Civil servants and military officers all speak English well enough to carry on a reasonably sophisticated conversation and in most cases well enough to conduct detailed and subtle negotiations. Many members of the Pakistani elite grew up speaking English along with one or two of the vernacular languages, and some of them have done so much of their schooling in English that it has become a more comfortable medium for professional discourse than the vernacular. For those Americans who speak some Urdu, it is a much appreciated icebreaker and an excellent way to convey respect for Pakistan and for its culture. To attempt to use it as the language of negotiations, however, would be tricky, and could be interpreted as belittling Pakistani officials' English.

Some politicians, and military and civil service officers from less prominent family backgrounds, are less comfortable in English but nonetheless expect to use it for all their contacts with Americans. Using an interpreter would involve a serious loss of face. Changes in recruitment patterns since about 1990 have increased the number of military officers in this category. If future political developments in Pakistan give greater prominence to regional politicians who are less confident of their English, the language issue may become more of a factor in U.S.-Pakistan relations. This would especially be the case in dealing with politicians who are less comfortable in Urdu than in other vernacular languages, such as the leaders of some of the religious parties, discussed more fully in chapter 6.

One experienced Pakistani analyst has suggested that commitments given in English are somehow regarded as less binding than those given in the vernacular. This may apply chiefly to those whose English is weaker or more recently acquired. In practice, the only way to address this is by being clear and specific about what is being agreed to.[20]

A Bazaar Culture, with an Elite Overlay

Bargaining is the norm when shopping in the bazaars in Pakistan. However, this is not a culture in which the art and sport of bargaining is half the fun.

---

20. This section draws on the authors' experience and on their interviews with Touqir Hussain, Tariq Fatemi, Riaz Khokhar, and Shuja Nawaz.

When Pakistanis bargain, they are looking for a good deal, but do not necessarily need to have a full dose of drama with it.

Most bargaining in Pakistani society takes place inside the web of social and power relationships that govern the rest of life. As in any bargaining culture, the normal rules of the game call for an initial offer which is too low (or high, depending on whether one is buying or selling) to be accepted. There is no implicit "standard playbook" that guides the rest of the process. In a bazaar encounter, bargaining can proceed by small increments or larger steps, and may or may not be punctuated by having the buyer walk out of the store. The buyer, playing up his position as the social inferior of the seller, may stress that "I am a poor man"—suggesting that the seller has an obligation to be generous.

Occasionally, however, the seller will refuse to name a price, and will simply say "whatever you think is right." This may happen, for example, when the transaction is between social unequals who have just begun to establish a personal relationship. This tactic once again is intended to create, and play on, a social obligation. It also follows the classic negotiator's dictum that whoever names his price first is at a disadvantage.

These bargaining patterns show up at the international level as well. Relatively technical negotiations—military supply contracts where the basic quantity of major items is fixed but ancillary details like spare parts are negotiable, for example, or the particulars of aid agreements—will usually proceed in fairly straightforward fashion, with both sides putting on the table starting offers that give very little away, and working out the details over a series of meetings. One important feature of the bazaar that figures in this type of negotiations is that a negotiator needs to be confident—and to persuade his own government—that he has gotten a good deal. The United States, in other words, needs to have some "give" in its starting position.

When the issue being negotiated touches the core of U.S.-Pakistan relations, however, the Pakistani side may simply wait for the United States to put its position on the table first. This generally indicates that the Pakistani side is trying to figure out how serious a commitment the United States is prepared to make, and that it is looking for something beyond a monetary figure. This was the case in the negotiations described in chapter 7, which set the terms of reference for U.S.-Pakistan relations after the Soviet invasion of Afghanistan and after 9/11. This approach is intended to maximize the sense of obligation felt by the United States. Once the basic agreement has been reached—in these two cases, once the Pakistani leaders decided that the United States was putting a serious relationship on the table—the rest of the process of negotiating the terms of engagement may go astonishingly quickly, as happened in 2001.

In a negotiation in which one side is asking for a favor, it matters how that request is conveyed. In traditional Pakistani society, for example, one does not send a younger son to ask an important or difficult favor of someone in authority. Success requires playing a high card—sending the eldest son or another person of comparable seniority. The person making the request, moreover, will usually show up with an entourage of "his people." Politicians are likely to carry this principle over into their official behavior. Nawaz Sharif, for example, often used his younger brother, Shahbaz, widely recognized as the most senior politician in his party (and his family) after Nawaz himself, when he wanted to request something from the United States. One of the most dramatic examples was Shahbaz's visit to Washington in the late summer of 1999. The ostensible purpose of the visit was to follow up on President Clinton's carefully qualified offer to "take a personal interest" in the Kashmir problem, but it was clear to the American officials involved that his main objective was to convey Nawaz Sharif's anxiety about the possibility of a military coup, and to persuade the United States to help stave it off. No one on either side mistook the importance of the message once Shahbaz had been chosen to deliver it.

When a special envoy comes from outside the circle of family or personal intimates, a Pakistani leader will often look for someone with recognized star power and a strong likelihood of impressing his American interlocutors. This is the more classic model of diplomatic envoy used by many countries. During the urbane and eloquent Sahibzada Yaqub Khan's long tenure as ambassador to Washington and as foreign minister, he played this role on several occasions: in 1990, he was unable to avert sanctions following Pakistan's development of a nuclear explosive; in 1999, he was more successful in preserving some elements of the U.S.-Pakistan relationship following the coup that brought Musharraf to power. The distinction between these two models for special envoys is that Shahbaz Sharif's task was to make his brother feel comfortable; Yaqub Khan's job was to make the Americans feel comfortable.

The rank and status of U.S. emissaries also matter. The United States often turns to senior military officers when there is sensitive business to be done in Pakistan. General Anthony Zinni, at that time commander in chief of the U.S. Central Command, was sent to Pakistan on at least three occasions during 1997–99, two of which we will examine more closely in subsequent chapters. Using a general for such a mission is a two-edged sword: the

Pakistani military clearly attaches significance to messages delivered by senior U.S. military officers; on the other hand, envoys in uniform may convey the unintended message that the United States attaches more importance to Pakistan's military than to its civilians. Especially when doing business with the military, it helps to be able to match the rank of a person of whom one is making a difficult request.

U.S. officials have access to Pakistanis well above their own rank, and have sometimes been extremely effective in "punching above their weight" in this fashion. Under Secretary of State Alan Larson, for example, worked directly with the finance minister in developing the economic dimension of the post-9/11 relationship, and by all accounts this was a very productive relationship.[21]

Who Needs Whom?

The United States and Pakistan do not always have the same perception about who is doing a favor for whom. Many Pakistani observers and most U.S. officials start from the premise that Pakistan is the supplicant: it needs U.S. military and economic aid. As will be seen in chapter 7, however, at key points in U.S.-Pakistan relations, Pakistan has been convinced that the United States needs it more than the reverse. This has a profound impact on the negotiating dynamic. It is likely to lead Pakistan to make the United States put its offer on the table first, and it has repeatedly led Pakistani leaders to assume that they could ignore U.S. warnings about legal strictures on aid, in the expectation that Pakistan's importance to the United States would override these.

This is a problem that may develop, not while the United States and Pakistan are negotiating the terms of their engagement, but after they have embarked on a partnership that is important for both. Throughout the 1980s, for example, Pakistan assumed that its collaboration with the United States in Afghanistan would always override U.S. concerns about its nuclear program. In 1990, however, the nuclear problem exploded the relationship. Officials throughout the Pakistan government who had assumed that the United States needed Pakistan more than the reverse—starting with President Ghulam Ishaq Khan—were caught off guard. The bitterness of the U.S.-Pakistani "divorces" has been much aggravated by Pakistanis' overcon-

---

21. This section draws on the authors' personal experiences and on their interviews with Prof. Anita Weiss, Paula Newberg, Mushahid Hussein, Tariq Fatemi, William Milam, Karl F. Inderfurth, Col. (ret.) David Smith, Col. (ret.) John Gill, Alan Larson, and Patricia Haslach.

fidence that they will always be able to override U.S. concerns that interfere with continuing the aid relationship.[22]

What Is a Commitment?

Underlying all these issues of style are two fundamental questions: what do the United States and Pakistan want to negotiate, and when is a commitment binding? The kinds of negotiations the United States has conducted in Pakistan run the gamut, and include highly technical military supply or textile trade agreements, broad understandings about the scope of the U.S.-Pakistani relationship during the three periods of closest U.S.-Pakistan cooperation, operational agreements on a variety of issues, including intelligence matters, understandings about aspects of Pakistani policy toward India and Afghanistan, and even looser agreements about Pakistan's internal politics.

Observers from both countries sometimes comment that the United States usually has tactical goals, whereas Pakistan has strategic ones. In fact, both countries are dealing at the tactical as well as the strategic level. What differs, however, is what they think they can deliver, or at least influence. One astute Pakistani observer told the authors that the United States approaches the world as a set of problems that can be solved. Thus, at both the strategic and the tactical level, the United States tends to look for concrete "deliverables" and "metrics," and measures its success or failure by whether those benchmarks are achieved. Pakistan, on the other hand, lives in a dangerous neighborhood and is skeptical of the willingness or ability of the United States to stay around for the long haul.[23] This has led Pakistani negotiators over the past six decades to try to draw the United States in on Pakistan's side in an effort to adjust the strategic balance in the region in Pakistan's favor in a fundamental way. Yet, given Pakistan's low view of U.S. reliability, its negotiators want above all to avoid giving away an asset Pakistan might some day need against India. The Pakistani state has been prepared to tolerate groups that pose a threat to its security and authority if the offenders are also reliably anti-Indian. Before the government and army cracked down on the Pakistani Taliban in early 2009, for instance, they had suffered over two years of deadly attacks on military and police targets. A crisp reestablishment of authority seemed out of reach or dangerous; better, in the view of

---

22. This section draws on the authors' experiences and their interviews with Touqir Hussain, Lt. Gen. (ret.) Javed Hassan, and Prof. Riffaat Hussain.

23. Mushahid Hussein, interview.

the government and army, to try to achieve some kind of ambiguous modus vivendi—and to keep the potential asset available against future need.

Some of the most important agreements between the United States and Pakistan are never written down. Examples include the basic understandings that cemented the periods of closest U.S.-Pakistan cooperation after the Russian invasion of Afghanistan in 1979 and after 9/11, as we will see in chapter 7. In these cases, the national leaders— Presidents Zia and Musharraf—gave their word, and passed instructions down the chain of command.

When there is a written agreement, the Pakistani negotiators are careful drafters. The written agreement may turn out, however, to be the beginning rather than the end of the process. One U.S. official who was involved in economic negotiations after 9/11 noted the contrast between the relatively easy process of getting something signed and the dilatory action by the Pakistani government when it came to providing information specified in the agreement. The Pakistan government keeps careful track of the written undertakings it has received from the United States, but as already noted, the mercurial history of U.S.-Pakistan relations is punctuated by occasions when the two sides had radically different interpretations of what those commitments meant. During the implementation phase, the significance of the two countries' divergent objectives becomes more apparent, and, as one longtime observer put it, Pakistan acts as a "marginal satisfier"—trying to gauge how much or how little it needs to do to maintain the parts of the U.S. relationship it most values.[24]

Even where the underlying agreement is one of broad principles, the implicit fine print may make a difference. Two retired U.S. officials commented separately that in any negotiation that touched on Pakistan's relations with Afghanistan or India, it was important to "seal off the exits"—to cover explicitly all the special cases or contingencies Pakistan might wish to exploit in order to get around an agreement. One of them ruefully commented that during an India-Pakistan crisis he had made the mistake of asking Musharraf to dismantle certain militant bases on the Pakistani side of Kashmir. Musharraf complied, but then established other bases in the same area. The next time, the official recalled, he made his request more specific: dismantle the bases, do not establish new ones, and make sure the total number goes down by an equivalent amount. He felt this had more satisfactory results, despite the obvious pitfalls of negotiating over numbers without an agreed

---

24. Marvin Weinbaum, conversation with authors.

baseline. The United States' quest for a clear metric did not eliminate the possibility of misunderstandings.

Symbols can take on a larger than life importance, and one key request sometimes preempts the whole agenda. A classic example is F-16 aircraft. The first shipment of these sophisticated planes was supplied to Pakistan in the early 1980s, and F-16s were the most concrete symbol of the revival of the U.S.-Pakistan alliance after the Soviet invasion of Afghanistan. When the United States cut off assistance to Pakistan in 1990 over its nuclear program, it canceled the supply to Pakistan of a new batch of F-16s. This quickly became the symbol of the U.S.-Pakistan breach. It took nearly a decade to work out how to reimburse the payments Pakistan had made for planes it never received. After 9/11, when the United States reengaged with Pakistan, Musharraf requested that the United States supply F-16s once again. The U.S. government was unenthusiastic, given the limited utility of fighter aircraft for counterinsurgency or counterterrorism missions, but it eventually not only agreed but supplied the planes on an expedited basis. The United States recognized that the symbolism of reversing the F-16 cancellation a decade earlier was of huge importance to Pakistan.[25]

Integrating Pakistan's Worldview

When one puts this cultural style together with Pakistan's narrative of insecurity, constant comparisons with India, and the unreliability that Pakistanis believe the United States has exhibited over the years, the result is a negotiating style that relies heavily on creating a sense of obligation—a guilt trip—in the minds of the U.S. negotiators. Pakistani negotiators emphasize both national pride and national vulnerability. They start from the premise that Pakistan is an aggrieved party. It is a manipulative style, aimed at creating an air of indispensability for Pakistan but mindful that the U.S.-Pakistan friendship could vanish at any moment. Above all, the Pakistani negotiator will have firmly in mind the asymmetry between Pakistan and the United States.

This approach has been quite successful in persuading the United States to back off unwelcome demands. However, that success has sometimes come to an abrupt end, as the United States found it necessary to take drastic action on account of an issue Pakistan thought it could finesse. The two major ruptures between Pakistan and the United States fall into this category. In

---

25. This section draws on the authors' interviews with Andrew Haviland, Patricia Haslach, Richard Armitage, Wendy Chamberlin, and Alan Larson.

1965, the falling-out was over Pakistani use of U.S.-supplied arms to start a war against India and its effort to foment insurrection on the Indian side of Kashmir. In 1990, the break came over Pakistan's nuclear program.

The next three chapters will explore the bureaucratic status, training, and culture of Pakistan's main negotiators, its military, and its civilian officials and politicians. All start from this common core, but, as will be seen, they use it in different ways.[26]

---

26. This section draws on the authors' experiences and on interviews with Col. (ret.) John Gill and Col. (ret.) Woolf Gross.

4

Navigating the Pakistan Government: Military and Intelligence

On July 26, 2008, the Pakistani press put banner headlines on a story reporting that the newly elected civilian government was changing the chain of command for the country's major intelligence agency, the Inter-Services Intelligence Directorate. ISI, technically part of the army but operating with the longer leash that is characteristic of intelligence organizations, would henceforth report to the Home Ministry, responsible for internal security and headed by a civilian. Within six hours, the army had announced that there would be no change in ISI's chain of command, and the government went along with this new announcement.[1]

This episode illustrates a basic fact about the power structure within the Pakistan government. The army is the power player, and when its direct interests are engaged, it can trump not only the civilian bureaucracy but the country's elected government. It is not often challenged as directly or ineptly as this, nor does it necessarily play its trump cards as heavily, but the power relationship is clear, and this has an impact beyond strictly military or national security issues. Even the terminology in common use in Pakistan underlines this point. "The Establishment," in Pakistan, really means the security establishment: the army, its related institutions, and those closely associated with them—not, as in the United States, the socially well connected and powerful.

Power relationships within the Pakistan government, together with the particular cultures of each of its major constituent parts, are the third major

---

1. Syed Irfan Raza, "Government Forced to Withdraw ISI Decision," *Dawn*, Islamabad, July 27, 2008, www.dawn.com/2008/07/28/top1.htm. The director general of the military's Inter-Services Public Relations told the press that the army chief and other defense authorities had not been informed in advance. "When we realized that the decision had been taken, we discussed the issue with the government and are thankful that there was *a realization of ground realities* and that our position was accepted," he said. (Emphasis added.)

influence on Pakistan's negotiating style. This chapter will review the institutional style of the military; the next two will take a similar look at the two major civilian categories—diplomats and civil servants, and politicians.

Dominating the Political Landscape

At least as far back as the mid-1950s, the Pakistan military has been the largest single player on the Pakistani political scene. Within the military, the army has the overwhelmingly dominant position; Pakistan's air force and navy are both smaller and much less engaged in politics. Even before Pakistan's first experience with military rule in 1958, General Ayub Khan, then commander in chief of the army, was the public face of Pakistan's foreign policy and the architect of its relations with the United States. The army remains the strongest institution in the country, with a powerful corporate culture and an unparalleled commitment and ability to protect its institutional interests. It worked hand in glove with the civil service during the military-led governments of 1958–71. But the civil service's role diminished during each of the subsequent military governments, and institutional relations between it and the military eroded.

Elected politicians have had the bumpiest ride and the most changeable level of influence on the governing of Pakistan. The elite character of the Pakistan Muslim League, the nucleus of the Pakistan movement before the partition of India, and the tragic death of two of Pakistan's early leaders— the founder, Mohammed Ali Jinnah, of tuberculosis in 1948, just over a year after independence, and his right-hand man, Liaquat Ali Khan, of assassination in 1951—stunted the growth of an effective political culture. The high point for civilian politicians came in the early 1970s under Zulfiqar Ali Bhutto. His legendary political skills combined with the army's devastating defeat in Bangladesh to give him a degree of control of government machinery not seen under any other civilian leader other than Jinnah himself.

The army has been willing, able, and often eager to shape domestic political developments, even if this did not involve directly taking power. It had a major hand in the removal of all Pakistan's civilian governments since 1958. Army leaders took over in bloodless coups in 1958, 1977, and 1999.[2] Earlier in the 1990s, the alternating civilian governments of Nawaz Sharif and Benazir Bhutto were removed through technically constitutional processes

---

2. In 1969, Field Marshal Ayub Khan, who led what was at least technically a constitutional civilian government as president, was forced to resign. He was succeeded, contrary to the constitution, by the army chief of staff, General Yahya Khan.

in which the military, while not taking power, played a decisive role behind the scenes. In the spring of 2009, the publicly acknowledged brokering role of the army chief resolved a brewing crisis between Asif Zardari's government and its principal civilian opponents, led by Nawaz Sharif. On two other recent occasions, the army's decision not to interrupt the political process was critical. In February 2008, the army, from which Musharraf had just retired, decided not to interfere with the parliamentary elections. Six months later, when the major political parties were preparing to impeach Musharraf for his actions as president, the army did nothing to prevent him from being forced out of office.[3]

The Military Family

Pakistan's army officers come through a rigorous winnowing process. From 15,000 applicants, the Pakistan Military Academy at Kakul selects about 350 cadets each year. In the class of 1979, 275 of these graduated. By the time the group is ready for promotion to major general, the number is down to 70 in the fighting branches, of whom no more than a handful will become lieutenant generals, eligible to become corps commanders, the elite group that runs the army.[4]

The largest number are from Punjab, the province that includes 56 percent of Pakistan's population[5] and has historically dominated all the ruling institutions—military, civil service, and politics. But the regional balance has shifted. In the 1979 "batch," 70 percent were from Punjab, 14 percent from the North-West Frontier, 12 percent from Sindh and Balochistan, and 1.3 percent from Azad Kashmir (the part of Kashmir administered by Pakistan).[6] By 1990, staffing in the army as a whole had shifted away from Punjab, now down to 65 percent, toward Sindh and Balochistan (15 percent) and Azad Kashmir (6 percent). After 1990 there was a further sharp decline in recruitment from Punjab, with enlistments down to 43.3 percent.[7]

---

3. Some analysts argue that the army had concluded that Musharraf had become a danger to the corporate interests of the army.

4. Stephen Philip Cohen, *The Idea of Pakistan* (Washington, D.C.: Brookings Institution Press, 2004), 97–98.

5. Government of Pakistan, Population Census Organization, "Population by Province/Region since 1951," www.statpak.gov.pk/depts/pco/statistics/pop_by_province/pop_by_province.html.

6. Cohen, *The Idea of Pakistan*, 98.

7. Pakistan Army GHQ, cited in Shuja Nawaz, *Crossed Swords: Pakistan, Its Army, and the Wars Within* (Karachi: Oxford University Press, 2008), 570–71.

There were also changes in social background in the army over the same period, though these are harder to define with precision. Shuja Nawaz's well-regarded study, which draws heavily on official documents he was able to obtain from army headquarters by virtue of being the younger brother of a deceased former chief of army staff, refers to the "Zia *bharti*," or "Zia recruits," who entered the army starting in 1978. He and other observers, both within the army and outside it, argue that this group was more religiously observant and more conservative than its predecessors.[8]

By the mid-1990s, among the officers assigned to the Army Staff College, only a small group consisted of officers from army families, the traditional military elite. These officers appeared to be headed for the most prestigious jobs; they also had the best education before entering the army, the best English, and the greatest exposure to the outside world. Perhaps one-third of the Staff College participants were from middle-class professional families with some army connections. A similar number were from families new to the army, from more modest backgrounds. For them, the army provided both economic security and social status. The remaining officers were more conservative and more politically Islamist in orientation. In general, as one proceeded along this continuum, the level of religious observance and political Islamist sensibility rose, while the level of English declined, as did exposure to, and sympathy with, the United States. Despite an effort to recruit the children of junior officers and NCOs, many of whom had a village background, the preponderance of the officers identified themselves with cities or towns rather than the countryside.[9]

The Pakistan army enjoys a privileged existence in Pakistan. Military officers are paid salaries that are roughly comparable to their civil service counterparts, but they have access to valuable perks not available to civilians, including plots of land on a preferential basis. Their children have a special school system, which over the years has moved up the educational scale and now includes universities run by the military. Their medical care is taken care of for life, and they enjoy the equivalent of a PX system for subsidized shopping. Retired officers are often in a favored position when it comes to postretirement jobs in public sector corporations and even in private business. Widows and children of deceased military personnel are entitled to full pensions, in contrast to the half pension available to civilians. Military retirees and institutions created for their benefit run a network of businesses that

---

8. Nawaz, *Crossed Swords*, 572.

9. Authors' interview with former international participant in Pakistan Army Staff College, Quetta; see also Cohen, *The Idea of Pakistan*, 106–09.

represent a major share of the Pakistan economy.[10] These expenses are not fully reflected in the published data on defense spending. Defense spending in 2008 constituted 3.3 percent of gross domestic product and 17.6 percent of the national budget, but pension expenses and some of the other quality-of-life benefits for the military are not included in these figures.[11]

Especially during periods of military rule, army officers occupy some coveted civilian jobs, including diplomatic posts. Some of these appointments are due to a personal relationship with the president or prime minister. These include two retired generals who successively served as Musharraf's ambassadors to the United States: Jehangir Karamat, whose forced resignation as chief of army staff opened the way for Musharraf's own appointment, and Mahmud Durrani, for whom Musharraf had once worked as a staff officer. In other cases, typically not involving service in major countries, generals may be assigned as ambassadors by civilian-led governments to move them farther from the political action (in the early 1970s, for example, Zulfiqar Ali Bhutto sent several powerful generals to minor European posts).

There is also a regular provision reserving 10 percent of civil service jobs for military officers converting to civilian service. These officers' army service counts toward their civil service seniority, so they are instantly senior to civilians who enter the civil service in the same "batch." Other officers are seconded to the civil service on a temporary basis. In contrast to this institutionalized involvement by military officers in the civil service, the army resists strenuously any involvement by civilians, whether civil service or elected politicians, in the military's internal affairs, including perks, assignments, and especially promotions. All these arrangements encourage a culture of entitlement, which can carry over into the attitudes officers bring to the negotiating table.[12]

The military protects its own. One of Musharraf's early decisions when he took power in 1999 was to establish the National Accountability Bureau, an anticorruption unit intended to punish corruption within the previous regime. But he was quick to exclude military officers from its jurisdiction. He

---

10. Hasan-Askari Rizvi, interview and correspondence with authors; see also Ayesha Siddiqa, *Military Inc.: Inside Pakistan's Military Economy* (Ann Arbor, MI: Pluto Press), passim.

11. World Bank Group, World Development Indicators, http://data.worldbank.org/indicator; see table 4.4 titled "Consolidated Federal and Provincial Government Expenditures" in Government of Pakistan, Ministry of Finance, "Pakistan Economic Survey 2007–2008," www.finance.gov.pk/survey/chapter_10/04_Public_Finance.pdf.

12. Nawaz, *Crossed Swords*, 575–77; Siddiqa, *Military Inc.*, esp. 204–42; Hasan-Askari Rizvi, interview.

noted that the military has its own internal system of discipline, which army officers regard as more rigorous than its civilian counterparts. Nonetheless, the impression among Pakistani civilians was that this was a way of sparing the military—but not civilians—public embarrassment. In this respect as in others, it appeared that the military was privileged.[13]

The bond among military officers is extremely strong. Officers remain connected to those who join the service with them—their "batchmates"— and often also retain long-term ties to former commanding officers and to subordinates who have worked closely with them. Like most armies, this one is hierarchical. Officers are accustomed to having one person in charge, and will generally not go against the wishes of "the chief." Pervez Musharraf, even after he had become president, spoke constantly of the importance of "unity of command," and seemed not to recognize the difficulty of reconciling this concept with the checks and balances inherent in civilian politics and constitutional government.

The leadership of the army, however, is not a solo performance. Most chiefs of army staff have worked with and through the corps commanders and other generals who hold key headquarters assignments. This group can be counted on to carry out the chief's orders, but the chief will generally try to create consensus rather than ram orders down the throats of his closest colleagues. During the early Musharraf years, this pattern was very much in evidence. Major policy decisions were usually preceded by a meeting of the corps commanders, and those meetings were publicized, so the collective leadership was publicly recognized. Toward the end of Musharraf's time as president the seniority gap between Musharraf and the corps commanders widened significantly, and the relationship between the army chief and his corps commanders evolved into a teacher-student relationship. Corps commanders who openly disputed the chief were shunted aside into less prestigious posts and denied significant government positions following their retirement from the army.

Retired officers are part of the military family. General officers may continue to live for years in cantonment areas in housing controlled by the military. Relations of seniority dating from the time of active service continue into retirement. Thus, in private conversations, President Musharraf continued to address retired officers who had been his superiors while they were on active duty as "Sir" (and, of course, the "Sir" was reciprocated).

---

13. Government of Pakistan, Ministry of Law and Justice, "Ordinance No. XVIII of 1999," www.pakistan.gov.pk/divisions/law-division/media/XVIII-1999.pdf.

Increasingly, retired senior officers now go on to serve after retirement in prestigious positions in Pakistan's version of the military-industrial complex, typically serving at least one and often two four-year contracts. Since these positions are controlled by the army chief, they serve as a subtle form of control on dissent within the senior ranks.

Retired officers share a strong nationalism, but especially among retired generals, many speak out about Pakistan's problems in ways they could never have done on active duty. The impressive list of retired generals who participate in dialogues with India and have published creative and forward-leaning analyses of what it would take to make peace included Mahmud Durrani, Jehangir Karamat (both former ambassadors to the United States), and Talat Masood. While it is unusual for retired officers to speak out on political controversies sensitive to the army, it happens from time to time. In July 2006, for example, six retired flag-rank officers joined another twelve politicians and retired civil servants in publicly issuing a declaration that urged Musharraf not to stay on as both president and army chief, an issue that was intensely controversial in the context of the national elections that were expected to take place the following year.[14] And retired officers are also more likely to take seriously the economic dimension of Pakistan's security.[15]

The "Sword Arm" of Pakistan

Besides being the senior service among Pakistan's military, the army has had the dominant political and negotiating role as well. Army officers are trained to remember at all times that the nation's security is in their hands. The bearing of military officers in their contacts with Americans is striking for its self-confidence. They are accustomed to having the dominant voice within the councils of government. They are also supremely sure that the army represents all that is best about Pakistan. They consider themselves the only true Pakistanis, above the competing regional and social loyalties to which their countrymen are subject. Like other Pakistanis, however, military officers are keenly aware of their colleagues' ethnic backgrounds.

---

14. "Report on the Dialogue on Civil Military Relations Advises the President against Combining the Office of the President of Pakistan with the Chief of Army Staff," Pakistan Institute of Legislative Development and Transparency (PILDAT), July 8, 2006, www.pildat.org/eventsdel.asp?detid=151.

15. Material in this section that is not otherwise sourced draws on the authors' interviews with Col. (ret.) John Gill, Col. (ret.) David Smith, Lt. Gen. (ret.) David W. Barno, Col (ret.) Woolf Gross, Shuja Nawaz, Prof. Riffaat Hussein, Mushahid Hussein, Riaz Khokhar, Hasan-Askari Rizvi, and Gen. (ret.) Jehangir Karamat.

The military asserts, and is usually granted, institutional primacy in shaping Pakistan's policy on national security issues. This includes not only military policy, personnel, supply, and management, but also policy toward India and Afghanistan, anything connected with the nuclear arsenal, and those aspects of relations with the United States and China that touch on these issues.

The military culture starts with a strong, assertive nationalism, instilled in military officers from the start, and reinforced in higher-level training. As one former commandant of the National Defense University put it, the curriculum emphasizes that Pakistan is "a national, not an ideological state," and that it makes its decisions based on Pakistan's interests. However, the thinking behind the articulation of those interests comes close to being a national ideology. One astute observer referred to the "standard national narrative."[16] The story is essentially the one described in chapter 2, but for military officers even more than for civilians, it ranks as an article of faith. It is based on the deadly threat from India and the inferiority of Indian compared with Pakistani culture.

The issue of Kashmir, in particular, is a question of honor. Military officers commenting on the proposals for a Kashmir settlement that have been under discussion in recent years, which involve leaving the prized area of the disputed state under Indian control, will ask how they can accept such a settlement after all the sacrifices Pakistan has made in pursuit of its larger ambitions.[17] The army is institutionally skeptical at best about India-Pakistan rapprochement.[18] Self-interest probably plays a role: better relations with India would prompt calls for a reduction in Pakistan's sizable military budget and would make the army less central to Pakistani concerns. Curiously, this does not necessarily extend to retired military officers, who have been some of the most articulate and effective participants in semiofficial India-Pakistan dialogue.

---

16. Nawaz, *Crossed Swords*, 574–75; Lt. Gen. (ret.) Javed Hassan, interviews with authors; Lt. Gen. (ret.) Javed Hassan, *India: A Study in Profile* (Rawalpindi, Pakistan: Army Education Press GHQ, 1990); Brig. (ret.) Feroz Hassan Khan, correspondence with authors, November 2009.

17. Interestingly, the one Pakistani leader who has deviated from this view by floating an approach to Kashmir calling for a territorial settlement that accepted the Line of Control was Pervez Musharraf. This suggests two things: that such unconventional proposals can only be floated from the top, and that the country's top generals have more flexibility to deviate from the standard position than do civilians. See fuller discussion in chapter 7.

18. As discussed in chapter 8, Musharraf deviated from this pattern and offered significant changes in Pakistan's Kashmir policy during the last few years of his presidency. This illustrates not so much a new flexibility in the army as the freedom he had, being both army chief and president, to redefine Pakistan's security requirements. The army does not seem to have continued this flexibility after Musharraf's departure from office.

Most Pakistanis are convinced that it is only nuclear weapons that ultimately deter India from walking all over Pakistan. For military officers bearing the burden of national security, this is central to their credo. Military officers also see the nuclear arsenal as an essential tool for protecting Pakistan against a sellout by the United States. For them, the nuclear arsenal is the ultimate guarantor of national sovereignty. By the same token, protecting the nuclear arsenal, not just against India but just as insistently against the danger that the United States might wish to disable it, is the classic example of a cause in which it is legitimate—and perhaps even a duty—to lie if necessary.

Pakistan's army has always been conscious of its role as the defender of the homeland for South Asia's Muslims. Until the Zia years, however, strong religious observance was the exception rather than the rule among army officers. Zia, first as army chief and later as president, fostered a much greater Islamic religious consciousness, encouraging officers to attend religious services and giving a much stronger religious tone to the guidance he provided army officers. Taken together with the army's institutional involvement with militant movements, which they cultivated as an asset against India and Afghanistan, this has brought the army politically closer to those forces in Pakistan that want to give a more explicitly religious Islamic character to the state. This helps to explain why the Pakistan army has at times been ambivalent about striking back forcefully at militant groups who wear the mantle of Islam, even when these groups have attacked it.

Also central to the institutional culture of the Pakistani military is professional pride. Its rigorous training program includes mandatory professional formation at roughly five and ten years of service. Two midcareer training choices are considered by insiders to be indicative of an officer's prospects. The most exacting is the Armed Forces War Course at the colonel/brigadier level, for which officers are selected based on their performance and career record. One observer described it as an incubator of strategic conservatism. The Army Staff College, Quetta, is similar to its American counterparts, and somewhat less rigorously selective. An officer has four chances to be selected.[19]

Especially in higher-level courses, officers attend lectures on Pakistan's foreign policy that build on the strongly anti-India ethos instilled in them from the time they join the military academy. In recent years, lectures on Pakistan's economic development have also been added to the curriculum. In

---

19. Brig. (ret.) Feroz Hassan Khan, correspondence with the authors.

general, however, this instruction seems to have had relatively little impact on officers' views of Pakistan's security priorities: in that realm, the threat from an antagonistic, well-armed India remains central. On this score, there is a strong drive toward uniform thinking among officers on active service.

One aspect of the Pakistan army's professional pride is a relatively restrictive concept of the tasks worthy of a first-class army. This is an army that has trained primarily for conventional warfare against another major force, India's. Other tasks, notably counterinsurgency, are looked on as unworthy of being the Pakistan army's primary mission. For the past two decades, Pakistan's military and intelligence services have employed militant groups as the tip of the Pakistani spear, stirring up trouble in Kashmir or Afghanistan, but this unconventional approach does not figure in the army's concept of its primary mission, and the military (and civilian) leadership of the country is reluctant to acknowledge publicly a tactic the outside world looks on as illicit. But this asymmetrical warfare does affect how the army is structured and how it addresses U.S. requests for more and better coordinated action along the Pakistan-Afghanistan border. More recently, as the United States and Pakistan have talked about beefing up Pakistan's counterinsurgency capacity, this task has been assigned to the Frontier Scouts,[20] a group separate from (and less prestigious than) the regular army. Its officers come from the army but its troops are locally recruited in the frontier areas.

The strategic culture Pakistani military officers absorb, both through formal training and from their senior colleagues, in practice discourages individual risk taking. Officers who make waves are not believed to fare well at promotion time. (This is hardly unique to Pakistan: it is characteristic of armies and other entrenched institutions in many countries.) In the Staff College, officers get good marks for providing "school solutions" to the problems they are asked to solve. Americans who have worked with Pakistani officers on courses in the United States have found many of them creative and ingenious, but have been given to understand that these traits are not much prized in the day-to-day work of the army.[21]

On the other hand, the army as an institution has undertaken some extraordinarily risky operations. The decision to send Pakistani troops into Indian-administered parts of Kashmir at Kargil in 1999 is a case in point. The authors of that operation planned a brilliant tactical move, but assumed, against all logic, that India would not respond in force, and failed to consider how Pakistan could turn tactical success into strategic gain. Their calcula-

20. Previously known as the Frontier Corps.
21. Authors' interviews with former U.S. participants at the Staff College.

tions were based primarily on their estimations of their own capacity, not on a clear assessment of what their adversary might do. They assumed that surprise could overcome even a substantial disparity in the overall size of Pakistan's forces compared with India's. [22] Kargil ended with the Pakistan army's return home under embarrassing circumstances. A quarter-century earlier, Pakistan's incursion into Indian Kashmir, Operation Gibraltar, which launched the 1965 war, had similarly failed to consider how India would respond. That engagement too ended with no strategic gains for Pakistan.

Risk taking in the army seems to be concentrated at the top, and in specialized units such as intelligence, which will be discussed later in this chapter, and the Special Forces. President Musharraf, who as army chief took the decision to move into Kargil, was a commando by background. His account of his years in public life refers with some pride to his early propensity to get in trouble and to his later willingness to take risks.[23]

Like many armies, the Pakistan army has a culture of secrecy. Military officers do not like to share information with civilian officials, even on subjects where control is shared, such as administration of the tribal areas. They resent civilian officials or the media making even careful and bland public statements about sensitive or embarrassing issues such as the weakness of government control in the tribal areas or the nuclear program. The decision to make public the broad outlines of the 2009–10 military budget was hailed as an extraordinary concession to the elected government. The military's handling of the media takes this institutional suspicion to extremes. In the case of the Kargil operation, the army and the government continued to describe it as a "mujahideen" operation long after its own involvement had become painfully obvious.

Thinly veiled contempt for civilians, and in particular for Pakistan's politicians, is also characteristic of Pakistan army officers. Military officers consider civilians soft, weak, and insufficiently dedicated to Pakistan's national security. They regard politicians as corrupt—an accusation that all too

---

22. See especially Peter R. Lavoy, ed., *Asymmetric Warfare in South Asia: The Causes and Consequences of the Kargil Conflict* (Cambridge: Cambridge University Press, 2009). Several of the essays in this volume, which is based on extensive interviews, document how intent the Pakistan army was on tactical gains, to the point of assuming away the strategic shortcomings of the plan. See especially chapter 3 (Feroz Hassan Khan, Peter R. Lavoy, and Christopher Clary, "Pakistan's Motivations and Calculations for the Kargil Conflict"); chapter 4 (Col. John H. Gill, "Military Operations in the Kargil Conflict"); and chapter 8 (James J. Wirtz and Surinder Rana, "Surprise at the Top of the World: India's Systemic and Intelligence Failure"). Wirtz and Rana in particular argue that the Pakistan army was acting in accordance with a long history of weaker powers using surprise successfully as a tactical device, but failing to translate this into strategic gains.

23. Pervez Musharraf, *In the Line of Fire: A Memoir* (New York: Free Press, 2006). Examples are spread all through the book; see especially p. 49.

often has been well-founded—and ineffective. Military officers contrast these traits with the vigor and probity they attribute to themselves. This glosses over some persistent reports of corruption within their own ranks, as well as the handsome perks they receive upon retirement, such as grants of valuable public land. Civilians during the 1990s occasionally referred sardonically to the "crore commanders," using the Pakistani term for ten million rupees in place of the title Corps Commanders.

There have been long periods, including most of the 1990s and the period following the election in 2008, when the military has taken a corporate decision to remain behind the scenes while the elected government runs Pakistan. This acquiescence in the civilian government's formal supremacy has in the past stopped short of a long-term commitment to make elected government work. The army's institutional view holds that civilians have messed up the governance of Pakistan and that the army, however reluctantly, may need to set things right again, as it so often has claimed to do in Pakistan's past. This further confuses the complex structure of authority within the Pakistan government.

The other side of the coin is a pervasive confidence that the army can, if need be, perform any task required for the governing of Pakistan, regardless of whether or not it is related to their military experience. This helps to explain why, in Pakistan's periods of military and quasi-military rule, both active and retired military officers have been placed in positions of responsibility for which they had essentially no experience but where they were expected to outperform and supervise civilians who had been working as senior officials for years. During the first four years of Musharraf's government, for example, colonels were assigned to "monitor" secretaries to government in the different civilian ministries, officials with 25–30 years' experience under their belts who made up the cream of the civil service crop. Musharraf and other military leaders have maintained that they made these arrangements to clean up corruption, a plausible claim but not the whole story. The record of military management of civilian institutions is at best mixed.[24]

Confidence Clashing with Reality

There is a disconnect between the universally shared professional confidence of the Pakistan army and Pakistan's record of unsuccessful military opera-

---

24. Material in this section that is not otherwise sourced draws on the authors' interviews with Col. (ret.) John Gill, Col. (ret.) David Smith, Lt. Gen. (ret.) David W. Barno, Col. (ret.) Woolf Gross, Shuja Nawaz, Gen. (ret.) Jehangir Karamat, Prof. Riffaat Hussein, Mushahid Hussein, Hasan-Askari Rizvi, and Brig. (ret.) Feroz Hassan Khan.

tions, including its wars with India and its operations after 9/11 in the tribal areas bordering Afghanistan. This is exacerbated by the absence of a "lessons learned" culture and can at times produce a kind of detachment from reality.

The clearest example came when newly installed president Zulfiqar Ali Bhutto ordered a rare review of army performance leading up to its most disastrous defeat, the loss of East Pakistan in 1971. A commission headed by former chief justice Hamoodur Rehman, including both civilian and military members, prepared a report, which was effectively buried for twenty-five years until an Indian newspaper revealed its findings. The Pakistan army's internal review, prepared by a team of eight officers, was confined to the unimportant military operations between India and West Pakistan, a thousand miles from the main battlefront. This report too was barely distributed either inside or outside the army.[25]

This aversion to critical scrutiny continues to this day. Chapter 8 reviews the negotiations with the United States that followed Pakistan's disastrous decision to send troops into Indian-administered parts of Kashmir at Kargil in 1999. These resulted in the withdrawal of the Pakistani troops following Prime Minister Nawaz Sharif's meeting with President Clinton in Washington. Although the retreat, and hence the strategic failure, were on public display, the one analytical account published by a government-funded think tank was basically an apologia for the operation.[26]

Overestimating their capabilities shows up in some officers' casual conversations as well. Many U.S. observers recall having been told that Muslim Pakistanis have martial qualities that are inherently superior to those of Hindu Indians.[27] Javed Hassan's study of India, long used in officer training, emphasizes the allegedly weak motivation and poor discipline in the Indian army.[28]

This affects the negotiating style of military officers, who on some occasions have made demands as if they were in control, when in fact they were by far the weaker party. The Simla negotiations with India that ended the 1971 war are a case in point. The brief prepared by the Pakistani military for Zulfiqar Ali Bhutto called for him to demand that India "settle the Kashmir issue according to the wishes of her people"—a phrase that in the Pakistani lexicon means allowing Kashmir to join Pakistan. This would have been difficult even if Pakistan had won the war, but coming only six months after

---

25. Material from Pakistan Army GHQ archives, cited in Nawaz, *Crossed Swords*, 311–15.

26. Shireen M. Mazari, *The Kargil Conflict, 1999: Separating Fact from Fiction* (Islamabad: Institute of Strategic Studies, 2003).

27. See also Cohen, *The Idea of Pakistan*, 103–04.

28. Hassan, *India*, 228–56.

Pakistan's defeat and the surrender of its army in Dhaka, it lacked any relation to reality.[29]

The system of avoiding institutional blame is so strong that it can make it difficult for the army to understand when it has failed, and why. No institution takes kindly to this kind of criticism when it comes from an outsider, especially a foreigner. This creates a significant communication problem for U.S. officials working with the army. They must either risk offending their Pakistani counterparts or appear to accept a sometimes unrealistic assessment of the army's abilities.[30]

"The American Generation" and Beyond

The officers at the summit of today's Pakistan army belong to what some have called the "American generation," those who came of age professionally during the years when many of Pakistan's most promising officers came to the United States for professional training. This practice was suspended in 1990, when the United States cut off not only assistance but most military training on account of Pakistan's nuclear program, as required by the Pressler Amendment. "Zia's recruits," the next generation, did not receive this exposure to the world, and to U.S. thinking. Military training in the United States for Pakistani officers resumed after 9/11, but the officers who participated in it have not yet risen to positions of major leadership.

Training in the United States did not necessarily lead the participants to favor U.S. positions, nor did it change their negotiating style to accord with U.S. practices. The officers of the "American generation" included many whose formative professional experience was the 1971 war that left Pakistan cut in half, and they saw the United States as a country that had stood by and allowed this to happen. Participation in U.S. training courses did, however, give the participants some familiarity with U.S. society and with the kinds of argument that make an impact on their American counterparts. The larger cultural gap that resulted from the suspension of these contacts may not be immediately obvious, given that negotiations often involve technical subjects that are less subject to cultural misunderstanding. But it is there nonetheless,

---

29. Nawaz, *Crossed Swords*, 328–331. In this case, Bhutto appears to have turned this advice on its head and persuaded Indian prime minister Indira Gandhi not to demand concessions on Kashmir lest he be overthrown by the military—a classic example of playing Pakistan's weakness as strength.

30. Material in this section that is not otherwise sourced draws on the authors' interviews with Col. (ret.) John Gill, Col. (ret.) David Smith, Lt. Gen. (ret.) David W. Barno, Col. (ret.) Woolf Gross, Shuja Nawaz, Gen. (ret.) Jehangir Karamat, Hasan-Askari Rizvi, Prof. Riffaat Hussein, and Mushahid Hussein.

and the resentment that arises from the accepted Pakistani narrative of U.S.-Pakistan relations may be accentuated among those who feel that they lost out on one of the attractive perks of military life when they were deprived of U.S. training.

When it comes to dealing with Americans, army officers feel an especially keen resentment of U.S. inconstancy, often described as "betrayal." It is driven especially by recollections of interruptions of U.S. military supply during the downturns in U.S.-Pakistan relations. Military officers are understandably focused on Pakistan's military needs—both general ones and the need for particular hardware—in their assessment of Pakistan's security. Their resentment is reinforced by a tendency toward black-and-white thinking that is shared by many military officers around the world. It is the military especially who insist that Pakistan "will not be dictated to," by India or by the United States. At the same time, at least in military supply negotiations, army officers really need to have a positive outcome. The United States, whatever its shortcomings in their view as an ally, is the most attractive source of top-of-the-line military equipment.

Army officers tend to assume that the Americans they are dealing with know little about Pakistan. More than any other Pakistan government representatives, military officers start their presentations to U.S. officials with a textbook brief on India-Pakistan and, in some cases, Pakistan-Afghanistan relations. They do not deviate from their cleared script, which in any case is probably quite close to their personal convictions. When Pakistani military officers attend meetings or training courses in the United States, they are punctilious about making sure their perspective is articulated in detail, including a full description of the Indian scheming that they believe lies at the heart of Pakistan's problems. They are likely to assume that American civilians know little or nothing of military affairs.

The institutional culture of avoiding blame or self-criticism shows up at the negotiating table as a strong tendency to blame the army's problems on the United States, and to try to make their American counterparts feel guilty about Pakistan's difficulties. The military, more than other parts of the Pakistan government, tend to levy specific demands in a negotiation. When military officers are leading the government, they also play hardball, insisting that unless all their demands are met, disaster of one sort or another will follow.

The military fields a fully staffed team for negotiations. A general will ordinarily have a colonel with him, taking copious notes and preparing a written record of the meeting. Generals and brigadiers do little of their own writing: [31] this is done by staff and reviewed by senior officers.

The bond among military officers carries over to dealings with the United States. Pakistani military officers generally look on the Pentagon as their "best friend" inside the U.S. government, a subject which will come up again later in the book. Colin Powell, as secretary of state, and his deputy Richard Armitage invoked the bond of "soldier to soldier" or "war wound to war wound" when they needed to address difficult issues with President Musharraf. Countless U.S. military officers have had the same experience in dealing with their Pakistani counterparts.

Because the Pakistan army has a privileged position in the government, and because it is a strong institution with a well-developed staff system, it often can get things done more effectively than civilian institutions. Even when it is not able to deliver, it usually can give the appearance of following through. It is tempting for U.S. officials to drift toward doing more and more business with and through the military, and to rely on U.S. military officers to deliver important messages to the Pakistan leadership. Sometimes this is necessary and appropriate, but, as noted in chapter 3, excessive reliance on the military to do civilian business tends to further undercut the effectiveness of Pakistan's civilian institutions. This has policy consequences that U.S. officials need to consider carefully. There is a fine line between keeping Pakistan's most powerful institution in the loop and reinforcing the disproportionate influence and political leadership role of the army.[32]

Negotiating Military Supply

The military dominates the policy process on a raft of issues important to the United States, including the overall shape of U.S.-Pakistan relations. On military supply, the military run the show, to the nearly complete exclusion of any civilians (with the very limited exception of the Finance Ministry). Participants in military-supply negotiations find the process very focused and pragmatic. Often, the basic numbers are predetermined: the United States is willing to sell a set number of items and the U.S. Foreign Military

---

31. In the Pakistani system, which reflects its British antecedents, "brigadier" is not considered a general officer rank.

32. Material in this section that is not otherwise sourced draws on authors' interviews with Col. (ret.) John Gill, Col. (ret.) David Smith, Lt. Gen. (ret.) David W. Barno, Shuja Nawaz, Gen. (ret.) Jehangir Karamat, Hasan-Askari Rizvi, Prof. Riffaat Hussein, Mushahid Hussein, William Milam, and Ryan Crocker.

Supply system sets the financial terms. The negotiations, described by one veteran of the process as "bazaar haggling," concern other details—the size and configuration of the spare parts package, the amount of training, and other issues that will determine whether Pakistan gets, as it sees it, as much bang as possible for the buck. The military may have a clearer concept of their bottom line than their civilian counterparts, and when they conclude that the negotiations are unlikely to meet their minimum requirements, they are also more likely simply to say "no."

In this setting, the Pakistan side tends to ask for as much as it possibly can, and to suggest that any offer short of its request will leave Pakistan unacceptably vulnerable and oblige it to take unacceptable risks on behalf of the United States. The basic approach is, as in so many other cases, the guilt trip.

The U.S. negotiating process is riddled with deadlines and technicalities, which presents a challenge for the less legalistic and less deadline-driven Pakistani military. One retired U.S. military officer recalled the scramble to make a payment in order to prevent a Letter of Offer from expiring. After increasingly anxious warnings on his part, his Pakistani counterparts called up at midnight on the final day to say they were sending a courier over to him with the check.[33]

The Military Elite

Three units within the military are regarded as the ultimate elite. The first and most powerful is the Directorate of Military Operations, headed by a two-star director general (DGMO). The officers who work for him regard themselves as the unit that runs the army. Most army chiefs have previously served as DGMOs. The most promising officers are recruited to work there. The DGMO reports to the chief of army staff.

Second, the Strategic Plans Division (SPD) of the army is in charge of the nuclear arsenal. The director, Lieutenant General Khalid Kidwai, has run the organization since its creation in 1999, and was asked to stay on beyond his 2006 retirement from the army. His principal associates are a small cadre of officers from the army and air force, many of whom also serve there for an extended period. SPD's elite status derives from its association with nuclear weapons, but is based on specialization. Officers who serve there for more than a few years, especially those on the technical side, can then expect to spend most of their careers there. They have enough specialized knowledge

---

33. Col. (ret.) Woolf Gross, interview.

to do the job—and SPD, famous for its secretive practices, does not want to extend that knowledge unnecessarily beyond its own ranks.

SPD has developed a strong planning culture, and prides itself on its ability to think ahead about different contingencies. Despite the culture of secrecy, it has provided its officers with surprisingly generous foreign exposure, so they are familiar with international thinking and best practices on both nonproliferation and safety and security issues.

SPD has conducted Pakistan's very discreet discussions with the United States on nuclear safety and security. It has also conducted the Pakistan military's so far unsuccessful campaign to persuade the United States to give Pakistan a civil nuclear cooperation agreement like the one concluded with India in 2008.

The nuclear dialogue in the two decades that preceded Pakistan's nuclear test (and preceded the creation of SPD) was carried on at a higher level, by the national leadership and the leadership of the army. U.S. officials trying to dissuade Pakistan from developing a nuclear weapon warned Pakistani leaders that they would lose their aid and military supply if the program exceeded the limits laid down by the U.S. Congress. These limits were not negotiated between Washington and Islamabad but spelled out in legislation binding on the U.S. government. Pakistan was determined to protect its program. In discussions with the United States, the Pakistani officials assured the Americans that they understood and would not cross the redlines U.S. officials had spelled out—assurances that were disingenuous at the start and untruthful toward the end: a clear case of "strategic deception" in the minds of the Pakistanis. In this case, however, Pakistan's assumption that its "true friends" in the CIA and the Pentagon would rescue them from the sanctions demanded by U.S. law led them not to take the U.S. message seriously. The United States' choice of messenger inadvertently reinforced this Pakistani instinct. At key points, the U.S. warnings were delivered by the ambassador or by State Department officials. Throughout most of the 1980s, CIA leadership was not used to convey or supplement this message. Pakistani officials who had been involved with the nuclear program recall that the only restrictions placed on their activity were not to test or to transfer nuclear weapons-related materials. The restriction on transfer may have been more show than reality: the Pakistan government's assertion that the transfers orchestrated by A. Q. Khan were an unauthorized rogue operation are widely disbelieved in Pakistan.

Toward the end of the decade, in 1989, President George H. W. Bush raised the nuclear issue during the first official visit by newly elected prime minister Benazir Bhutto, and arranged for her to be briefed on the Pakistani nuclear program by Director of Central Intelligence William Webster. By sharing with Bhutto information on the nuclear program, the United States hoped that she would be able to get the program under control. This clearly did not lead Pakistan to dial down the program: the following year, the United States cut off aid because it could no longer certify that Pakistan did not possess a nuclear explosive. Indeed, it has been argued that Bush's nuclear briefing appeared to the military as a violation by Bhutto of the understanding she had reached with them and President Ghulam Ishaq Khan before taking power—that she would not become involved with the nuclear program and would leave it to the president and the military. It may ultimately have contributed to her removal by Ghulam Ishaq Khan and the army just over a year later.[34]

Inter-Services Intelligence

The third elite organization within the military is Pakistan's principal intelligence agency, the Inter-Services Intelligence Directorate. ISI has played a major role both in the country's history and in U.S. dealings with Pakistan. Created early in Pakistan's history as one of several military intelligence institutions, it came of age during the 1980s, when Pakistan and the United States together were supporting the mujahideen fighting against the invading Soviet army in Afghanistan. ISI's role as implementing agency for this operation gave it prestige, prominence within the Pakistan army, government, and public, and an enhanced budget, including generous funding provided by both the United States and Saudi Arabia. By the time the Soviet army left Afghanistan, ISI had unquestioned dominance among Pakistan's intelligence agencies.[35]

ISI has the reputation of being a "state within a state," able to operate outside other civilian or military authority. This is misleading. It is part of the army. Its director general is subordinate to the chief of army staff in the chain of command, but he also reports directly for certain purposes to the presi-

---

34. This section draws on authors' interviews and correspondence with Polly Nayak and Feroz Hassan Khan.

35. Nawaz, *Crossed Swords*, 577–579. Steve Coll's careful study *Ghost Wars* (New York: Penguin, 2004) also includes many important insights into ISI's role. Newspaper reports assert that U.S. intelligence sources continue to supply a major portion of ISI's budget (see Greg Miller, "CIA Says It Gets Its Money's Worth from Pakistani Spy Agency," *Los Angeles Times*, November 15, 2009, www.latimes.com/news/nationworld/world/la-fg-cia-pakistan15-2009nov15,0,4066853.story). ISI has also had a major role in domestic politics, providing advice to the national leaders on how to undercut their opponents and shoring up the standing of the military. We will discuss this further in chapter 6.

dent or prime minister, depending on which of these is the more powerful. ISI is staffed from the army. Its top leadership is drawn from senior officers who are on the fast track and have not necessarily been involved in intelligence work earlier in their army careers. Chief of Army Staff Ashfaq Pervez Kayani's immediate past assignment was as director general of ISI. His successor at ISI had previously served as director general of military operations. Its other senior officers are considered very able and entrepreneurial, and many go on to positions as corps commanders.

Other ISI officers spend much of their careers in the organization. These officers are the backbone of the directorate and become deeply involved in operations. They may not get promoted beyond colonel, but they have a policy influence that goes well beyond their rank. Zia took a personal interest in the staffing of ISI and was said to telephone officers personally to ask that they join the directorate.[36] U.S. officials who have worked closely with ISI are unanimous in arguing that the organization is subject to orders through the chain of command. However, ISI leaders have more discretion than other army officers, and have often been quite selective about how much detailed information they passed to their superiors. This is partly a mutually agreeable effort to preserve "plausible deniability" and partly a practice designed to protect traditional ISI assets such as insurgent groups, which may be out of favor either with the national leadership or with Pakistan's international friends.[37] It is widely reported that some retired ISI officers continue to maintain contacts with the clients they dealt with when they were on active duty. This introduces an even murkier area into ISI's operational style.

ISI's professional formation and attitudes are similar to those of the rest of the army, only more so. Its officers are intensely suspicious of India, and the commitment to "strategic depth" is strongest in ISI. Like other Pakistanis, especially in the army, ISI officers have a strongly developed sense of honor and are quick to accuse others of "selling the country too cheaply." Officers who serve there are waiting for the next "American betrayal." They are supremely confident that they understand better than anyone—even better than the rest of the army—what Pakistan's security requires. ISI is a risk-taking organization that manages its risks in part by assiduous efforts to cover its tracks. Its institutional culture is more religious than the rest of the army.[38]

ISI has a reputation for high-handedness, and its special status has provided the opportunity to settle scores behind a veil of operational secrecy.

---

36. Authors' interview with retired U.S. official.
37. Authors' interviews with retired U.S. and Pakistani officials.
38. Authors' observations and interviews with retired U.S. officials.

This helps explain the fearful and suspicious tones in which Pakistanis sometimes speak of the organization. Shuja Nawaz recounts an incident in which physical assaults and other abuse were visited on a much-decorated Pakistan army brigadier and his family by ISI plainclothes operatives. The incident was apparently in retaliation for an altercation between the children of a senior ISI official and the brigadier's grandchildren. The episode embarrassed the army and drew a rare public apology from the military spokesman, but there is no indication of disciplinary action against ISI or the individuals responsible.[39]

In keeping with its intelligence mission, ISI cultivates secrecy and practices deception. ISI officers are wary of Americans who "know too much." They insist on keeping control of operations that touch on Pakistan's vital interests and try to prevent their U.S. counterparts from getting too deeply involved. ISI insisted, for example, on keeping full operational control of the supply of weapons and money to the Afghan mujahideen fighting the Soviet army. One retired former ISI chief's description of those years—tinged with a strong sense of accomplishment and not a little nostalgia—is instructive. The United States, Saudi Arabia, and Pakistan, he said, all had clearly delimited tasks: the Saudis and the United States supplied funds, the United States managed the funds, and Pakistan spent them. Pakistan retained the discretion to modify the agreed-on lists of whom they would support, confident that the United States would not complicate this congenial working arrangement with too many questions.[40] In short, his account described a rather one-sided working relationship, based on limited information flows and putting money into a "black box." It is hardly surprising that this evoked nostalgic memories.

The agreements between ISI and the CIA during these years were usually worked out one-on-one between the heads of both organizations, based on a handshake. There were no notetakers. U.S. officials familiar with this period observed that ISI routinely deceived them, typically by overstating the degree to which they were honoring U.S. requests. ISI officers appeared surprised when they were found out.[41]

Deception was, intentionally or not, a two-sided affair. Pakistani officers believed that they had assurances from their U.S. counterparts that Pakistan's nuclear program would not stand in the way of further cooperation. This of

---

39. Nawaz, *Crossed Swords*, 579. The source is noteworthy: Nawaz's elder brother, Gen. Asif Nawaz Janjua, served as chief of army staff and died under mysterious circumstances.

40. Authors' interview.

41. Authors' interviews with retired U.S. and Pakistani officials.

course turned out to be wrong. CIA did develop its own independent links to Afghan insurgents, much to the anger of ISI when it found out.[42]

The relationship between ISI and its American counterparts is remarkably resilient. Because agreements are reached and implemented in the shadows, cooperation can continue—and new negotiations take place—even during periods when U.S.-Pakistan relations are badly strained. After the 1990 aid cutoff, for example, the United States approached ISI to suggest that they collaborate on antinarcotics work. ISI was not enthusiastic, but surely interpreted the request as evidence of their own importance to the United States, and as a way of keeping Washington in their debt: once again, the art of the guilt trip.

ISI is a relentless practitioner of realpolitik. It has no "enduring alliances" (though it does have enduring hostility toward India) and will pursue its own interests even if those fall afoul of the United States' or another friendly country's. Operational negotiations with ISI reflect personal relationships— the close ties Ambassador Robert Oakley cultivated with the officers who headed ISI during his time in Islamabad come to mind, as do the personal relationships CIA chief William Casey built with his counterparts and with Zia. But these coexist with deception in the line of duty. ISI officials tend to treat the U.S. government as a mirror image of their own, and to regard the CIA not just as the friendliest agency but as an institution capable of trumping, and deceiving, the rest of the U.S. government.

Pakistan, the United States, and Afghanistan

Afghanistan has been the entry point for two of Pakistan's three periods of close relations with the United States and the generous military assistance that went with it. The most important collaborations between ISI and the CIA dealt with Afghanistan, during the 1980s and after 9/11. ISI was, under the close direction of President Zia, the dominant voice shaping policy toward Afghanistan, and the CIA was similarly the primary bureaucratic player, but not the only one, on the U.S. side. During the post-9/11 period, the U.S. structure for negotiating and implementing policy was much more complex, with the Defense and State Departments as major players. In the Obama administration, the president's special envoy, Ambassador Richard Holbrooke, became the most prominent personality on the U.S. side. The Pakistan government's structure for dealing with Afghanistan changed

---

42. Ibid.

much less: the regular army became a more prominent player, but ISI still had the lead.

Triangular negotiations involving the United States, Afghanistan, and Pakistan became a staple of U.S. policy during this period. As noted earlier, Pakistan and the United States are working together on the basis of certain shared objectives, but behind these lie significant differences in their purposes and tactics. If the U.S. priority is to prevent Afghanistan from becoming an ill-governed haven for terrorists, Pakistan's is to preserve its influence there. The expectation that the current U.S. security involvement in Pakistan and Afghanistan will come to an end at some relatively early point is almost universal in Pakistan's military and especially in ISI. So for them, Pakistan's goal is to have the best possible position in Afghanistan the morning after the U.S. withdrawal they consider inevitable.

Especially since 9/11, the United States has wanted to be involved in the Pakistan-Afghan dialogue, especially when relations between Islamabad and Kabul are strained, as is often the case. For its part, Pakistan has once again sought to keep the Americans from getting too close to its networks and relationships. To this end, it emphasizes the cultural uniqueness of Afghanistan and the adjoining Pashtun-dominated areas in Pakistan and argues that because Pakistan understands these areas and the United States does not, U.S. officials should give Pakistan primacy. During the 1980s, when the United States ran its operations in Afghanistan through ISI, this approach was by and large successful.

The Pashtun factor is woven into the way Pakistan thinks about and makes policy toward Afghanistan. Pashtuns make up about 15 percent of Pakistan's population, including virtually the entire population of Khyber Pakhtunkhwa and about half the population of Balochistan, the two provinces that border Afghanistan, plus over three million Pashtuns resident in Karachi and smaller populations scattered around the country.[43] Pashtuns have traditionally dominated Afghanistan, and Pashtuns from both countries share a conviction that the British-drawn 1893 Durand Line dividing them is arbitrary. Partly in deference to the sensibilities of its Pashtun population, Pakistan has been solicitous of the tradition of Pashtun predominance in Afghanistan, and particularly of the tribes that have members on the Pakistani side of the border. At the same time, it is this same Afghan Pashtun group that has historically supported the call by successive Afghan governments for the transfer of Pakistan's Pashtun areas to Afghanistan.

---

43. CIA, "Pakistan," *The World Factbook*.

Pakistan has usually assigned Pashtuns to many of the key government and military posts that have responsibility for the frontier areas and for Afghanistan. The officers who staff ISI's Afghan operations are disproportionately Pashtuns. So are senior civil servants with responsibility for Khyber Pakhtunkhwa and the tribal areas. Pakistan's ambassador in Kabul has almost always been a Pashtun.

In practice, Pakistan often has difficulty dealing with the tribal structure and cultural milieu in Afghanistan and the tribal areas. For non-Pashtun Pakistanis, the tribal areas are alien territory, and even Pashtuns from a cosmopolitan background may not be as familiar with the ins and outs of these tribal societies as they claim to be. And non-Pashtun Pakistanis are often regarded as outsiders in that tightly bound society. General Ashfaq Pervez Kayani was quoted as telling Condoleezza Rice, in connection with proposals that Pakistan take a more aggressive posture toward the tribal areas, "Madame secretary, they call us all white men."[44] But the United States has difficulty countering the argument of cultural familiarity.

Pakistan believes it faces higher stakes in Afghanistan than the United States. In contrast to the 1980s, however, the presence of U.S. troops puts Afghanistan, and Pakistan's policy there, at the very center of the U.S. foreign policy stage. U.S.-Pakistani tensions over Afghanistan are much more public and more anguishing than they were in an earlier era. Nor does the United States share Pakistan's perception of Afghanistan as an extension of the Indian threat. The United States is prepared to be sensitive to Pakistani concerns on this score, but only up to a point. At the same time, the United States has been careful not to encourage India to become involved in Afghan security and political matters.

Many observers believe that the dominant ISI role and the intensity of Pakistan's concerns about a widely anticipated "next divorce" with the United States result in a dual Pakistani policy, in which the stated objective of the government is to stabilize Afghanistan, but the real priority is to ensure that Pakistan's friends are at the center of the Afghan government. ISI and the army are especially attracted to this more ambitious goal. Until recently, this "rainy day" policy treated the Taliban as a strategic ally for Pakistan, or at least a potential asset that Pakistan may need to use in its epic rivalry with India. Pakistan's decision to go after its internal insurgents in the Pakistani counterpart to the Taliban movement in May 2009 suggests that at least the Pakistani elements of the Taliban movement have attracted the enmity of

---

44. Cited in Miller, "CIA Says It Gets Its Money's Worth."

the Pakistan army. However, it does not indicate any lessening of Pakistan's desire to ensure a pliant regime in Kabul.

During the 1980s there was no "triangular diplomacy" as such, but Afghanistan was the lead issue in bilateral discussions between the United States and Pakistan, and the basis for their resumed alliance. Following the establishment of the post-9/11 Afghan government headed by Hamid Karzai, the United States became very interested in establishing trilateral linkages in an effort to secure the porous border and also to establish better relations between the Pakistani and Afghan leadership.

A Tripartite Commission involving primarily military representatives from all three countries began meeting in 2003. According to U.S. officials who were involved, it had some success as a relationship-building exercise, but little operational impact. Relatively senior officials attended, including three-star generals from all three countries. For the Afghans, the commission was an opportunity to enlist the United States on their side. American participants felt that the Pakistanis saw themselves and the U.S. team as real military comrades, with the Afghan team in a subordinate position. Meetings usually included briefings on military operations. The group spent a great deal of time working on the press release that would be issued at the conclusion of the meeting. Typically, the Americans provided the first draft. Much of the meeting was taken up with drafting changes, in which the major issue often was how to describe the boundary separating Afghanistan from Pakistan, the Durand Line, which no Afghan government has recognized as an international frontier. Afghanistan wanted to avoid characterizing it as a border; the Pakistani participants wanted to emphasize that it was a border.

The commission spawned lower-level committees. The narcotics committee had some serious discussions, although the Pakistan army was not keen to get more deeply involved in drug issues. The intelligence committee seems to have morphed into a more elaborate joint border intelligence entity. The committees' success in expanding personal relationships should not be dismissed: both Afghanistan and Pakistan run on personal relationships. But in general, this was a classic encounter of action-oriented Americans with Pakistanis and Afghans whose main objective was to avoid giving anything away.[45]

More recently, Richard Holbrooke has orchestrated a series of higher-level tripartite meetings among political figures. This had actually started when President George W. Bush invited Presidents Karzai and Musharraf

---

45. Authors' interview with retired U.S. official.

to dinner together at the White House in September 2006. It was a painful event, as the television coverage made clear. Both guests looked as if they wanted to be on opposite sides of the moon. The personal chemistry between the top leaders became more promising after Asif Zardari became president of Pakistan in August 2008. In May 2009, a group of Afghan and Pakistani cabinet ministers came to Washington for meetings with each other and with their U.S. counterparts. This was once again predominantly a relationship-building effort, and it seems to have been fairly effective. It is not clear, however, how much impact this will have on the military- and intelligence-dominated issues that ultimately determine policy between Afghanistan and Pakistan.

Pakistan's negotiating approach toward Afghanistan in these triangular encounters is different from the one it uses with the United States. Pakistan is the dominant power, and Afghanistan the "younger brother." Pakistanis continue to regard Hamid Karzai's government as excessively influenced by Afghanistan's non-Pashtun tribes. One American observer commented that Pakistanis behave in joint Afghan-Pakistani meetings as if they, rather than the Afghans, "represented the Pashtuns."[46] Especially in military meetings, such as the Tripartite Commission, the Pakistani participants seem to regard the U.S. officers as their real counterparts, and the Afghans as having lower status. Pakistan's well-developed sense of grievance underpins its approach, as does its conviction that India is threatening Pakistan by the back door from Afghanistan. The relationship with Afghanistan's political leaders is intensely personal.

Pakistan's approach to the United States in these encounters follows the pattern we have seen elsewhere, especially for issues dominated by the military and ISI. Pakistani negotiators' strong presumption is that Pakistan understands these issues far better than Americans ever will, and that with time, they can ultimately have their way. The overlay of suspicion, the predominant sense of grievance, and the expectation of U.S. fickleness are all there, together with the realpolitik that characterizes ISI's approach to the world.

---

46. Authors' interview with retired U.S. official.

5

Diplomats, Civil Servants, and the Problem of Authority

Pakistan's civilian government services grew out of the hierarchy of civil services established by the British, the steel frame that ran the government of India in the days before partition. In independent Pakistan, however, they have been outflanked and outranked by the military.

In British days, the elite Indian Civil Service was the core group. In independent Pakistan, the Civil Service of Pakistan inherited that mantle. The Pakistan Foreign Service shared its elite standing as well as the prominent social background and good education of its members. During the first two of Pakistan's military-led regimes, between 1958 and 1971, the civil service was a partner of the military in running what they hoped would be a good technocratic government. In each of the subsequent periods of military-led rule, the role of the civil service diminished. This reflected the impact of populist administrative reforms in the 1970s that replaced the elite branches of the civil services with less competent and confident organizations. More fundamentally, it stemmed from the military's growing contempt for civilians of all stripes.[1]

This chapter will examine in turn the diplomats and civil servants who form the sinews of Pakistan's government and carry out many of its negotiations with the United States. These officials share many of the same negotiating traits as their military colleagues, but with one striking difference: whereas military officers are supremely— perhaps overly—confident, not just of their ability but also of their standing to make national decisions, civilian officials are often to some degree feeling their way, testing how much authority they will be able to exercise. On matters of national security, civilian officials may at times be able to block a negotiation, but the military and in some cases the national leadership must be on board to say

---

1. Charles H. Kennedy, *Bureaucracy in Pakistan* (Karachi: Oxford University Press, 1987), 54–88.

"yes." Shifting authority patterns have an impact on how Pakistani civilian officials approach their task.

The Civil Services: Best and Brightest, or Second Fiddle?

Recruitment to the foreign service and the civil service both start with the rigorously competitive Federal Public Service Examination. Assignments to a particular ministry or specialized service are based on a combination of merit and the preference of the candidate. Before the reforms of the 1970s, the foreign service could count on recruiting a major proportion of the high scorers on the exam. Following the reforms, an affirmative action program was grafted onto the system to expand recruitment from underrepresented areas, including rural Sindh, Balochistan, and the tribal areas. More important, the job market changed. Private sector opportunities available to bright young Pakistanis with a university education and good English expanded markedly in the 1990s, luring candidates away from government service. Within the government sector, most of the top ten candidates on the annual exam went elsewhere. In 2008, the most popular destinations were the police and the District Management Group, the group within the civil service that most closely approximates the Civil Service of Pakistan that preceded the reform. Also popular were Customs and Audit and Accounts, seen as more lucrative. The government tries to have women compose 10 percent of the recruits into each ministry.

Recruitment to officer-level positions in either the civil service or the foreign service requires at least a bachelor's degree; a master's is common. Recruits come from a mixed social and educational background, which in practice tilts toward urban populations and the middle or upper middle class because of the educational requirements. New entrants are less likely than they once were to have been schooled abroad or in Pakistan's most prestigious universities. Almost all have excellent English. Those whose English is weak are at a serious disadvantage, and the government training institutions do not include remedial English.[2]

Pakistan maintains a Civil Services Academy that conducts basic training for new entrants into both the civil service and the foreign service. President Musharraf's government assigned as its director a retired three-star general, Javed Hassan, who had previously served as commandant of the National Defense University. Both men clearly wanted to bring to the civil-

---

2. Ambassador Fauzia Nasreen, director general of the Foreign Service Academy, interview with the authors.

ian arm of government the more structured and more vigorous approach to training that was used in the military. Under General Hassan's leadership, the academy instituted a number of mandatory courses, mostly focusing on the "tradecraft" involved in managing government services. The training includes presentations on Pakistan's history and its security interests; negotiation is not directly part of the curriculum. Hassan commented that he wanted to provide training—that is, development of professionally relevant skills—rather than education, which the newly recruited officials should in any case be bringing to the table.[3]

The Pakistan Foreign Service still attracts a talented group despite changes in the job market. Recruits who joined the foreign service in the 2008 batch had degrees in law, literature, international relations, and engineering. Assignments within the service are usually controlled by the foreign secretary, the senior foreign service officer in the ministry, who effectively runs the organization. The most coveted assignments are those in major English-speaking countries and China. Service in India is recognized as professionally important, and some of the service's best officers are assigned there, but it is often a rather unpleasant experience.[4]

The Pakistan Foreign Service Academy, established in 1981, conducts courses both for Pakistani diplomats and for participants from other developing countries. New recruits go through a brief orientation with their civil service counterparts, followed by a year-long course. For most, this is the only formal training they will receive during their career. The participants' grades in the entry-level course will determine their seniority when they move to regular assignments, a sure formula for increasing their attention to the training task. The curriculum includes lectures on the subjects one would expect to find in a diplomatic training institute, including the theory and practice of diplomacy, international relations, law, politics, and economics, and Pakistan's foreign policy and international economic relations. It also includes writing exercises and simulations of the sort that are much more common in American schools than in Pakistan.

---

3. Lt. Gen. (ret.) Javed Hassan, interviews with the authors. The different philosophies of training in the military and in the civilian branches of government service track with the experience of other countries. Teresita Schaffer, who served as director of the U.S. Foreign Service Institute from 1995 to 1997, found a very similar dichotomy in the United States: for the military, training was a distinct activity to which people were assigned full time; in the culture of the State Department, apart from language training and other similarly clear-cut skills, most officers believe that their most valuable training is obtained on the job, in real-life crises. The directors of diplomatic academies in other governments report very similar experiences.

4. Ambassador Fauzia Nasreen, interview, and Abdul Sattar, interview.

The exercises used to train Pakistani diplomats in negotiation involve conducting informal consultations and negotiating resolutions in a simulated United Nations setting. The skills and dynamics needed for bilateral diplomacy are covered more in lectures than in exercises. These exercises do not appear to be intensive or elaborate enough to develop a real institutional "playbook" on how to conduct negotiations. However, the guidance the academy's director seeks to leave uppermost in students' minds is that they need to know their brief and know "where Pakistan stands" vis-à-vis their negotiating partners. With respect to the United States, the training emphasizes the need to be "as truthful as possible" and to recognize that the Americans they deal with are usually in a hurry.

Those at the top of Pakistan's diplomatic service in many cases joined the service with a higher level of education than today's recruits. For many years, the Pakistan Foreign Service sent all its junior officers for a year's training to the United States, to the Fletcher School at Tufts University. This program ended in 1963. Since then, training has been less regular, but a cooperative training arrangement has been established with the Netherlands Institute of International Relations at Clingendael.[5]

Foreign Service officers who serve as ambassadors, or in the ministry at the level of secretary or additional secretary, are urbane and impressive. Having dealt with foreigners for their entire career, they may be more nuanced and sophisticated than military officers in their discussion of Pakistan's place in the world and its rivalry with India. At the same time, they have probably spent twenty years or more keeping score on the comparative standing accorded India and Pakistan, and this has left them with a keen nose for any signs of disrespect. This attitude becomes apparent especially in times of high tension.

Foreign Service officers, more than other Pakistani negotiators, like to build arguments around the principles of international law.[6] This can come across to their American counterparts as academic, impractical, and ponderous. U.S. efforts to respond with the kind of legal arguments that are more meaningful to them—typically involving the constraints on U.S. action imposed by U.S. law or legislative procedures—similarly produce at least inward groans on the Pakistani side. Legal discussions are an essential part of

---

5. The information on current recruitment and training of Pakistani Foreign Service officers is drawn from the authors' interview with Ambassador Nasreen and from the Foreign Service Academy booklet, *28th Specialised Diplomatic Course for FSP Officers: Guide for the Participants.*

6. See, for example, Abdul Sattar, *Pakistan's Foreign Policy 1947–2005: A Concise History* (Oxford: Oxford University Press, 2007), 13–15, and Agha Shahi, *Pakistan's Security and Foreign Policy* (Lahore: Progressive Publishers, 1988), 7. Both authors served as both Pakistan's foreign secretary and foreign minister.

many negotiations, but if one is searching for a solution, both sides would do well to minimize this aspect of their discussions.

This emphasis on concepts of international law and obligations can take surprising forms. For example, in contrast to the usual Pakistani effort to maximize the U.S. supply of aid and military equipment, Pakistan's top diplomat of the day, Agha Shahi, urged President Zia to refuse concessional military assistance during the negotiations with the United States that followed the Soviet invasion of Afghanistan in 1979. He felt that accepting concessional terms would make Pakistan beholden to the United States in ways he found risky or unacceptable.[7]

Pakistani diplomatic officials, especially those who have served at the United Nations or in other multilateral organizations, are also very sensitive to Pakistan's standing as a member of the Non-Aligned Movement (NAM) and other developing-country organizations. This reflects in part the fact that India kept Pakistan out of the NAM for decades. It is also a way of trying to diversify Pakistan's diplomatic "protectors" beyond the United States. Pakistani diplomats are similarly very solicitous of the sensitivities of Pakistan's Muslim friends. All of these arguments—diversifying Pakistan's sources of support as well as the legal arguments—come back to one of the central tenets of Pakistan's approach to negotiating with the United States: that Pakistan must be exceptionally vigilant in managing a basically asymmetrical relationship.

Like other senior Pakistani officials, Foreign Service officers come to negotiations well prepared. They usually operate on the basis of specific cleared instructions. How much leeway they have to expand on these depends on the individual involved and his or her standing with the national leadership. Pakistan's senior diplomats tend to be exacting negotiators of language. Who does the drafting is not necessarily a major issue, but officials in the Foreign Service will continue until (and sometimes beyond) the last minute trying to improve the language. If the agreement in question can be interpreted to have an implied comparison with India, this will be a particular focus for attention.

One of the great frustrations of Pakistan's talented diplomatic corps is that their institution does not really control the heart of Pakistan's foreign policy. The Ministry of Foreign Affairs (MFA) has a stronger institutional structure than many other ministries, and a more elaborate system for internal clearances. Historically, however, the national political leadership and the military have had the deciding voice regarding relations with the United

---

7. Shahi, *Pakistan's Security and Foreign Policy*, 178. Shahi's view was not shared by the military.

States and on the issues that drive ties with Washington: the nuclear program, relations with India, and Afghanistan.

The ministry's relations with the national leadership have often been difficult. However, some of its senior officials—foreign secretaries in Islamabad and diplomats overseas—have been extraordinarily adept at navigating the waters of Pakistan government authority. Two former foreign secretaries told of episodes in which they talked presidents or prime ministers out of an action they had planned to take. These were examples of skillful personal negotiation and networking; there was little or no carryover to the next foreign secretary.[8]

Aside from the diplomats, the most important civil servants with whom U.S. officials regularly negotiate are Pakistan's senior economic officials. In earlier years, these were people who had studied abroad and came to the service with advanced degrees in economics from Oxford, Cambridge, or comparable U.S. universities. The government did not provide training in negotiations, nor did it offer "senior training" as preparation for the most senior jobs.

The Ministry of Finance is the most sophisticated and prestigious of the economic ministries, and the finance secretary (or secretary-general) is usually the most senior civil servant not only in his ministry but in the economic ministries as a whole. Americans who have worked on finance issues have found its top civil servants exceptionally well qualified, sophisticated, businesslike, and pragmatic. They were also less prickly about the United States than some of their colleagues in other ministries. Many of these officials had experience in Washington and had dealt with the U.S. government as well as the World Bank and International Monetary Fund. This gave them broad experience with the world of international finance.

Senior finance officials have a more economically driven view of Pakistan's interests. Their priority is Pakistan's economic health, typically starting with the country's balance of payments and its modern sector, but also including "poverty alleviation." The constant comparison with India is less of a factor when negotiating with economic officials. These officials are of course very well aware of the success India has enjoyed since 1990, but they see in this record an experience that Pakistan should emulate, not a threat to Pakistan's status or national security. They also see improved economic performance as a major security benefit for Pakistan. By virtue of their experience and their broad responsibility for Pakistan's aid receipts, finance officials usually see

---

8. The discussion of the negotiating style of Pakistani Foreign Service officers draws on Shahi, *Pakistan's Security and Foreign Policy*, and on the authors' interviews with Robert Oakley, former U.S. ambassador to Pakistan; Phyllis Oakley, a former U.S. embassy official in Pakistan; Shamshad Ahmed, former foreign secretary; and Tariq Fatemi, Abdul Sattar, Riaz Khokhar, and Shahryar Khan.

their negotiations with the United States as part of a larger picture. They are typically trying to reach not just an agreement with the United States but a broader package of agreements—on the size of aid programs, or the shape of an IMF program, or on rearranging debt payments—that involves other players, and in which U.S. support for Pakistan with those other players is only one of the variables. Far more than Pakistan's other officials below the level of president or prime minister, they are thus willing to enlarge the scope of negotiations in order to "get to yes."

At the same time, these officials want to maximize Pakistan's flexibility. They will resist conditionality in aid agreements (whether with the U.S. government or with other international donors); they will press for aid to be given in the form of cash or quasi-cash, rather than projects. They understand the mechanics of these processes and will be diligent about making sure their hands are not tied any more than is necessary. They are looking for "help without advice," as one former U.S. official put it to the authors.

Pakistan's national leaders, both military and civilian, respect the expertise of the top finance officials, at least within their area of responsibility. The finance ministry alone among the civilian ministries has at least a minor voice in the financial mechanics (if not the substance) of military procurement. Most of Pakistan's national leaders look on economics as an intimidating "black box," and rely heavily on those with the specialized knowledge to see inside it. For military officers, economic progress is a desirable national goal, but ranks as a national security issue only when the country's economic problems reach a crisis point. Finance secretaries cultivate close relations with the national leadership. They are better able than most unelected Pakistani civilian officials to reach an agreement and make it stick.

The top finance officials are the cream of the civil service crop. Observers in both Pakistan and the United States have commented that the level of sophistication and training further down in the civil service ranks is less impressive, and is falling. Lower-ranking officers are less secure in their government positions and more concerned about running afoul of their superiors or the military. The most immediate consequences for negotiations with the United States are reduced willingness and ability to make decisions and to make agreements stick, and a less nuanced view of Pakistan's international interests.

A handful of Pakistan's finance ministers have basically been technocrats. The clearest example is Shaukat Aziz, Musharraf's finance minister and later prime minister. A former Citibank official, he played a central role in the economic negotiations with both the United States and the

IMF following Musharraf's takeover and after 9/11. These negotiations had a dynamic similar to working with top finance ministry officials, except that Aziz had more power and greater discretion, both by virtue of his ministerial position and especially because of the confidence the president had in him personally. The respect in which he held his ministry's senior officials also enhanced their stature.[9]

Navigating the Pakistan Government: The Problem of Authority

Civilian officials and those who negotiate with them have to deal constantly with the problem of overlapping and conflicting authorities within the Pakistan government. The divisions fall along three axes: between civilians and the military; within the civilian world, including divisions among ministries and between the civil servants and the politicians; and between personal networks and the institutions of the Pakistan government.

As noted, the army holds the high cards on anything touching security, which it interprets to include nuclear policy and Pakistan's relations with India, Afghanistan, and the major outside friends, principally the United States and China. Others may articulate policy or even negotiate within this realm, but no agreement connected to national security can stick without the support of the military. Even civilian prime ministers venture into these areas at their peril and need to take the army with them. Military leaders at the national level have used the corps commanders to create and enforce consensus within the army. Civilian leaders have generally brought the army into their deliberations through the chief of army staff. It is common for major Pakistani delegations going abroad to include a military adviser or two. Efforts to create an institutionalized voice for military recommendations on national policy, most recently the legislation creating a National Security Council with mixed military and political membership, have not resolved this problem. Civilians have seen the council as a thinly disguised military intrusion into policy; the army viewed it as an inadequate substitute for a direct policy role, and in practice continued to weigh in, if necessary outside the regular policy process, whenever it felt its interests were at risk.

---

9. The section on senior finance officials and on Prime Minister Shaukat Aziz draws on the authors' own experience and their interviews with Mueen Afzal, retired secretary-general of finance; Alan Larson, former U.S. under secretary of state for economic and business affairs; Patricia Haslach, former economic counselor, U.S. embassy in Pakistan; Andrew Haviland, former economic counselor, U.S. embassy in Pakistan; and William Milam, former U.S. ambassador in Pakistan.

In the normal workings of government, the institutional asymmetry between the civilian ministries and the military can be a real impediment to decision making, and confuses Pakistan's international interlocutors. Civilian agencies recognize that they need to touch base with the army on issues it cares about, but the reverse is not true. Senior Pakistani civilian officials complain that they are often not briefed on meetings between senior American visitors and military officials. These problems are especially acute during periods of military rule. They are compounded by the U.S. practice of making sure that all its senior officials, whether military or civilian, touch base with Pakistan's military leadership in addition to whatever civilian calls they make.

Civilian institutions are in the shadow of the army, but there is little formal liaison between them. The military officers Musharraf stationed in civilian ministries as "monitors" reported on activities in the ministry but provided little coordination or two-way communication. The principal exceptions to this rule, as already noted, are the top officials in the finance ministry, who have expertise that is important to the military in arranging the financing of their major purchases, and who have sometimes been able to make personal relationships at the top that give them a freer hand.

The influence and authority of the Ministry of Foreign Affairs is uneven and depends a great deal on the personal relations between its leaders and the national leadership. Foreign ministers vary in the degree to which they control foreign policy and in their closeness to the national leadership. Some have been the central figure in foreign policymaking, but others have had primarily a personal or political role. In the "permanent government," however, the key official is the foreign secretary. A close relationship with the president or prime minister can give a foreign secretary remarkable access and influence. On the other hand, when the national leadership either does not like the foreign secretary or considers him too hidebound, the MFA is bypassed. Three foreign secretaries have become foreign ministers, all in either military or "interim" governments.

The MFA and the Pakistan Foreign Service have skills that can give them a strong role in crafting the formal brief on which negotiations are based and in transmitting information through the Pakistan government. Foreign Service officers tend to be good drafters. After India's nuclear weapons tests in 1998, the MFA set up a kind of secretariat to manage the overwhelming flow of information on international reaction to the tests and to get Pakistan's position out to the diplomatic corps and the press. It is the only civilian institution in Pakistan capable of this kind of organization. This capacity does not enhance its status compared with the military, however.

For decades, the MFA has seconded a couple of officers, one of them quite senior, to the office of the prime minister, a much prized assignment that several of Pakistan's most distinguished diplomats have held. The officers in question quickly became associated in the minds of their colleagues and others with the particular leader who held office at that time. The young diplomat who served as the prime minister's notetaker under Zulfiqar Ali Bhutto came back as the senior MFA liaison officer when Bhutto's daughter was prime minister. The senior MFA liaison officer in Prime Minister Nawaz Sharif's office was appointed ambassador to the United States, only to be kicked out by Musharraf following his seizure of power, on the assumption that he was too close to Sharif.[10]

Record keeping is uneven. One observer with close ties to the military noted that no written records were kept of the 1999 visit to Washington of Shahbaz Sharif, brother of the then prime minister, described in chapter 3. One reason for this was that the military had concerns that Sharif might have said some things they disagreed with, which they did not want "minuted."[11]

The relationship between elected politicians who serve as ministers and the staff of their ministry varies greatly. The institutional loyalties of officials working in a particular ministry run through the secretary—the senior civil servant or Foreign Service officer in the ministry—rather than the minister. This reflects the way formal authority runs in Pakistan. Agreements on behalf of the Pakistani state are normally signed by the secretary, with the minister looking on, rather than by the minister him- or herself. The secretaries represent the permanent government, whereas the ministers represent the government of the day. The secretary may work closely with the minister, and when that happens, the two may be "networked" over the long term. In some cases, these relationships can significantly enhance the secretary's influence—on a personal rather than institutional level. A handful of additional officials in the ministry may develop a serious professional relationship with the minister, either by serving in the minister's office or by virtue of involvement in an issue of great personal interest to the minister. These people become bridges between the minister and a somewhat wider circle of subordinates.[12]

---

10. This discussion of civil-military liaison and of the MFA draws on the authors' own recollections and their interviews with Prof. Riffaat Hussein, Riaz Khokhar, Tariq Fatemi, Maleeha Lodhi, William Milam, Robert Oakley, Wendy Chamberlin, and Gen. (ret.) Jehangir Karamat.

11. Prof. Riffaat Hussein, interview.

12. The discussion of relations among civilian agencies and politicians draws on the authors' recollections and on interviews with Prof. Riffaat Hussein, Tanvir Ahmed Khan, Riaz Khokhar, Tariq Fatemi, and Wendy Chamberlin.

A handful of Pakistani civilian officials in senior positions, including several ambassadors to the United States and some foreign secretaries, have been able to exert far greater influence than this description of civilians in the military's shadow would suggest. Networking is the key to maintaining authority as a civilian in this military-dominated system. Other important characteristics are establishing direct personal relations with the military leadership, persistence, and the ability to deliver the goods, in this case key favorable decisions from the United States.

Pakistan's ambassadors in Washington have often been unhappy with the quality of information they got through the MFA, particularly when the military was involved in the issue they were concerned about. As a result, the Pakistani ambassadors who were most often described as effective all developed their own sources of information. Retired generals serving as ambassador already had links to the military and personal ties to President Musharraf or Zia. They had to work a little harder to get the MFA to respond to their requests for support. Their network into the MFA was built on the ties between their deputies, who were Foreign Service officers, and the foreign secretary.

Civilian ambassadors had to develop two kinds of networks. The first reached into the different parts of the military. One ambassador spoke of the vital importance of being able to call the director general of ISI directly in order to get information on controversial military operations that the MFA was unable to provide, such as the Kargil operation. Another had made it a point to stay in Islamabad for several weeks before going out as ambassador to the United States, to make sure that the necessary connections were in place not just with the MFA but with the military, including ISI. The military resisted the new ambassador's request to see the entire file on U.S.-Pakistani nuclear discussions, and the MFA was hesitant to push too hard, but eventually the file was made available. Both these ambassadors, as well as those who came out of the military, made it a point to telephone the top personalities in the military as well as the prime minister and president on a regular basis. These ambassadors believed they had developed a strong enough relationship that they were able to deliver bad news when the occasion required it, a rare trait in the Pakistani system.

The same techniques were used by a handful of effective foreign secretaries, though it seems to have been more difficult to sustain them from a position inside the government apparatus in Islamabad. A couple of former foreign secretaries were apparently close enough to Nawaz Sharif to be able to discuss some of the country's most sensitive issues with him. This was not impossible, but it was harder to do, in military-led governments, partly because foreign secretaries all come from outside the military family, and partly because generals at the national helm usually used a military-style staff structure that was more effective than the equivalent civilian mechanisms in discouraging contacts from further down the chain of command.

These were personal successes, however, not institutional ones. Whatever access one ambassador had achieved would not carry over. The next incumbent would have to develop his or her own network and forge an independent relationship with the national and military leadership.[13]

During periods of transition, either between political governments or between military- and civilian-led ones, the country's policy leadership on the civilian side effectively passes to the senior secretaries in the government ministries. Relatively few major policy decisions are made during these times, and senior bureaucrats will measure their authority carefully before making any decisions. But especially on issues that are not central to the military, secretaries can take advantage of a transition to make important decisions, for example on economic issues, and get them adopted before the end of the transition brings the political process back in full force.

Gaming the U.S. System

Pakistanis negotiating with the United States have to do more than navigate their own system. They must also "game out" how the U.S. system works. Pakistan's ambassadors in Washington are the key figures in deciphering the U.S. system, with its confusing array of government departments, executive-legislative relations unlike those in any other country, and a high-profile and influential media scene. In "working Washington," they start as usual from their convictions about Pakistan's place in the world and the nature of its ties with the United States, and they continue to work within their own complex authority structure. But the cultural context and the networking skills that are so critical in Pakistan are supplemented and sometimes overridden by a focus on fitting into the U.S. system and appealing to U.S. values.

The Pakistan embassy in Washington is one of the largest Pakistani missions in the world. Over the years, Pakistan has sent somewhat more professional diplomats as ambassadors to Washington than retired generals or noncareer officials. Almost without exception, ambassadors from all three

---

13. This passage on personal networking draws on the authors' recollections and on their interviews with Riaz Khokhar, Maleeha Lodhi, Mahmud Durrani, Tariq Fatemi, Abida Hussein, Gen. (ret.) Jehangir Karamat, Shahryar Khan, Wendy Chamberlin, William Milam, and Husain Haqqani, Pakistan's ambassador to the United States.

groups have been effective in Washington, and have been heavy hitters in their own government. Two of the career diplomats who served as ambassador to the United States subsequently became foreign minister, three later served as foreign secretary, and several others spent decades as ambassadors in Pakistan's most sensitive posts. As illustrated in the previous section, the most effective ambassadors have developed remarkable skills in networking within their own system.

In comparison with U.S. embassies overseas or with the embassies of some of the larger developing countries, Pakistan's embassy in Washington is very centralized. The ambassador has most of the action. Specialized issues may be handled by others, though the ambassador will keep a hand in anything important. The economic minister, for example, is responsible for relations with the IMF and the World Bank as well as with the United States. The ambassador will not try to take over this portfolio, but will remain informed and weigh in as needed.

The substantial role of the military carries over to Pakistani missions overseas. The defense attaché, usually a brigadier who goes on to more senior army jobs, has a lot of latitude and a wide circle of contacts in the Pentagon. In negotiations over the specifics of military supply, he is likely to be a central figure. Like his counterparts in other Pakistani posts, he is expected to keep tabs on his colleagues in the mission on behalf of the Pakistani military.[14]

Pakistanis assessing how the U.S. government will behave and how to approach it tend to project onto the U.S. government some of the features of their own. Thus, they assume that winning over a small number of officials at the top will solve their problems, and that their key relationships are with the White House, the Pentagon, and the intelligence community. Pakistani officials, especially military and intelligence officials, look on the Department of Defense and the CIA as the agencies most committed to relations with Pakistan. During the periods of closest U.S.-Pakistan relations, military and intelligence cooperation have been at the heart of the relationship. Relations with the CIA have been the preserve of Pakistan's intelligence chief more than of the ambassador in Washington. The officials responsible for negotiating military agreements with Washington know the U.S. Defense Department well.

The State Department is respected by Pakistan's diplomats but regarded as less friendly, especially during periods of cool relations between the two

---

14. This passage on the Pakistani embassy in Washington draws on the authors' recollections and their interviews with Maleeha Lodhi, Riaz Khokhar, Maj. Gen. (ret.) Mahmud Durrani, Gen. (ret.) Jehangir Karamat, Patricia Haslach, Alan Larson, and Woolf Gross.

countries. Other civilian organizations, especially the economic agencies, get involved only as particular issues come up. For Pakistanis, as for most other foreign diplomats in Washington, the multiplicity of actors on the U.S. government stage can be a bit bewildering, and many agencies are not involved on a consistent enough basis for Pakistanis to be able to feel confident about taking their measure.

The most difficult "constituency" in Washington, from Pakistan's point of view, is the Congress. At times, the Congress has been a major source of support for Pakistan. The golden years came during the late 1980s, when funding for the Afghan mujahideen fighting the Soviet Union was at its height, and Congressman Charlie Wilson had taken on the task of obtaining maximum funding and sophisticated weapons for them and for their Pakistani backers.

More frequently, however, Congress has been seen as the source of Pakistan's woes, or at least as the source of unpleasant surprises. Congress has come to symbolize the inconstancy of the United States. The Pressler Amendment, enacted in 1985 to make possible the renewal of a major aid program for Pakistan, led to an aid cutoff in 1990, and the many other sanctions that were either threatened or applied to Pakistan—deriving from its narcotics problem, the activities of Islamic extremist terrorists, and illegal trade in nuclear-related material—were the result of congressional action and the subject of intense congressional interest. Pakistani civilian and military officials discussing the U.S.-Pakistan negotiations that followed India's nuclear test made a point of saying that Pakistan was looking for security guarantees from the United States, but that such guarantees could only be considered reliable if they were enacted into law.

The Israeli and Indian lobbies in Congress are a particular concern for Pakistan. Not surprisingly, given their generally India-centered frame of reference for negotiations and their penchant for conspiracy theorizing, Pakistani officials see these two groups as colluding against Pakistan. A great frustration is the difficulty of getting time with members of Congress, either for Pakistan's Washington-based diplomats or for high-ranking visiting government officials and parliamentarians. Senior Pakistanis are not comfortable meeting with congressional staff. One former ambassador commented that he felt that being obliged to deal with staff rather than members was a sign of disrespect to his country.[15]

---

15. This section draws on the authors' personal recollections and on their interviews with Touqir Hussain, Riaz Khokhar, Maleeha Lodhi, Lt. Gen. (ret.) Javed Hassan, and Abida Hussain.

A Pakistani Success Story: Reimbursement for F-16 Payments

Pakistanis negotiating in Washington find two arguments especially valuable in winning over U.S. officials. The first is fairness, which they recognize as a key value in American culture. Second, they will when possible appeal to U.S. law. As discussed earlier, Pakistanis find U.S. officials excessively legalistic. But when the law is ambiguous, or when Pakistani negotiators are able to find legal cover for a "fairness" argument, they find this an effective technique.

Both figured prominently in Pakistan's campaign to obtain reimbursement of the money Pakistan paid for the F-16 aircraft whose delivery was banned by the 1990 sanctions triggered by the Pressler Amendment. After the sanctions went into effect, Pakistan continued making payments, in the hope that something would end the aid ban. After several years, it stopped paying and asked for its money back. The U.S. government, consistent with its standard contracting provisions, refused on the grounds that all Pakistan's payments had already been passed on to the manufacturers of the aircraft. Since the U.S. government no longer held the Pakistanis' funds, it could not reimburse them.

Pakistan's diplomats began working this issue as a "fairness" question. People who had worked on it in the U.S. government considered the refusal to reimburse as fundamentally unreasonable, and Pakistan tried hard to bring this unfairness to the attention of the U.S. political leadership. President Clinton, whom two Pakistani ambassadors in a row described as impressed by the fairness argument, had initiated a search for a solution, but it proceeded at a desultory pace. Publicly released correspondence between Lee Hamilton, then the ranking minority member of the House Foreign Affairs Committee,[16] and Secretary of State Madeleine Albright and National Security Adviser Sandy Berger emphasized the fundamental injustice of not refunding Pakistan's money. This certainly improved the atmospherics for Pakistan's case.[17]

Recognizing that persuasion was not producing results, Ambassador Riaz Khokhar looked for a more compelling approach. He engaged a lawyer, Lanny Davis, who had earlier served in the Clinton White House. At Davis's suggestion, Khokhar floated to the administration the idea of taking the U.S. government to court. He made clear that he much preferred to

---

16. From 1995 to 2007, the committee was called the House International Relations Committee.

17. Hon. Lee H. Hamilton, of Indiana, in the House of Representatives, "U.S.-Pakistan Relationship Worth Repairing," *Congressional Record* 144, no. 46 (April 23, 1998): E666-E667, http://fdsys.gpo.gov/fdsys/pkg/CREC-1998-04-23/html/CREC-1998-04-23-pt1-PgE666-2.htm.

work things out diplomatically, but argued that he "trusted the fairness of the U.S. courts." The U.S. side pushed back. However, once the administration became convinced that Pakistan might win in court—and might even win a judgment awarding them principal and interest on their payments—the search for a mechanism for reimbursement began in earnest.

The United States eventually decided to draw on a special Justice Department fund established to settle potentially losing lawsuits against the U.S. government, supplemented by an in-kind payment in the form of food aid to make up the gap between what the Justice Department could fund and the Pakistan government's payments. It was a businesslike negotiation, without public drama. Pakistan had relied primarily on tactics that were powerful motivators for Americans but that were not necessarily part of its own normal negotiating practices. The Pakistanis used a U.S. lawyer, gained leverage from the U.S. legal process, and negotiated a pragmatic solution to the problem.[18]

Working the Congress: The Brown Amendment

The importance of networking and the approach Pakistan has used to work with the Congress are illustrated by its participation in securing passage of the Brown Amendment in 1996, which restored some of the economic assistance that had been cut off by sanctions in 1990. In this case, Pakistan was working with the Clinton administration, which had decided that restoring economic assistance to Pakistan was necessary in order to engage Pakistan on issues important to the United States.

Once again, the "fairness" argument was central, and once again the Pakistani ambassador, then Maleeha Lodhi, worked hard to understand the U.S. system and to fit her advocacy into it. Her approach also exhibited the networking skills and emphasis on personal relationships that work so well in the Pakistani system. She developed a close working relationship with the then secretary of defense, who was the strongest champion of this legislation within the administration. One former senior defense official noted that Lodhi was one of the few foreign ambassadors able to see the secretary whenever she needed to.

The embassy had engaged lobbyists to amplify its congressional outreach, but in this case, Lodhi thought she would be her own best advocate and worked hard to enhance her own direct access to the members of Congress

---

18. The account of the reimbursement issue draws on interviews with Riaz Khokhar, Karl F. Inderfurth, Maleeha Lodhi, and Robin Raphel.

critical to passage of the legislation. Pakistan's traditional friends in Congress had been Republicans, whose interest was sparked initially by the Cold War and more recently by their interest in supporting the Afghan mujahideen during the 1980s. With a Democratic White House and a Republican Congress, Pakistan's historical friendships complemented the administration's natural working relationships with its fellow Democrats in Congress. Lodhi's own impressive public persona was a tremendous asset. In frequent appearances in public and on television, she put the best face on Pakistan's position, with an elegant speaking style and a refreshing dose of candor that added to her credibility. She also mobilized the Pakistani-American community to supplement her efforts.

Lodhi also "marketed" Benazir Bhutto, then in her second stint as Pakistan's prime minister. As an intelligent, attractive, modern Muslim woman leader, educated in the United States, Bhutto had tremendous appeal in Washington, and more generally among the American people.

Lodhi believed that India was trying to block the legislation. Also concerned about opposition from pro-Israeli sources, she asked National Security Adviser Sandy Berger to request the American Israel Public Affairs Committee (AIPAC), the strongest pro-Israel lobbying group, to stay neutral and not urge its congressional supporters to oppose the Brown legislation.

The legislation signed into law in February 1996 was carefully circumscribed. It permitted resumption of some economic assistance and made one-time provision for delivery of previously contracted military equipment (other than the F-16 aircraft) whose delivery had been prevented by the aid cutoff in 1990. But it was the first break in the wall of sanctions, and Pakistan's efforts were a significant factor in getting it through the Congress.[19]

Pakistan's diplomats have a mixed record when it comes to that other vital piece of Washington tradecraft, using the media to bolster a political approach to the U.S. government. Two ambassadors who were former journalists were brilliant at it: polished in their presentations, tireless in their relationship building both with key reporters and with commentators interested in Pakistan, equally quick with sound bite and written commentary, and savvy about dealing with media personalities critical of Pakistan.

Military officers seem more uncomfortable with the media. Perhaps the most painful example comes not from a Washington-based diplomat but from a 2006 visit of President Musharraf to Washington. Musharraf, normally deft in his public appearances with the press, denied a *Washington Post*

---

19. This account draws on the authors' interviews with Maleeha Lodhi, Robin Raphel, and Bruce Riedel.

story about offensive remarks he had made about Pakistani women in a conversation with the paper's editorial board. Unfortunately for the president, the newspaper had his remarks on tape. Musharraf's discomfiture at being caught in this kind of controversy may have contributed to an even more embarrassing verbal confrontation with two Pakistani women in New York two days later—also, to his chagrin, in full view of the media.

This kind of public contretemps is unusual. It is an extreme version of two common problems Pakistani diplomats in Washington face in their media relations. The first, familiar to politicians and diplomats everywhere, is the temptation to say things to one audience that will be unwelcome to others—in this case, to present a U.S.-friendly view to the American media, only to have it undercut by the Pakistan government's official statements in the press or in political forums at home.

The second problem is confusing packaging with substance. During difficult times, Pakistani officials correctly worry about the image of their country presented in the U.S. media. To the extent that criticism of Pakistan reflects real concerns or policy differences, however, the typical remedy—a stepped-up pace of contacts between embassy officers and the press, for example, or a blizzard of e-mails to the Pakistani community and other well-wishers—does not address these. The substantive problems are unfortunately more painful to address.

6

Pakistan's Politicians

Pakistan has spent about half its independent life under elected civilian-led governments. Despite the dominant role of the military, civilian politicians have always had a highly visible place in its government except for brief periods immediately following military coups. They have led most government ministries and participated in the bicameral Parliament, where they have enacted legislation, served as conduits for popular requests, and distributed patronage to their friends and constituents. Politicians have played comparable roles at the provincial level. Their power and authority have varied over time, however. Not surprisingly, they are substantial during periods of civilian rule but drop off sharply when a military officer leads the country either as head of a martial law or quasi-martial law regime or as a constitutional, elected ruler.

Pakistan's constitution, often suspended and amended but still in place nearly four decades after its unanimous adoption in 1973, provides for a parliamentary system in which the lower house of the legislature (the National Assembly) is popularly chosen and the upper house (the Senate) is elected primarily by the provincial legislatures. The constitution as originally written made the prime minister the primary national leader. The president, elected by Parliament and the four provincial assemblies, was to be a figurehead with limited power and authority.

In practice, power has shifted back and forth between the president and the prime minister. Following each of Pakistan's four military coups, the chief of army staff who seized power appointed himself president either immediately or within a year or two, and exercised full executive authority in that capacity. In 1988, President Zia's handpicked prime minister, Muhammad Khan Junejo, decided despite Zia's reservations to sign the Geneva

Accords, which set up a framework for Soviet withdrawal from Afghanistan. The prime minister's defiant action was a major factor in Zia's decision the following month to dismiss Junejo, dissolve Parliament, and order fresh elections. During the 1990s, when elected governments headed by Benazir Bhutto and Nawaz Sharif alternated in power, civilian presidents working with the military were instrumental in removing them before the end of their terms as prime minister. Following the defeat of President Pervez Musharraf's governing party in the landmark February 2008 parliamentary election, a prime minister again became the most powerful figure in the formal government. Pakistan returned temporarily to the model of presidential primacy with the election of Asif Ali Zardari as president following Musharraf's resignation six months later. But within little more than a year it was clear that effective power had once again shifted back to the prime minister, depite Zardari's continuing role as leader of the country's governing party.

These shifts in effective power between the president and the prime minister have sometimes, but not always, been reflected in constitutional amendments that altered the distribution of authority between them. The most important—and controversial—of these amendments is the provision empowering the president to dismiss the government and Parliament, as Zia did when he forced out Junejo. This provision has been in and out of the constitution several times. Civilian prime ministers, fearing usurpation by the military and its allies, have usually wanted it out.

Following Zadari's accession as president in August 2008, the issue became a sore point between him and his major civilian political opponent, Nawaz Sharif, and its fate served as a barometer of Zardari's power and of his relations with the military. Sharif, who had removed the provision when he was prime minister in the late 1990s—only to see it restored by President Musharraf—wanted it taken out again. Zardari, while professing to agree, thought the power might become useful and for two years stonewalled efforts to bring about change. In November 2009 the government introduced legislation shifting the leadership of the National Command Authority (NCA), the body responsible for nuclear and other major security decisions, from the president to the prime minister, and two months later the army public relations office announced that Prime Minister Gilani had presided over the NCA for the first time. This did not change the constitution, but it was a clear sign that Zardari had lost the army's confidence and that the army had forced a change in the chain of command.[1] The Eighteenth Amendment to

---

1. Tahir Niaz, "Control over Nuclear Activities: NCA Bill Tabled in National Assembly," *Daily Times*, November 12, 2009, www.dailytimes.com.pk/default.asp?page=2009\11\12\story_12-11-2009_pg1_1; Tahir Niaz,

the constitution, an omnibus measure adopted in April 2010, formalized the change in power that had already taken place, and returned the authority to disband Parliament to the prime minister, making that official the most powerful figure—or at least the most powerful civilian—in the Pakistan government.[2]

The story of this shift in power is an apt metaphor for the ambiguities of constitutional rule in Pakistan. The requirements of the constitution not infrequently collide with the drive for power on the part of both civilian and military leaders, setting off serious confrontations. The recent rise as a major political factor of the judiciary, long either manipulated, disregarded, or over-awed by military and civilian governments alike, has further complicated the way Pakistan is governed.

This chapter reviews the structure of Pakistan's politics, the modus operandi of its politicians, and the way these affect negotiations with the United States. It takes a closer look at one key negotiation that took place when Pakistan had a civilian-led government: the failed U.S. effort in May 1998 to dissuade Pakistan from testing a nuclear weapon following India's test. It then examines U.S. engagement in Pakistan's internal politics and U.S. contact with Pakistan's religious politicians, whose operating style differs in important respects from the other Pakistani negotiators described herein.

Political Parties

Two major political parties have held power at the national level. The Pakistan Muslim League was the party of the country's founder, Mohammed Ali Jinnah, who won independence for Pakistan in the 1947 partition of British India. The Muslim League has been a major political force from the start. Its name, with its patriotic symbolism, has been adopted by a succession of political players, some of them operating at the same time as bitter rivals using a variant of the same name.

The Musharraf era left Pakistan with two Pakistan Muslim Leagues. One, marginalized during Musharraf's time but subsequently the more powerful of the two, is dominated by former Prime Minister Nawaz Sharif, and is hence called the PML-N (for Nawaz). Sharif had been a provincial politician during the Zia years. After Zia's death in 1988, he built up his

"NA Passes National Command Authority Bill 2009," *Daily Times*, January 29, 2009, www.dailytimes.com.pk/default.asp?page=2010%5C01%5C29%5Cstory_29-1-2010_pg7_5; "16th NCA Meeting," Press Release, Inter-Services Public Relations, January 13, 2010, www.ispr.gov.pk/front/main.asp?o=t-press_release&date=2010/1/13.

2. Irfan Ghauri, "NA Unanimously Passes 18th Amendment Bill," *Daily Times*, April 9, 2010, www.dailytimes.com.pk/default.asp?page=2010\04\09\story_9-4-2010_pg1_1.

party with assistance from ISI, which wanted to ensure that there was a strong (and, they hoped, successful) counterweight to Benazir Bhutto on the national scene. By the time Sharif's second stint as prime minister was over, his relationship with the army had gone very sour. Sharif's effort to fire Musharraf gave the immediate impetus for Musharraf's coup, and for Musharraf's subsequent legal action accusing Sharif of attempted hijacking on the grounds that Sharif had forbidden an aircraft carrying Musharraf home from an international visit to land in Pakistan.

The second Muslim League was originally developed by Musharraf as his civilian political base, drawing much of its membership from opportunistic or disaffected members of Sharif's party. It is known as the PML-Q, in which the Q represents Jinnah's honorific title Quaid-e-Azam (Great Leader). It carried on, with reduced numbers and influence, when Musharraf left office.

The other major party is the Pakistan People's Party (PPP), founded in the 1960s by Zulfiqar Ali Bhutto, later Pakistan's president and prime minister. Both the PPP and the PML-N are dominated by a powerful family, a familiar phenomenon in the politics of South Asia. The PPP is the domain of the Bhutto dynasty, now headed by Asif Zardari, who inherited the leadership mantle on the assassination of his wife, Benazir Bhutto, in 2007. The Sharifs, Nawaz and his younger brother Shahbaz, who has served several times as chief minister of Punjab, an office roughly comparable to a U.S. governor, dominate the PML-N. While both parties have strong and talented personalities in their upper ranks, in practice people from outside the family face a glass ceiling. The families, unwilling to let go, have managed to retain tight control even when their leaders are in exile. Party regulars are rarely prepared to challenge this arrangement. They fear that without the family to hold adherents together the party would fragment. Both the Bhuttos and the Sharifs are grooming the next generation of dynastic leaders. Benazir Bhutto's and Asif Zardari's son Bilawal, now a student at Oxford, shares the chairmanship of the PPP with his father but does not yet play any serious role in party affairs.

Both the PPP and the PML-N also have a regional core. The PPP is strongest in the Bhutto home province of Sindh, especially in the countryside, and in southern Punjab. It has smaller representation in the other provinces. The PML-N is basically a Punjabi party, but given Punjab's position—it is home to some 56 percent of Pakistan's population and has almost always dominated the government and the army—this gives it national standing. This is especially true at times when the Sharifs project themselves as symbols of a larger national cause, as has been the case at least since mid-2008.

This neat party identity is complicated by another characteristic of Pakistan's political parties: the tendency of many politicians to gravitate toward power. The propensity to form a "king's party" goes back to Pakistan's earlier decades. It has especially come to the fore when military rulers whose governments are taking on constitutional trappings have felt the need to establish a civilian political base. Politicians whose loyalties have shifted with the times include some of the country's best-known personalities. They are rarely apologetic for turning their coats and make no serious effort to explain their switch in terms of policy or ideology. They see it as a way to win office and the perks that go with it, nothing more. The PML-Q, described above, is the most recent example. The support from ISI that the PML-N enjoyed in its early years, too, is a recurring phenomenon in Pakistani politics.

Any elective system has its share of patronage barons. In Pakistan this group has been especially prominent in successive king's parties. The familiar Pakistani derogative—"*lota*," referring to a pot that is used for personal hygiene—is often applied to this group. Patronage is vital for all politicians; for this group, it is the only game in town. Each of the country's military rulers initially undertook to put them out of business. Each wound up hiring them.

Many politicians come from the social elite, from families that are prominent in a particular district or province, often landowning families with a quasi-feudal relationship with the rural population in the constituencies they represent. This is true not just of the large parties but also, and perhaps especially, of tiny parties whose political standing is entirely based on their ability to deliver votes in one or two constituencies. Some of these families have hedged their bets by placing members in rival parties. In both large and small parties, politics is often a family business, with constituencies passing from elder to younger members.

Some politicians have the same high level of education, cosmopolitan background, and excellent English as the country's top diplomats and civil servants. Benazir Bhutto, urbane and sophisticated, with degrees from Harvard and Oxford, is the most obvious case in point. In an earlier generation, her father was another prime example. Some have relatives living outside Pakistan—in the United States, Britain, or the Gulf. Many do not, however, and more important, educational qualifications and international experience are irrelevant to their ability to win elections.[3]

Regardless of a politician's educational background, going on the campaign trail plunges the sophisticated, cosmopolitan politician and the homespun rural baron alike into the web of social relationships described in chapter 3. The politician's network will include both the rich and powerful figures of a constituency and the less prominent but well-connected people who he hopes will deliver the bloc voting needed to carry the election. In his constituency, a politician attracts swarms of well-wishers and favor seekers pressing into his palm notes requesting a job for a relative, assistance in getting a loan, or a helping hand in resolving a local dispute. This is the source of political power and the stuff of Pakistani politics. In comparison, some of the policy issues that animate U.S.-Pakistan relations seem dry, bloodless, and sometimes incomprehensible on the hustings—and often irrelevant in the voting booth. All the social obligations described in chapter 3—hospitality most prominently among them—apply with special force to the politician.

Politicians who participate in negotiations with the United States or deal with American officials rely on personal relations to an even greater degree than the other Pakistani groups examined in this book. The personal network is the heart of any political system. In a country with weak institutions, and especially with weak political institutions, it is the only thing one can rely on. Politicians will often urge American officials posted in Pakistan to visit them in their constituencies, to see political Pakistan up close (and to dramatize their own importance). The American visitor becomes both a fascinated tourist and a bit player in an epic with thousands of "extras" that might have been scripted by Cecil B. DeMille. At least until recently, having a prominent American in tow has been a plus for an aspiring Pakistani politician.

This highly personal approach affects how politicians operate when they hold ministerial office. Military officers will have a staff, but politicians, especially when serving as prime minister or chief minister, have a kind of court, with personal friends, loyalists, and sometimes relatives playing especially important roles. Politicians, far more than senior civil servants or military officers, rely on special envoys to carry important messages for them, and tend to pick for that role family members or other people outside the government system. A classic example was Nawaz Sharif's decision to send his brother

---

3. Musharraf instituted a requirement that candidates for Parliament have at least a bachelor's degree, ostensibly as a way to upgrade the sophistication of the country's Parliament. This was widely seen as a means of getting rid of some political old-timers who did not support him. The announcement that followed, stipulating that a degree from a madrassah would be deemed equivalent to a bachelor's, was greeted with cynicism.

Shahbaz to Washington in the summer of 1999, discussed in chapter 3. Asif Zardari's most trusted advisers consist mainly of personal friends or school chums; many have no obvious training or credentials for their positions.

Like most Pakistanis, politicians are usually strongly nationalist, sharing the widely held view of the danger of India and the inconstancy of the United States. Since 9/11 and especially since about 2005, there has been a stronger edge to anti-Americanism among them, and a real effort to show that there is daylight between the United States and Pakistan. This need not disrupt or discourage their personal relationships with Americans.[4]

Most U.S. negotiations with Pakistani politicians take place at the top, with elected prime ministers. When dealing with policy issues, prime ministers use the government resources available to them, often supplemented by special representatives or go-betweens. However, the negotiation typically bears the prime minister's personal stamp. It is not just an interaction between two governments but also part and parcel of the daily tugging and hauling over political power in Pakistan, both among political parties and with the military. The intense discussions that followed India's nuclear weapons tests in 1998, when the United States put on a full-court press to try to dissuade Pakistan from following suit, illustrate how this process can work.

The Nuclear "Mission Impossible"

On May 11 and 13, 1998, India exploded five nuclear devices in the Thar Desert, and announced that it was now a nuclear weapons state. On May 28 and 30, Pakistan set off six similar nuclear explosions. In the two-and-a-half weeks between those dates, the United States mobilized a high-level—and ultimately unsuccessful—campaign to dissuade Prime Minister Nawaz Sharif from testing. The U.S. negotiators knew they had an uphill task, and in hindsight it appears that the end result was never in doubt. But the way the negotiations unfolded illustrates how a civilian political leader, very much a product of Pakistan's political culture, dealt both with his own government and with the powerful U.S. negotiators. The direct participants in the negotiations included Pakistan's senior diplomatic officials, while the military watched closely. But the key person was Prime Minister Nawaz Sharif.

The nuclear issue was already a hardy perennial between the United States and Pakistan. U.S. aid had been cut off twice because of Pakistan's

4. This discussion of Pakistani politicians draws on the authors' recollections from service in Islamabad in the 1970s and in the State Department from 1979 to 1984 and 1987 to 1992, and on their interviews with Prof. Anita Weiss, Karl F. Inderfurth, William Milam, and a series of retired Pakistani diplomats.

nuclear program before the Reagan administration enthusiastically restored it when the Soviet invasion of Afghanistan made Pakistan a "frontline state" for Washington. In 1985, the U.S. Congress, wanting to avert the cutoff of aid to Pakistan required by existing nuclear sanctions legislation, enacted the Pressler Amendment. This legislation provided that virtually all economic assistance and military supply would be cut off in any year in which the president could not certify that Pakistan "did not possess a nuclear explosive device." In 1990 the administration of George H. W. Bush found itself unable to make the required annual certification, and aid was stopped, to the Pakistanis' surprise and mortification.[5] Nonetheless, Washington continued to use its (reduced) clout to discourage Pakistan from moving beyond its widely recognized capability to develop nuclear weapons to the point of actually building and testing them.

Like everyone else, American officials recognized that once India tested, Pakistan would want to follow suit. Five decades of rivalry with India, the country's chronic insecurity, the army's strong views and vigilance about anything connected with India, the feeling the military shared with Sharif that Pakistan's national honor was at stake, the concern that a decision not to test would be interpreted to signify that Pakistan was incapable of doing so, and, perhaps most important, Sharif's fear that not testing could lead to his political downfall, all combined to make the pressure to go ahead virtually irresistible.

The United States pushed hard. Deputy Secretary of State Strobe Talbott, the key American official in the negotiation, thought three arguments would be critical for the success of his efforts: (1) by not testing, Pakistan would "occupy the high ground in the eyes of a nervous world"; (2) it stood to inherit the aid that donors would divert from India, an important consideration for an economically strapped country; and (3) it would obtain from the United States the F-16 planes that had remained undelivered because of the 1990 aid cutoff.

President Clinton kicked off the diplomatic campaign with a personal approach by telephoning Nawaz Sharif. Talbott reports that the president sought to "whet [Sharif's] appetite," and also offered Sharif an official visit to Washington, always an important attraction for Pakistani leaders. Sharif's response was inconclusive. Talbott quotes Clinton as saying, "You can almost hear the guy wringing his hands and sweating."

---

5. The Pressler Amendment also required the president to certify that continuation of U.S. assistance would materially reduce the likelihood that Pakistan would acquire nuclear weapons capability. The first certification, however, was the one that got most of the world's attention.

Talbott headed immediately for Islamabad with a civilian-military team. The delegation was airborne so fast that the Pakistanis asked it to delay to give them time to think through their approach. Talbott noted that a call to Pakistan Army Chief of Staff General Jehangir Karamat from General Anthony Zinni, the commander of the U.S. Central Command and a member of the negotiating team, led the Pakistanis to withdraw their request for a delay.[6]

As it awaited Talbott's arrival, the Pakistan government was debating whether to test. This process was initially complicated by Sharif's absence in Kazakhstan when the news of the first Indian tests broke. He curtailed his visit and hurried back. The fact that a civilian government was in power, not a martial law regime, meant that civilians as well as military officers were participating in the debate, broadening and complicating the decision-making process. The Defense Committee of the cabinet met, with the participation not only of the key ministers but also of the foreign secretary and the military service chiefs. The civilian leaders clearly recognized that both their political opponents and the military would judge them by whether they had upheld the honor and the security of Pakistan—and that standard would be hard to meet without a nuclear test. The Foreign Ministry was in charge of "message control," sending guidance to its diplomats overseas and calling in the Islamabad-based diplomatic corps.[7]

The Pakistani foreign minister greeted the American visitors with a recap of Pakistan's bitter view of India's constant hostility and a stiff dose of "I told you so." He and his colleagues recalled that Pakistan had warned the United States that the newly elected Hindu-nationalist Bharatiya Janata Party–led government in India would test. The American participants remember the meeting as tense and passionate, the Pakistanis as cordial. But it clearly did not change any minds.[8]

The meeting with the foreign minister was followed by one with General Karamat, which Talbott describes as less contentious. Karamat and Zinni were able to draw on their "soldier-to-soldier" bond. Karamat heard the visitors out and made clear that the decision would be made by the civilian government, which was "wrestling" with the issue. He also conveyed indirectly that the visitors' arguments really had not addressed the national security questions that he had to deal with.[9]

---

6. Talbott, *Engaging India*, 56–59.

7. Authors' interviews with Shamshad Ahmad, Tariq Fatemi, and Gen. (ret.) Jehangir Karamat.

8. Talbott, *Engaging India*, 60–61; Shamshad Ahmad, interview; and Tariq Fatemi, interview.

9. Talbott, *Engaging India*, 61–62.

The final meeting in this series was with Nawaz Sharif. Talbott describes Sharif as exhausted, under intense pressure, and tremendously worried. He was concerned about popular reaction, which he clearly thought would be harsh if Pakistan did not test. He worried that India would "get away" with its test: it would suffer neither significant political nor economic consequences. Toward the end of the meeting, Sharif asked everyone but Talbott to leave the room. Talbott chose this moment to give him a handwritten note from Secretary of State Madeleine Albright urging that he hold firm. Sharif asked, "How can I take your advice if I'm out of office?"[10]

The Pakistanis had not presented a list of demands. They wanted to hear what the United States had to offer. This was apparently Nawaz Sharif's decision: according to one of his confidants, he felt that asking for aid when Pakistan's security was at stake would be demeaning. (He might also have calculated that his government could get more by letting the Americans open the bidding.)[11]

What the Pakistani team was listening for was not in the United States' brief, however. They wanted to hear that Washington was going to make India's decision to test prohibitively expensive, politically and otherwise, for New Delhi. The legal sanctions the United States had imposed on India were not game changers. Talbott had repeatedly condemned India's test— but his condemnation had been made in private and hence did not impress his hosts. The statement that came out of the summit meeting of the G-8 group of industrialized nations a few days later did criticize India; Talbott's account describes the text with evident satisfaction on that score. But from Pakistan's point of view, the statement was a dud. It included no consensus by the G-8 countries to cut off aid. This confirmed Sharif's view that India would not significantly suffer because it had tested. Sharif had written to the G-8, so he must have felt stung by their mild action.

Both Talbott and Pakistani participants in the meeting recalled that the Pakistani side had raised the possibility of the United States weighing in on Kashmir. According to Bruce Riedel, a senior member of the National Security staff who played an important role on the team, "the one area Sharif hinted that would make a difference was Kashmir. If the United States and the international community committed itself to a major effort at peace keeping in Kashmir then he might have the cover not to test."[12] Talbott

10. Talbott, *Engaging India*, 63–65.

11. Shamshad Ahmad, interview, and Tariq Fatemi, interview.

12. Bruce Riedel, background paper, Institute for the Study of Diplomacy at Georgetown University, Washington, D.C., May 2007. In the paper, Riedel concludes that "Clinton saw this [suggestion] as a trap. While he was personally very interested in trying his hand at resolving Kashmir in order to defuse

quotes Foreign Secretary Shamshad Ahmad as urging the United States to mediate the dispute. His response, that the United States would certainly take a look at the issue, did not impress (nor in light of the United States' record on Kashmir should it have).

One might have expected that a negotiation that touched so directly on Pakistan's security and its most acute national fears would have included proposals for a U.S. security guarantee for Pakistan. This does not seem to have been part of the discussion, however. Pakistanis who were involved in the decision have commented that such a guarantee could only have been taken seriously if it took the form of legislation enacted by Congress.[13] This reasoning obviously reflected their perception that earlier U.S. security assurances had been useless in the crunch.

After the U.S. team left Islamabad, there were further telephone calls between Clinton and Nawaz Sharif. A more detailed U.S. offer was put forward in one of these calls. General Zinni made a second trip to Pakistan and again met Karamat as well as the prime minister.

The new proposals from the United States were discussed again in the Defense Committee of the cabinet. General Karamat recalled having sought and received assurances that economic sanctions following a test would not cut into other aspects of Pakistan's defense budget. Pakistan's consensus was hardening around the view that "there is no economic price for security." What finally moved the government from debate to action was an intelligence report in late May that Israel and India were planning to attack Pakistan's nuclear sites. A number of observers inside and outside Pakistan had serious doubts about the veracity of the report, but the specter of India-Israel collusion—even in a report of highly doubtful provenance—was more than any Pakistani leader could withstand.[14] Sharif called Clinton to apologize for "disappointing him." The tests took place right after that.[15]

The personal approach President Clinton took would normally have appealed to the Pakistanis. However, the manner in which Washington put its cards on the table did nothing to erase Pakistan's conviction that the United States was an unreliable partner. In the end it was the elected civilian prime

---

tensions in the subcontinent, he knew that a high visibility effort was a non-starter for India and would be refused, leaving him exposed and ineffective."

13. Talbott, *Engaging India*, 59–65; Shamshad Ahmad, interview; and Tariq Fatemi, interview.

14. According to one highly authoritative source in Washington, there was no genuine report of India-Israel collaboration, and the Israeli embassy denied it (Walter Andersen, in communication with the authors, March 2010). Andersen was head of the South Asia office in the State Department's Bureau of Intelligence and Research at the time of this negotiation.

15. Authors' interviews with Tariq Fatemi, Shamshad Ahmad, and Gen. (ret.) Jehangir Karamat.

minister who decided to test. But the military were always there, at the heart of the internal debate if not in all the meetings with civilian American visitors. Most observers doubt the military would have stood still for a decision not to test. Washington for its part both recognized and underscored the military role by meeting with General Karamat and by giving General Zinni such a prominent role.

In the end, this negotiating effort proved to be, as Talbott wrote, "mission impossible." The nub of Pakistan's approach was the threat the country perceived from a nuclear-armed India. Pakistan's leaders felt the United States did not understand how greatly India's test had magnified this historic dread. Viewed from that angle, the United States' response relied too heavily on economic assistance and did not make India pay for its nuclear sins, or at least not pay enough. To have any chance of success, the United States would have had to tailor its approach to Pakistan's Indo-centric view of the world, make India a virtual international pariah, offer Pakistan much more ironclad security guarantees than it had been prepared to provide even during the heyday of the U.S.-Pakistan alliance, and pledge to take a meaningful role in resolving the Kashmir dispute (and, at least in Pakistan's view, to resolve it to Pakistan's satisfaction). This would have represented a vast change for Washington in both style and substance, one that would have put U.S. policy in the region at the service of Pakistan. The Clinton administration was not willing to do this.

The United States and Domestic Politics

On several occasions going at least as far back as the late 1980s, the United States became deeply involved in negotiations on internal Pakistan politics, brokering deals between national leaders and their principal opponents or between political leaders and the military. The impetus for U.S. involvement has come from both sides at different times. For the United States, the motivation has been to encourage democracy and to mitigate the poisonous rivalries that characterize Pakistani politics. For the Pakistani participants, the goal was to preserve or attain power, and in some cases to use the power and influence of the United States to strengthen their own position in the negotiations they were carrying out with their domestic rivals.

In 1988, after the death of President Zia ul-Haq, U.S. ambassador Robert Oakley was deeply involved in persuading the army to allow elections to take place and, after the victory of the PPP, to allow Benazir Bhutto to take office. Oakley recalled that he had worked out an understanding on what issues would remain under the control of the army, including the nuclear program, Pakistan's policy toward Afghanistan, and all institutional questions regarding the military, especially promotions. These and other initiatives earned the ambassador the sobriquet of "viceroy," an allusion to the title used by the ruler of the British Indian Empire.[16] But such behavior was certainly not unique to him.

After Benazir Bhutto took office in 1989, she had difficult relations with the army, the civilian opposition headed by Nawaz Sharif, and the entrenched bureaucratic establishment led by Ghulam Ishaq Khan, a senior civil servant who had become president. Bhutto repeatedly sought Oakley's help in resolving contentious issues. Bhutto's decision to work with the United States reflected her close relations with the ambassador, but was probably also influenced by her personal ties with President George H. W. Bush, who had known her father, had children about her age, and seemed to have established a somewhat paternal relationship with her during her first visit to the United States as prime minister in 1989. Bhutto's approach to using the United States to help with her domestic problems was similar to Pakistan's national approach to foreign policy and to negotiations, as described in chapter 2: she was looking for a counterweight, in this case to army generals and the president, who she feared might be conniving with the political opposition to drive her from office. The fact that Bhutto was deposed at the insistence of the military after only a year and a half in power indicates that her fears were not frivolous.

More recently, the United States became deeply involved in a nearly three-year negotiation between President Musharraf and Bhutto, then in exile, to work out the conditions under which she might return and participate in Pakistan's political life. A close adviser to Musharraf simultaneously approached the British high commissioner and the American ambassador in 2006. Contacts between Musharraf's advisers and Bhutto had been taking place for some time. Bhutto wanted to return to Pakistan to take part in the elections that were supposed to take place in late 2007, in the hope that the electorate would bring her back to power. Musharraf's stated interest was in moving Pakistan back to a real political process in a controlled fashion, giving him an ally—in his mind, a subordinate one—from among the regular political parties in addition to the "king's party" he had created. He had earlier made overtures to one of the religious parties. The approach to the PPP

---

16. Robert Oakley, interview. Oakley was the subject of a regular satirical column called "Viceroy's Journal," published by the *Friday Times*, a sophisticated English-language weekly from Lahore. The name of the column recalled the memoirs of Lord Wavell, one of the last of the British rulers.

seemed designed to give Musharraf a major secular party as an ally and to avoid giving an opening to Nawaz Sharif and his Muslim League.

Once it was clear that Musharraf and Bhutto both personally wanted the United States and Britain involved, both countries' diplomats met on a regular basis with both sides. The Americans and British met separately with their Pakistani interlocutors but coordinated their approaches closely. The contacts with Musharraf were for the most part carried out through his advisers; Bhutto did her own negotiating. Both Pakistani personalities mistrusted each other and saw an international role as a way of improving the odds that whatever agreement they reached would be implemented. Bhutto sought a U.S. guarantee, which the U.S. side told her was impossible. The stuff of the negotiations concerned both the legal conditions under which Bhutto might return to Pakistan, such as the terms of any immunity she might receive from prosecution on corruption charges and the possible repeal of the legislation limiting prime ministers to two terms, and the management of the upcoming elections.

As one would expect, the negotiations took place in an atmosphere of basic mistrust. However, the misgivings were in some ways more institutional than personal. Musharraf doubtless shared the army's suspicious attitude toward the PPP, but there had been few opportunities for him and Bhutto to clash personally, and in any event he saw her as vastly preferable to the other mainstream political leader, Nawaz Sharif, whom he had accused of trying to kill him. On Bhutto's part, there was deep distrust of the army going back to the military's overthrow and execution of her father and reinforced by her own experiences as prime minister. But once again, it was not primarily personal. Musharraf and Bhutto were said by knowledgeable observers to have used ISI director general Kayani as a go-between. The fact that Kayani had served as Bhutto's deputy military secretary when she was prime minister and had not been been involved in crackdowns against the PPP made him acceptable to her.[17]

The negotiations were more formal than has sometimes been the case on domestic political issues. The two sides exchanged formal papers, which they did not give to their American interlocutors. Not surprisingly, as Musharraf's political standing weakened following his decision to fire Chief Justice Iftikhar Muhammad Chaudhry in March 2007, Bhutto's price for an agreement went up. Both she and Musharraf, moreover, had allies and party members who stood to lose politically if the negotiations succeeded. This may have

---

17. Amir Mir, "Who Is General Ashfaq Kiyani?" Reuters IntelliBriefs, October 5, 2007, http://intel-libriefs.blogspot.com/2007/10/who-is-general-ashfaq-kiyani.html. Official documents spell the general's name "Kayani," but it is often spelled (and pronounced) "Kiyani."

contributed to the rather limited results of the negotiations. Bhutto returned to Pakistan in October 2007, but the only formal result of the negotiations was Musharraf's promulgation of the National Reconciliation Ordinance, which granted immunity to her and others. Questions about what office she might aspire to were deferred until after the elections, which both sides thought they could win. As things turned out, it was Musharraf who guessed wrong on this point. By then Bhutto had tragically been assassinated.

For our purposes, a few points illustrate the negotiating patterns in this high-stakes game. First, it's all personal. Both negotiating partners wanted to use the United States to overcome the fundamental mistrust between them. They both had misgivings about U.S. intentions on Pakistan's security issues, but nonetheless believed that the United States' desire for stability and at least the outward appearances of democracy could neutralize some of their disagreements with one another.

Second, the American participants repeatedly found themselves in an awkward position: they were implicitly or even explicitly blamed when one of the negotiating partners did not deliver on what the other considered a commitment. President Musharraf's carefully hedged responses to Bhutto's repeated requests for immunity are a case in point.

Finally, the negotiations were about power, but they never really cut through the complex questions of authority that bedevil civil-military relations in Pakistan. The only issue that was formally resolved was legal immunity. This suggested that Musharraf was looking for a way to allow Bhutto to return without achieving her principal objective of becoming a full participant in the political fray and a candidate for prime minister, from which she remained barred by the no-third-term provision of the constitution.

In an interesting coda to this episode, after the installation of a new civilian government following the 2008 elections, Asif Zardari again brought the United States into his effort to succeed Musharraf as president. This was not done through the officials who had brokered between Musharraf and Bhutto; by this time, these officials wanted to bow out of Pakistani domestic politics. Instead, Zardari approached the high-profile U.S. ambassador to the United Nations, Zalmay Khalilzad, an old acquaintance. For Pakistani politicians accustomed to operating at the top, reaching for a VIP connection comes as naturally as breathing, and there is an assumption that the U.S. government, like its Pakistani counterpart, can readily be swayed by such contacts.[18]

18. See Helene Cooper and Mark Mazzeti, "U.N. Envoy's Ties to Pakistani Are Questioned," *New York Times*, August 25, 2008, www.nytimes.com/2008/08/26/washington/26diplo.html?_r=1&scp=1&sq=helene%20cooper%20mark%20mazzetti%20august%202008&st=cse; and Robin

This type of negotiation also illustrates Pakistan's tendency to attribute wildly exaggerated powers to the United States and to miscalculate as a result. Often, these presumed powers are considered malevolent, as seen in the conspiratorial explanations Pakistanis proffer for the ups and downs of the normal negotiating process. But sometimes, as in these examples, political or national leaders want to mobilize the oversized power they attribute to the United States for their own reasons. When American officials try to help, this may lead to an exaggerated assessment of how much the United States is prepared to do, not so much for Pakistan as for a particular leader. It can also produce a backlash against "U.S. interference."

The end result may be miscalculation and disappointment. At the end of the day, despite its stated desire to promote democracy in Pakistan, the United States was not able to prevent the military from forcing Benazir Bhutto to leave office in 1990 or the three ousters of elected governments with the support of the military that followed later in the decade. The obvious sympathy the United States (and President George W. Bush personally) had for Musharraf during much of the post-9/11 period did not prevent his supporters from losing the election in February 2008. And despite publicly expressed U.S. support for Musharraf's remaining as a central part of the postelection political makeup, the political parties forced him from office under threat of impeachment six months later. Worse, the political parties themselves fielded leaders Washington knew to be deeply flawed. Washington had to live with this.[19]

Religious Politicians

Pakistan's religious politicians have a complicated and in some cases ambivalent relationship with the government and indeed with the Pakistani state. The largest of the religious parties, the Jamaat-e-Islami (JI), opposed the creation of the state of Pakistan in 1947, and to some extent the religious parties still carry the baggage of that decision. They have held power at the provincial level in the North-West Frontier Province (since renamed Khyber Pakhtunkhwa) and have participated in the provincial government of Balochistan. With the exception of a brief period in which one of the religious parties participated in the Zia ul-Haq government, they have never held power at the national level. But because of the magnetic pull of Islamic issues in Paki-

---

Wright and Glenn Kessler, "U.S. Brokered Bhutto's Return to Pakistan," *Washington Post*, December 28, 2007.

19. The passage on U.S. involvement in domestic negotiations draws on the authors' recollections and on interviews with Robert Oakley, Daniel Markey, Ryan Crocker, Richard Boucher, and other U.S. and Pakistani officials.

stani politics, national governments have had to take them into account and have at times quietly encouraged them, as Musharraf did in his early years in power. Despite their weakness at the national level, they have also served as handy bogeys who could be represented to Americans as a potential threat to U.S. interests in Pakistan. Some of the religious parties also have informal links to militant organizations that have attacked the state. The state's delayed and initially ambivalent response to these attacks is due in no small measure to fears of an Islamist backlash sparked by the religious parties.

The religious parties are even more suspicious of the United States than are other Pakistanis. High-level contacts with the United States have been relatively limited. When leaders of these parties have visited Washington, they have had little exposure to the U.S. government. The Obama administration's special envoy, Richard Holbrooke, met with leaders of two religious parties in Pakistan in August 2009, their most senior contact with a Washington-based U.S. official.

More often, U.S. contacts with the religious parties have taken place at the provincial level, especially in what is now Khyber Pakhtunkhwa Province, governed from 2002 to 2007 by a conglomerate of six of these parties, the Muttahida Majlis-e-Amal (MMA). Some of these encounters have been negotiations in the conventional sense, typically over implementation of aid projects. More often, they have been efforts to explain what the United States is trying to do in Pakistan. But there have also been MMA outreach efforts designed to explain or justify their position to the international community. Shortly after they came to power in the province in 2002, MMA leaders organized a kind of "show and tell" with U.S. and other foreign diplomats from Islamabad as part of a broader effort to assuage fears that they would implement a pro-Taliban agenda. These contacts as well as U.S. dealings with provincial politicians representing ethnic nationalists from areas that are routinely at odds with the federal government—Pashtuns or Baloch—may provide some useful lessons on what to expect if the Islamic right comes to play a larger role in Pakistani government and politics in the future.

The mainstream Pakistani political parties differ on whether and how Pakistan should implement Islamic law (sharia), and how it should deal with insurgents who are acting under the banner of Islam. Most politicians associated with mainstream parties will be very careful about the public positions they take on these sensitive matters. The government's decision to take military action against the Pakistani Taliban in the Swat Valley in early 2009 was delayed in part because it was difficult to get sufficient public political support for this action.

For the religious parties, support for Islamic causes is a given. They tend to take a very hard line on India, though parties with links to the Deobandi movement have occasionally tried to position themselves more centrally on India-related issues. But the Islamic parties' ideological core revolves around Pakistan's Islamic identity more than the India-centric concepts described in chapter 2. The religious parties play on other parties' unwillingness to criticize anything Islamic. Each of the constituents of the MMA tries to position itself as more Islamic than its colleagues. During the Musharraf years, the MMA was technically in the opposition but often in quasi-alliance with the government and shifted—sometimes uneasily—back and forth between the two roles and between Islamic and general governance issues. The religious parties are adept at using their Islamic identity to intimidate governments nervous about a backlash in the streets, including on issues important to the United States. Anti-Americanism has become a reinforcing bond among these parties.

The religious parties have been described as "natural opposition parties." During their stints in government, however, they have not necessarily put their Islamic legal agenda at the top of their action list. During the time when the MMA governed Khyber Pakhtunkhwa, it took only limited actions to bring in sharia. Its big gestures focused mostly on removing women's pictures from billboards and other public demonstrations of Islamic austerity. This austerity did not extend to financial probity: the government was widely regarded as corrupt.

Moreover, the different religious parties have different ethnic identifications and priorities. The JI, with a strong urban base and many adherents in Punjab, is passionate about Kashmir and is interested in government at the center. It is also the party most interested in legal Islamization. The Jamaat-e-Ulema-e Islam (JUI), centered in Khyber Pakhtunkhwa, is more concerned with Afghanistan and with Pashtun ethnic issues. In its dealings with the central government, it is more interested in patronage and in protecting its Pashtun base and its madrassa network. Many of the JUI's provincial legislators prefer to speak Pashto rather than English or even Urdu. This may complicate the Pakistan government's dealings with them, as well as those of the United States.

These different priorities of individual parties are accentuated by differences in style. The JI tends to be more intellectual and more rigid, and is closer to the global "Islamic movement." It is internally more democratic. The JUI breathes fire and has a strong track record of activism, but is more open to accommodation and the give-and-take of politics. The fact that their leader has been known to his detractors in Pakistan as "Maulana Diesel" suggests that Pakistani observers believe financial give-and-take is part of the deal. The JUI dominated the MMA government in Khyber Pakhtunkhwa, and significantly, they succeeded in having their leader named leader of the national parliamentary opposition during the Musharraf years.

More than other Pakistani negotiators, politicians from Pakistan's Islamic religious parties distinguish sharply between private conversations and their public posture. This has been a particular problem with the JUI, which has relatively little experience at the national and international level but a long track record in provincial office and a reputation for patronage politics. Both World Bank and U.S. officials have had the experience of thinking that they had a general understanding, only to have the provincial official they were dealing with make contrary statements to the press. Americans feel betrayed when this happens. When asked to explain this apparent contradiction, party officials profess to be surprised at the foreigners' dismay, commenting that they have to represent "the voice of the people" in their public statements. They maintain that in private, and on narrower, more specific issues, they are able to reach agreement. But the public/private distinction can be a trap: an agreement that they are not willing to acknowledge in public may not be reliable.

The Islamist parties generally, and the JUI in particular, are very sensitive to their status inside the Pakistani political setup. They are regularly engaged in several implicit negotiations at once—with the central government in Islamabad, with the relevant provincial government when they do not control it, and with the mainstream political parties. They are sensitive to how they are portrayed in the press. The image they seek to put forward is strongly religious and anti-American: being media savvy does not make them "moderate."

The United States occasionally becomes part of the religious parties' negotiating mix but is rarely their most important negotiating partner. The religious parties have tried to keep themselves in the middle of the Pakistani action on a number of issues important to the United States. They opposed the Musharraf government's reform of laws pertaining to women. They have pressed hard, and fairly effectively, to prevent the bureaucracy and the courts from taking decisive action against militant organizations such as the Lashkar-e-Taiba. They have been Pakistan's most vociferous proponents of "peace deals" with the Pakistani Taliban, in spite of the fact that some of their leaders have faced Taliban threats. These positions reflect their views but also enhance their standing as Islamic leaders. Religious-party leaders got involved in the unsuccessful negotiations over the militant takeover at

Islamabad's Red Mosque in the summer of 2007. In this case, their negotiations got no real results, but they probably felt that the failure of Musharraf's meager political efforts and the bloody outcome of his military operation left them looking good. It is not always easy to distinguish between posturing and real objectives, but their concept of the requirements for "Islamic leadership" probably means that U.S. negotiators will need a powerful constellation of other allies in order to prevail over the religious parties in any bargaining in which the latter are directly involved.

Most important from the U.S. negotiators' perspective, the Islamist parties are able to achieve a publicity value that goes way beyond their modest support in the Pakistani electorate. They have never collectively polled more than 11 percent of the votes in a national election. Only in 2002 did they exceed that share of seats in Parliament. That election, widely regarded as deeply flawed, was the first one in which they were able to coalesce, reportedly with ISI encouragement. They also benefited from the absence from Pakistan of the leaders of the two major secular parties. And yet their ability to wrap themselves in the banner of Islam and their presumed "street presence" has put a brake on the government's willingness to follow through on issues where there is an Islamic angle, real or contrived. Pakistani governments have used this threat on many occasions to avoid making commitments important to the United States. American diplomats need to be wary of this tactic, especially if the Islamic parties regain the momentum they lost when they were badly defeated in the 2008 election.[20]

The Pakistani Taliban and the Islamic extremist organizations represent another world, a long step beyond the characteristics of Pakistan's Islamic religious parties. The available evidence about how they deal with the established governments against which they are conducting insurgent movements—Afghanistan and, for some of them, Pakistan—indicates that they consider themselves at war, and that deception and blatant disregard of commitments are perfectly acceptable ways to proceed. Imtiaz Ali, a journalist who covered multiple efforts by the Pakistan government to negotiate a cease-fire in troubled parts of Pakistan's tribal areas or the Khyber Pakhtunkhwa, argues that each of the agreements between militant groups and the Pakistan state since 2004 was violated by the militant group within days

---

20. The discussion of the religious parties draws on the authors' interviews with Gerald Feierstein, U.S. embassy in Pakistan, Imtiaz Ali, and Joshua White. See also Joshua T. White, "Vigilante Islamism in Pakistan: Religious Party Responses to the Lal Masjid Crisis," *Current Trends in Islamist Ideology* 7 (November 2008): 50–65, and Joshua T. White, *Pakistan's Islamist Frontier: Islamic Politics and U.S. Policy in Pakistan's North-West Frontier*, Religion and Security Monograph Series no. 1 (Arlington, VA: Center on Faith and International Affairs, 2008).

of its conclusion. On each occasion, the Pakistan government tried again, partly because of the visceral revulsion at treating Pakistani Muslims as an enemy, and partly because of the help the militants were able to obtain from a few sympathetic provincial civil servants. The United States has assumed, at least since the 1980s, that Pakistanis are better able than Americans to interpret what they were being told by militant groups and to obtain satisfactory results. (The Pakistanis have encouraged this deference.) The record of Pakistan's efforts to negotiate control of its own territory suggests that this may be a herculean task for Pakistanis as well.[21]

---

21. Imtiaz Ali, "Negotiating with the Taliban: Is Reconciliation Possible in Afghanistan and Pakistan?" (seminar presentation, United States Institute of Peace, Washington, D.C., July 10, 2009), www.usip. org/newsroom/multimedia/video-gallery/negotiating-the-taliban-reconciliation-possible-in-afghan-istan-an-0, and interview. For another look at the operating style of the Taliban in both Afghanistan and Pakistan, see the five-part series by David Rohde, "Held by the Taliban," *New York Times*, October 18–22, 2009.

7

Negotiations at the Top

Pakistan has on three occasions become a key strategic ally of the United States. In each case the two countries formally negotiated military and economic aid packages, but their real objective was to define the relationship. All three negotiations were carried out with the direct involvement of the top national leadership in Pakistan and at very senior levels, sometimes including the president himself, in the United States. On the Pakistani side this high-level participation affected both the substance and the process of negotiations. The personalities, backgrounds, and styles of the Pakistani leaders differed and the domestic and international political environment in which they operated varied. Even so, there were common elements in the way Pakistan dealt with the United States that illustrate how Pakistan conducts negotiations at the top.

This chapter examines these negotiations, with particular emphasis on the two most recent ones. The first took place in 1954 under the leadership of General (later Field Marshal) Ayub Khan and brought Pakistan into the U.S.-led Cold War alliance system. In 1980–81, following the Soviet invasion of Afghanistan, first the Carter administration and then the Reagan administration negotiated a new security relationship with the government of General Zia. Two decades later, after the al-Qaeda attacks of 9/11, the George W. Bush administration once again negotiated a revived relationship with Pakistan.

Significantly, all three negotiations were spearheaded in Pakistan by military officers either as army commander in chief (Ayub) or as presidents of military-dominated regimes in which they concurrently headed the army (Zia and Musharraf). These soldiers brought to the negotiating table approaches sometimes different from those of Pakistan's civilian leaders.

The three generals shared the characteristics and worldview of military negotiators. They also had great confidence in their ability to trade on their personal relations with military and civilian leaders in the United States. All three were primarily interested in lining up a powerful partner against India. To achieve that end they were prepared to sign on to the U.S. campaign of the day, whether it was designed to fight Communists in the 1950s and 1980s during the Cold War or Islamic extremists after 9/11 in the "global war on terrorism." But their commitment to these U.S.-led efforts never came close to matching the primary concern they gave to the threat they perceived from India.

Ayub, Zia, and Musharraf tried to distinguish themselves from civilian government leaders by projecting a bluff, forceful candor in dealing with their American counterparts. They wanted to be perceived as people who told it like it was, even when they were being palpably deceptive. This "soldierly" style came naturally to them as Pakistan military officers. But they also probably believed that it would give them more mileage in negotiations and other dealings with their American interlocutors—and would contrast favorably with American impressions of Pakistan's politicians, whom they all held in contempt.

Ayub Khan

As army commander in chief (1951–58) and, following a military coup, as president (1958–69), Ayub was the first to use this "bluff-soldier" approach in his dealings with the United States. He did so with great effectiveness, and was relentless in bringing Pakistani demands and concerns to the attention of senior American civilian and military officials, not least Presidents Dwight D. Eisenhower, John F. Kennedy, and Lyndon B. Johnson. He found a natural rapport with Eisenhower as a fellow general, and won his respect and admiration. He did not mince words either in his meetings with his American interlocutors or in the public diplomacy he deftly conducted to bolster his negotiating positions. He was forthright in demanding an answer when he came to the United States in 1953 seeking American military hardware.[1] He was just as blunt when he famously told a joint session of

---

1. Dennis Kux has a fascinating account of Ayub's blunt ways. "In September 1953, the general took matters in his own hands, transforming a routine trip to the United States to inspect army facilities into a campaign for a positive decision on the arms issue. One day during his visit, Ayub stormed into [Assistant Secretary Henry A.] Byroade's office in the State Department, frustrated by his inability to get a firm answer on arms aid from the Americans. 'For Christ's sake,' Byroade recalled Ayub's saying, 'I didn't come here to look at barracks. Our army can be your army if you want us. But let's make a decision.'" Kux, *Disenchanted Allies*, 57.

Congress eight years later that "the only people who will stand by you are the people of Pakistan—provided you are also prepared to stand by them." During the U.S.-British-sponsored negotiations that Pakistan conducted with India in 1962–63, he privately told the American ambassador that the positions Pakistani officials were taking was "damned nonsense."[2]

Ayub made it a point to cultivate senior American military figures as well as top policymakers, influential congressmen, and journalists. As one American diplomat admiringly recalled: "[Ayub] would do the most beautiful briefing for anybody from the United States of significance who came out, in which he gave a rationale for Pakistan's military program, its force composition and disposition."[3] In dealing with the U.S. embassy in Pakistan, he took full advantage of the "clientitis" of a succession of ambassadors, most of whom became his firm admirers and sympathetic supporters of his policies. He also understood the usefulness of aggressive outreach to the pro-Pakistan lobby in the Pentagon, where his own status as a military officer helped his cause.

Ayub no doubt recognized that U.S. policymakers appreciated his outspoken man-to-man style (and that they compared it favorably with the conduct of Pakistan's Indian rivals). It reflected both his personality and training, and until his last years in office it served him and Pakistan well.

Ayub Khan was still in power when the U.S.-Pakistan alliance unraveled during the 1965 India-Pakistan war. Two of the military men who later succeeded him as president, Zia and Musharraf, faced different problems as they sought to work with American leaders to reinvent the relationship following the Soviet invasion of Afghanistan in 1979, and again after the al-Qaeda attacks on the U.S. mainland in 2001. But each in his own way brought a military officer's perspective to the negotiations that led to the revival of strong bilateral ties. Each also brought to the table a striking confidence that he could outwit and outmaneuver his American interlocutors, overcoming significant differences in national priorities. These negotiations also illustrate characteristics described in the earlier chapters, such as an ability to persuade their American counterparts to move from commitment to implementation along a route favorable to Pakistani interests, skill at turning Pakistan's potential vulnerabilities into a source of negotiating strength, and, above all, talent for convincing the United States that it owed Pakistan for the risks Pakistan was taking—the guilt trip.

---

2. Howard B. Schaffer, *The Limits of Influence: America's Role in Kashmir* (Washington, D.C.: Brookings Institution Press, 2009), 87.

3. John O. Bell, oral history statement, Association for Diplomatic Studies and Training, June 17, 1988.

Zia ul-Haq

Zia ul-Haq's personality differed sharply from Ayub Khan's. He was modest and self-effacing, perhaps the last words one would use to describe Ayub, and did not have the latter's commanding presence. Unlike his secular-minded predecessor, Zia was a devout Muslim who energetically promoted Islamic values and institutions during his eleven years in power. But despite his quiet, rather secretive nature and seeming humility, he too presented himself as a blunt, plain-speaking military man. His famous dismissal of President Jimmy Carter's offer of military and economic assistance as "peanuts" is a good example of this. Zia's effort to project that attractive persona—attractive at least to the Americans he dealt with—achieved only limited success. Many of them thought him devious, quite prepared to lie unabashedly when he considered that useful. His repeated denial of Pakistan's nuclear activities and ambitions was widely considered the most flagrant evidence of this. Discussing Zia's handling of American accusations on nuclear matters, Arthur Hummel, the U.S. ambassador to Pakistan in 1977–81, recalled that Zia "was a good actor. He expressed indignation and alarm and swore that none [of the accusations on the nuclear issue] could possibly be true."[4] Ronald Spiers, who followed Hummel in Islamabad, thought Zia's deviousness a reflection of Pakistani culture. He "was as honest with me [on the nuclear issue] as he could be."[5] But misgivings about Zia's truthfulness appear to have had little if any serious impact on U.S. policymaking after the Soviet army rolled into Kabul in December 1979.

Like Ayub, Zia used a personal touch and carefully cultivated influential Americans. He stepped up his contacts with senior Americans once the Soviet invasion of Afghanistan made Pakistan an attractive prospect for favorable U.S. attention. To quote Ambassador Spiers: "He had countless meetings with Congress members, cabinet members, and other U.S. dignitaries, most often in his modest little home, which had been the home of the Pakistan Army chief of staff."[6] The pitch Zia gave them when the Soviet army loomed on Pakistan's western border was a familiar one that was often replicated by his military subordinates. According to Spiers, who must have sat through the briefings more often than he would have liked, "[Zia] would display a map on which he superimposed a red area which was the part

---

4. Arthur Hummel, oral history statement, Association for Diplomatic Studies and Training, April 13, 1994, http://memory.loc.gov/cgi-bin/query/D?mfdip:2:./temp/~ammem_1HoZ.

5. Spiers, oral history statement.

6. Zia never moved into the impressive presidential residence. There were many reasons for this. But his meeting important Americans at his modest home surely helped allay any concern on their part that they were sending large sums of U.S. taxpayers' money to support Pakistan government officials' lavish lifestyles.

of Asia occupied by the Soviets. He would then discuss how Pakistan was being squeezed between India and the Soviet Union." In the ambassador's view, "he really believed this strategic view of the world and was genuinely concerned with the 'red horde' knocking on his door. He also believed that India would attack him some day."[7]

U.S.-Pakistan relations were troubled during the early years of Zia's government. The general had seized power in a bloodless coup in July 1977 when he overthrew the elected government of Prime Minister Zulfiqar Ali Bhutto. Zia's pursuit of a nuclear program put him at odds with Carter's focus on nuclear nonproliferation. Carter's interest in "regional influentials"— including India but not Pakistan—added another source of tension. Zia's government made matters worse when it failed to intervene as demonstrators attacked and torched the U.S. embassy in Islamabad in November 1979, killing two American and two Pakistani staff members and nearly roasting to death another forty trapped inside the burning building.

The Soviet invasion of Afghanistan in late December 1979, five weeks later, transformed the situation overnight. Instead of a near-pariah flouting Carter's global policies, Pakistan suddenly became a frontline state in the struggle against dangerous Kremlin expansionism. Zia's standing skyrocketed. As General K.M. Arif, his chief of staff, acidly put it, "The arch critics of the autocratic military ruler of Pakistan began to woo him. They suddenly discovered Zia's hitherto unknown 'sterling qualities' and the special importance of Pakistan in the changed circumstances."[8]

Carter called Zia on the morning of the invasion to offer support in the face of what Washington considered a serious threat to Pakistan. He reaffirmed the 1959 bilateral agreement that pledged American support for the Pakistanis against Communist aggression. Significantly, it was Carter who phoned Zia to volunteer support, not Zia who called Carter to ask for it. Carter's urgent call must surely have suggested to Pakistanis that as the Soviets moved into Afghanistan, Washington needed Pakistan more than Pakistan needed the United States. Through their well-informed embassy in Washington, they were quite aware that Carter, who had sought to end the longtime Cold War focus of U.S. foreign policy, had been surprised and politically embarrassed by Moscow's invasion and was trying to embrace the strong anti-Soviet approach that he had earlier spurned.

Carter quickly proposed to send Deputy Secretary of State Warren Christopher to Islamabad to work out the terms of a revived bilateral security

---

7. Spiers, oral history statement.
8. Arif, *Working with Zia*, 314.

relationship. The Pakistanis were guarded in their response. History had led them to question American reliability. They did not share Carter's sense of urgency and saw risks in tying themselves closely to Washington. Their well-advertised concern that a security relationship with the United States would bring Moscow's wrath down upon them became a major bargaining chip they repeatedly used in later negotiations. Deflecting the proposed Christopher mission, Zia suggested instead that Foreign Minister Agha Shahi go down to Washington from New York, where he was to lead the Pakistan delegation in a special UN General Assembly session convened in early January 1980 to deal with the Afghanistan crisis. The administration agreed.

Before Shahi reached Washington, Zia consulted with his military and civilian advisers to frame Pakistan's response to the Soviet invasion and Carter's offer of American support. Opinion was divided on both issues. As General Arif recalls,

> The choices available to Pakistan were hard. Firstly, she could accept the fait accompli [of Moscow's military occupation of Afghanistan] as she lacked the capacity to challenge the Soviet Union. Secondly, she could provide open and full support to the Afghan freedom struggle, despite the risks involved. And, thirdly, she could give overt political, diplomatic, and humanitarian support to the refugees with covert assistance to the Mujahideen.[9]

Not surprisingly, those who argued for a soft line cited the alleged unreliability of the United States.[10] Zia quickly decided to adopt the third option. This remained his government's policy throughout the Afghanistan war.

Shahi met in Washington on January 12, 1980, with Carter, Secretary of State Cyrus Vance, National Security Adviser Zbigniew Brzezinski, and other senior American officials. The previous week the president had publicly declared his administration's intention to provide military and economic assistance to Pakistan and reportedly won the backing of key members of Congress for emergency legislation needed to lift the aid ban imposed in April 1979 because of Pakistan's nuclear program.

Shahi and his delegation, which included many military advisers, presented to the American side a lengthy, unprioritized wish list of equipment running into the billions of dollars that Pakistan wanted from the United States. This was the first time since the Soviet invasion that they had submit-

---

9. Ibid.

10. According to Arif, the other arguments the soft-liners made were the inherent weakness of Pakistan, the ambivalent attitude of India on the invasion, the possibility of India and Afghanistan acting in concert against Pakistan, and, of course, the grave risk of incurring the active hostility of a neighboring superpower. Even though the soft-liners lost the battle, these arguments were useful to the Pakistanis in the negotiations.

ted a request. According to the *New York Times*, administration officials said that before Shahi came to Washington the Pakistanis seemed to be waiting to see what the United States would offer.[11] Thomas Thornton, a senior National Security Council official who participated in some of the discussions, noted that "the American side saw [the Pakistani request] as an opening position and quickly relegated [it] to working-level discussion. These were meaningless since the issue at stake was a political one."[12] He recalled that the Pakistanis "throughout the coming year . . . avoided making detailed and, from the American point of view, viable requests for military hardware. The Americans were never able to find out just what the Pakistani priorities were."[13] Several retired U.S. military officers commented that in their experience, "the Pakistanis usually asked for the moon."[14]

For all the air of crisis, the administration's response was modest. All the administration would offer the Pakistanis was a tentative two-year aid package, equally divided between military and economic assistance, totaling about $400 million. Before the meeting with Shahi, Carter had decided not to provide the F-16s that the Pakistanis wanted and some of his own advisers had recommended. Vance's brief made it clear that the proffered assistance did not signify "any lessening of the importance the United States attaches to nuclear non-proliferation."[15] The administration rejected Shahi's call for an upgrading of the 1959 bilateral mutual security agreement. The Pakistanis wanted the agreement changed into a mutual defense treaty, which would give the pledge formal congressional blessing through the ratification process. Vance told Shahi that he was willing to ask for a congressional vote reaffirming the agreement. Shahi considered this a step forward, though not as good as a treaty.

The talks ended inconclusively with the understanding that they would be resumed in Islamabad. The American negotiators had not come close to agreeing to the high opening gambit Shahi had brought with him to Washington. Nor had Shahi significantly lowered his extensive (and expensive) demands. The American side had quite evidently failed in this first round to answer successfully the question they had recognized as Pakistan's key

---

11. Graham Hovey, "Carter Vows to Help Pakistan," *New York Times*, January 13, 1980.

12. Thomas Thornton, "Between the Stools? U.S. Policy toward Pakistan during the Carter Administration," *Asian Survey* 22, no. 10 (October 1982): 970.

13. Ibid., 977.

14. Interviews with authors.

15. State Department talking points for Secretary Vance's meetings with Agha Shahi, January 12, 1980, obtained by Dennis Kux through the Freedom of Information Act and cited in Kux, *Disenchanted Allies*, 249.

concern: "whether the credibility and magnitude of U.S. support is sufficient to offset the real danger of Soviet intimidation as well as the potential damage of close relations with the United States to their nonaligned Islamic credentials."[16] But they could not be sure if the Pakistanis were just hanging tough, or if they were so worried about their security that they needed a much more favorable U.S. response, or something in between.

Zia provided a significant clue. When the leaked report of the $400 million package reached Pakistan, Zia made his famous "peanuts" remark.[17] He went on to say, "I have not heard it officially, but if this is true . . . it is terribly disappointing. Pakistan will not buy its security with $400 million." In an interview with American journalists he declined to name a figure for the American aid he wanted, but he indicated that it had to be much more than $400 million.[18] According to a Pakistani diplomat close to the action, the Ministry of Foreign Affairs and everyone else in the government believed that Pakistan needed to play hardball, given the stakes involved. He recalled that they were convinced Pakistan could do better.[19]

Reacting to Zia's comment, a State Department spokesman stated that "the $400 million figure is seen in Washington as only part of a larger package also involving nations friendly to Pakistan." He said that the United States was discussing the matter with other countries.[20]

The action now moved to Islamabad. Carter approved Brzezinski's proposal that he join Christopher in leading the American delegation because, according to the national security adviser, the president agreed "that it would signal to the Pakistanis that our approach was not merely a diplomatic one but that we were prepared to deal seriously with the security dimensions of the challenge."[21] Journalists who accompanied the delegation were told en route that it intended to make clear to the Pakistanis that the administration would ask Congress for an open-ended aid commitment beyond the

---

16. State Department scope paper for Shahi visit, undated but presumably January 8 or 9, 1980, obtained by Dennis Kux through the Freedom of Information Act and cited in Kux, *Disenchanted Allies*, 248.

17. Zia does not seem to have intended to personally insult Carter, who was a Georgia peanut farmer. He was just using what he thought was American idiom that would be understood in Washington. The episode demonstrates the peril of using another country's vernacular without recognizing the way it could be twisted, as the American media could not resist doing in this case.

18. William Borders, "Pakistan Dismisses $400 Million in Aid Offered by U.S. as 'Peanuts,'" *New York Times*, January 18, 1980.

19. Authors' interview with a retired Pakistan Foreign Service officer.

20. Bernard Gwertzman, "U.S. Still Plans Aid in Spite of Criticism by Pakistani Ruler," *New York Times*, January 19, 1980.

21. Zbigniew Brzezinski, *Power and Principle* (New York: Farrar, Straus, and Giroux, 1985), 448.

two years already pledged but would not increase the $400 million prom-
ised for 1980–81. The Pakistanis would also be told that the United States
did not intend to force them into a pro-Western alliance and was willing
to let the Islamic countries take the lead in the area. A final point was that
the new bilateral ties Washington was trying to develop did not mean that
it had lost interest in trying to dissuade President Zia from detonating a
nuclear device.[22]

The talks failed to achieve a breakthrough. Although Brzezinski reportedly
suggested that the two-year figure could be raised somewhat, this was still
"peanuts" to Zia. The Pakistanis continued to ask for a much bigger assistance package, which they coupled with a request that the U.S. assurances to
Pakistan be interpreted to apply as well to an Indian attack. This the Americans rejected; they said their commitment was limited to an attack by the
Soviet Union. How serious the Pakistanis were in making this request is de-
batable. According to Ambassador Hummel, a participant in the talks, "while
they pushed the idea of a commitment on India and a NATO-type treaty,
they knew very well they wouldn't get anything like that."[23]

Nor did the American negotiators offer F-16s or heavy armor, another
important negotiating aim for the Pakistanis and evidence that their negotiating strategy was developed with India in mind. In the view of Assistant
Secretary of Defense David McGiffert, another participant, "it was perfectly
clear that their [Pakistanis'] orientation as far as equipment was concerned
was what would be useful on the Indian border. They weren't interested in
the sort of thing we thought they needed to secure the Afghan border."[24]
Though they welcomed the willingness of the American negotiators to waive
the nuclear-triggered sanctions, the Pakistanis would have been happier if
the U.S. side had not continued to harp on the nonproliferation issue.

Brzezinski has written that as the negotiations faltered and then failed,
the Pakistanis backed away from the idea of a close security arrangement.
They contended that in light of the two sides' inability to agree,

> their security interests would be better served by a broad understanding with the
> United States, reinforced by the public U.S. reaffirmation of the 1959 assurances,
> but with Pakistan publicly distancing itself from the United States and collaborat-

22. Bernard Gwertzman, "High-Level American Delegation Arrives in Pakistan for Security Talks,"
New York Times, February 1, 1980.

23. Diego Cordovez and Selig S. Harrison, *Out of Afghanistan* (New York: Oxford University Press,
1995), 57.

24. Ibid., 57.

ing more closely with other Moslem countries in opposing the Soviet occupation of Afghanistan.[25]

In a private conversation, Zia told Brzezinski that such an approach would best serve both American and Pakistani interests.

In effect, Zia was walking out of the store to recalibrate the bargaining. According to Brzezinski, the president also confided that "on more sensitive matters he did not want to deal with the State Department, which he viewed as motivated by an anti-Pakistani bias."[26] The *New York Times* reported from Islamabad that while Brzezinski and Christopher were regarded by the Americans as delegation co-chairmen, "General Zia clearly saw Mr. Brzezinski as the leader, since the dinner was in his honor and he spoke constantly with him, rarely speaking to Mr. Christopher."[27]

Thornton, who was a member of the delegation, succinctly summed up what had gone wrong:

> Both sides had misjudged badly. The Americans overestimated the extent to which Pakistan had rethought its role following the Soviet attack; the Pakistanis erred in believing that the American offer could be bargained upward. Disagreements over individual elements of the proposal were less important than the fact that Pakistan sought a totality of commitment that the United States could not reciprocate. The basis for a deal was lacking, and since the Americans had made their offer as a package, it fell as a package.[28]

General Arif, who also participated in the negotiations, offered a Pakistani perspective. He wrote later that "the Carter administration misjudged the resilience of Pakistan. It had concluded that the Soviet pressure on Pakistan and her security compulsions in the face of her economic difficulties would compel her to backtrack and agree to a bilateral relationship with the United States, more or less on U.S. terms."[29]

The Brzezinski-Christopher visit to Islamabad was the Carter administration's last serious effort to develop a mutually acceptable U.S.-Pakistan security relationship. In the year that followed—Carter's last in the White House—the Zia government increasingly lost hope that he would meet

---

25. Brzezinski, *Power and Principle*, 448.

26. Brzezinski, *Power and Principle*, 449. This must have been music to the ears of the national security adviser, who in his memoir made no secret of his low regard for what he considered the soft positions taken by the State Department on U.S.-Soviet issues. Whether Zia's reported attitude was shared by other senior Pakistanis who negotiated with Americans is not known. But certainly Arthur Hummel, the career diplomat who served as U.S. ambassador to Pakistan at the time, enjoyed a warm relationship with his Pakistani interlocutors.

27. Bernard Gwertzman, "Leaders of Pakistan Meets Carter Aide," *New York Times*, February 3, 1980.

28. Thornton, "Between the Stools?," 971.

29. Arif, *Working with Zia*, 338.

their requirements. The Pakistanis made it clear through both diplomatic and public channels that they were not interested in the limited level of military assistance Washington proposed. They accepted the economic aid portion of the package and the administration's generous debt rescheduling offer, however. Carter himself seems to have had no regrets. When the State Department recommended to the White House that additional funding for Pakistan be worked into the tight budget then being put into final form, the proposal drew a sharply negative personal reaction from the president.[30]

During the visit Zia did agree to Brzezinski's proposal to expand covert intelligence cooperation on Afghanistan between ISI and the CIA. This co-operation had begun following the coup that brought the Communists to power in Kabul in 1978. Brzezinski discussed it with Zia when he visited Islamabad. Carter approved a broader covert action program days after the Soviet invasion. Negotiations with the Pakistanis on the program were carried on through intelligence channels. It is difficult to assess how the matter figured in the negotiation strategy of the two sides as they wrestled with arms supply, security guarantees, and economic assistance issues.

At the end of the day, the Zia government remained unconvinced that the United States under Carter wanted a security relationship with Pakistan sufficiently robust to balance the danger it posed to Pakistan's interests. These impressions shaped its negotiating strategy. As 1980 wore on, it became even clearer that Zia was looking for a better deal from the Republicans, led after their midsummer convention by Ronald Reagan, a confirmed cold warrior of long standing. When Zia came to the White House briefly in October following a UN gathering, he went so far as to rebuff Carter's offer to include the prized F-16s in an arms package for Pakistan. According to General Arif, who accompanied him to the meeting, Zia told Carter, "I do not wish to burden you with Pakistan's problems at a time when you are preoccupied in an election campaign. Let us defer this issue until after the . . . elections."[31] By then Zia had evidently concluded that Reagan would win the race and that as president after January 20, 1981, he would be more sympathetic to Pakistan's negotiating position.

Zia was right on both counts. After taking office following his landslide victory over Carter, Ronald Reagan and his outspokenly anti-Communist colleagues were eager to enlist Pakistan as a key partner in a stepped-up effort to make life difficult for the Soviets in Afghanistan and eventually force them to withdraw. One of the first things the new administration did was

---

30. Personal recollection of one of the authors.

31. Arif, *Working with Zia*, 338.

to launch a major review of Pakistan policy and put together a $3.2 billion five-year package to reconstruct bilateral ties. Ambassador Hummel, who had cabled incoming Secretary of State Alexander Haig urging him to take prompt action, was brought back to Washington to help shepherd the effort. Intense bureaucratic activity and consultations with Congress followed over the next few months. This preceded any serious negotiations with the Pakistanis about the levels and types of aid and became the basis on which the administration later conducted them.

For their part, the Pakistanis do not appear to have pressed Washington for early action. They seem to have been content to wait for the Reagan administration to make the first significant move. They calculated that the administration, eager to counter the Soviet hold over Afghanistan, could be relied on to provide them an attractive package that met both their broad political needs and their military and economic assistance requirements as they defined them. They were sure that the Americans needed them more than they needed the Americans.

They had good reason for their confidence. The new administration was not hampered by the hang-ups that had complicated Carter's efforts to restore U.S.-Pakistan ties. It was not concerned with Pakistan's domestic political arrangements. It was prepared to wink as Zia continued Pakistan's nuclear program. It was eager to do more than Carter had done to promote anti-Soviet ferment in Afghanistan. The administration shrugged off the shrill Indian reaction to American supply of sophisticated military equipment that the Pakistanis could use much more readily against them on the plains of the Punjab and in the Arabian Sea than against potential Soviet aggression through the Khyber Pass. Those in Congress and elsewhere who were skeptical about providing Pakistan with high-performance F-16s, modern heavy tanks, and Harpoon ship-to-ship missiles were told that these were needed to bolster Pakistani self-confidence. The administration argued that the Pakistanis needed such confidence if they were to cooperate in the struggle against the Soviets in Afghanistan. It also claimed that a Pakistan well armed with conventional weapons was more likely to restrain its nuclear ambitions.

But the Pakistanis did not take the administration's support for granted. When a delegation headed once again by Agha Shahi came to Washington in April 1981 in another bid to negotiate the terms of the new bilateral relationship, the Pakistanis played the same card of past American unreliability that they had used in Carter's day. General Arif, who again accompanied the foreign minister, recalled that in the group's meeting with Secretary Haig, "[the secretary] was apprised of Pakistan's apprehensions about the incon-sistency of U.S. support in the past. It was conveyed to him that a mutual relationship, lacking durability and dependability, was unlikely to serve the long-term cause of peace and friendship."[32] In other words, you let us down before and it will cost you plenty to get us to work with you again.

The administration for its part made the same argument to skeptics in Congress and elsewhere: if the United States wanted to overcome the Paki-stanis' suspicion of its trustworthiness, it needed to demonstrate to them explicitly that it could be counted on. The Pakistanis were of course aware the administration was taking this line with its domestic constituencies.

The Pakistanis made the nonproliferation issue a major point in the nego-tiations. Zia gave the new administration advance public warning of the im-portance to Pakistan of its ongoing nuclear program and its determination to continue it. He told columnist Joseph Kraft of the *Washington Post* in March that the most important condition the United States needed to fulfill to dem-onstrate its "credibility and reliability" as an ally was "giving up its opposition to Pakistani plans to develop nuclear energy for 'peaceful purposes.'"[33] Shahi stressed this point to Haig in Washington a few weeks later. According to Dennis Kux, who interviewed Shahi, Haig, and Arif, the secretary replied that "the issue need not become the centerpiece of the U.S.-Pakistan relation-ship" as it had been earlier. But Haig warned the delegation that if Pakistan detonated a nuclear device, the reaction in the U.S. Congress would make it difficult to cooperate in the way the Reagan administration hoped.[34]

This was a position the Zia government could live with. It did not deter the Pakistanis from continuing to develop their capacity to build nuclear weap-ons. The conversation Shahi's delegation had with Haig and other evidence led them to calculate—correctly—that the administration would prefer to ignore or play down any evidence that they were moving ahead with their nuclear program as long as they did not conduct an actual test. When from time to time they were challenged about the program they routinely lied.[35] Given the high priority the Reagan administration gave to undermining the

---

32. Ibid., 341.

33. Joseph Kraft, "In Pakistan, Unlikely Support," *Washington Post*, March 10, 1981.

34. Kux, *Disenchanted Allies*, 257

35. Ambassador Spiers, one of those lied to, offers an interesting explanation if not a justification for Pakistani mendacity. Discussing the effort of Ambassador-at-Large Vernon Walters to confront Zia with evidence of Pakistani nuclear activities, Spiers recalled, "I tried to tell Walters that he wouldn't get very far because that was contrary to the culture in which he [Zia] was raised. Zia would not have viewed his negative response as lying: it would have been what we would call a 'white lie,' that is an answer that would spare us embarrassment or hurt. In the Pakistani culture, that was perfectly innocent behavior: we just couldn't understand it." Spiers, oral history statement.

Soviets in Afghanistan and the lesser importance it gave to curbing Pakistan's nuclear ambitions, the American side was not inclined to pursue the matter. The Pakistanis surely understood this.

The toughest bargaining between the two sides was over the type of weapons systems the United States would provide. The Pakistanis wanted forty high-performance, state-of-the-art F-16 fighter aircraft, which until then Washington had provided only to its closest allies. Some policymakers had problems with this. Ambassador Spiers thought that "it was silly for the Pakistanis to waste their money on equipment they really didn't need."[36]

But for the Pakistanis, the F-16 had a symbolic significance that transcended its usefulness as a weapons system (to be employed primarily against India). Against the background of America's wavering past support, it became for them a test and an emblem of the Reagan administration's steadfastness, as Pakistani negotiators repeatedly pointed out. The Pakistanis wanted to get the first batch of aircraft within a year, a schedule that the U.S. Air Force said was difficult to meet. When a technical delegation from Pakistan visited the United States in July 1981 and was told that the time frame for initial delivery could not be less than twenty-seven months, General Arif, the delegation's leader, replied "that it was incomprehensible that the United States could not provide at least some aircraft [earlier]. . . . Early delivery would demonstrate U.S. concern for the security imperatives of Pakistan." The general said that if the American side stuck to its position, "I [will] return to Pakistan to report the failure of the talks to the government."[37] When this tactic failed and the delegation left Washington without an agreement on early delivery, Zia personally wrote Reagan to urge shipment of at least some of the planes within a year. Zia's arguments and the words he used to express them closely paralleled Arif's. They must by then have become familiar to the American side. Reagan conceded the Pakistani demand.

The Pakistanis were also upfront in their insistence that they would not take any advice on internal affairs. This was an easy one for the administration to accept. Haig was quick to tell the Shahi delegation that it was for Pakistan to resolve its domestic problems. The United States stuck to this position throughout the Reagan years. Although the administration occasionally called for the holding of repeatedly delayed elections and expressed modest concern about the increasingly Islamic character of Zia's govern-

---

36. Spiers, oral history statement. But in his oral history interview, Spiers also conceded that the planes "certainly gave the country a shot in the arm. The acquisition of the aircraft became a symbol of national virility. It is hard to believe how emotionally important that wing of planes became."

37. Arif, *Working with Zia*, 342.

ment, this was all basically lip service. The administration's care not to offend Zia by calling undue attention to the way he ruled fitted in well with Reagan's policy of confining U.S. criticism of the governing practices of other countries to those behind the Iron Curtain. The Pakistanis were obviously aware of this and acted accordingly.

Although Shahi led both Pakistani delegations to Washington and he and his foreign ministry colleagues played a prominent role in them, the army called the shots. Shahi was always accompanied by military officers, most notably General Arif but many others as well. He said later that he did not agree with the policy directives he received from Islamabad, where Zia was closely involved in developing negotiating strategy on the major issues. According to Ambassador Hummel, Shahi was "basically unhappy with getting too close to the United States and with tweaking the Soviets."[38] The foreign minister wanted a bigger role for the United Nations in resolving the Afghanistan issue than Washington did.

Shahi seems to have been gradually moved away from center stage in the negotiations. He told the American journalist-scholar Selig Harrison in a 1990 interview that

> I became convinced [when the negotiations were reaching their conclusion in June 1981] that Zia was using me as a front man for diplomatic window dressing and for bargaining purposes. . . . I had less and less control over policy, which was increasingly guided by the desire to please Saudi Arabia and the United States. We should have shaken hands with the Americans, not embraced them.[39]

What the foreign minister seems to have meant is that Zia used Shahi's well-advertised skepticism about a renewed American connection to persuade the U.S. side that it had to be more forthcoming in meeting Pakistani demands. Shahi resigned as foreign minister in February 1982.

Shahi's unhappiness stemmed in part from his opposition to the close cooperation on anti-Soviet activity in Afghanistan between ISI and the CIA. This covert program, in which arms funded by the United States and Saudi Arabia were funneled through ISI to the mujahideen freedom fighters in Afghanistan, was handled in Islamabad on the American side by the ambassador and the CIA station chief. The director of central intelligence, William Casey, an avid supporter of the program, visited Pakistan clandestinely from time to time. Ambassador Spiers recalled that he, Casey, and the station chief would meet with Zia and the ISI director general.

---

38. Quoted in Cordovez and Harrison, *Out of Afghanistan*, 66.
39. Cordovez and Harrison, *Out of Afghanistan*, 67.

The Pakistan foreign ministry was kept completely in the dark and was not even aware of Casey's visits.

The intelligence program, greatly expanded over the next seven years, became one of the mainstays of the revived relationship. The Pakistanis always insisted that they alone would deal with the mujahideen and allocate arms, supplies, training, and other support among the different mujahid groups. The American side accepted this. It was further evidence of how in the Zia-Reagan era the United States needed Pakistan more than Pakistan needed the United States—and both sides acted accordingly.

Agreement on the $3.2 billion military and economic aid program was announced on June 15, 1981, following a two-day visit to Pakistan by James L. Buckley, the under secretary of state for security assistance. The two governments' joint declaration stated that the program represented the Reagan administration's commitment to "assist Pakistan in meeting unprecedented threats" through rapid delivery of equipment to strengthen the Pakistani armed forces. It noted that Pakistan would remain a nonaligned Islamic country and was not entering into any "new alliance" with the United States. This language reflected the position Zia had taken with Brzezinski in February 1980 when the Pakistan president had backed away from his government's earlier call for an upgraded alliance between the two countries.

Significantly, the joint statement made no reference to the nuclear issue. Announcing the agreement in Washington, a State Department spokesman reiterated the familiar argument that "this administration believes that by addressing those security concerns which have motivated Pakistan's nuclear program and re-establishing a relationship of confidence with it offer the best opportunity in the long run for effectively dealing with its nuclear program." Although the administration had not yet won congressional support for the waiver of nonproliferation legislation that was required for resumption of assistance to Pakistan, it was urgently moving to do so. It got the necessary approval later in 1981. The *New York Times* account of the agreement also carried an assurance by a State Department official that "our aid to Pakistan is certainly not aimed at India. The United States is not fueling an arms race." The administration had repeatedly made these points to help sell the Pakistan program.[40]

The Pakistanis held off formally accepting the agreement until September 1981, when the Reagan administration assured them it had worked out a plan to speed delivery of the F-16s. The arrangement provided that six of the

---

40. Juan de Onis, "U.S. and Pakistan Reach an Agreement on $3 Billion in Aid," *New York Times*, June 16, 1981.

forty planes would be sent to the Pakistan air force within a year. Announcing Pakistan's formal acceptance, the foreign ministry stated that "we wish to reiterate that [this] does not affect in any way our commitments as a member of the Islamic Conference and the nonaligned movement or our well-known position on major international issues." The Pakistanis reported that Under Secretary Buckley, who had returned to Pakistan to clinch the deal, gave Zia a personal letter from Reagan affirming American acceptance of Pakistan's policies and stating that the United States recognized Pakistan's refusal to become linked in any kind of security alliance with the United States.[41]

It was the beginning of a beautiful friendship that lasted until the George H. W. Bush administration was obliged to suspend military and economic aid to Pakistan in 1990 because it could no longer certify as required by the Pressler Amendment that Pakistan did not possess a nuclear device and that U.S. assistance would reduce the risk of its doing so.

Pervez Musharraf

Like Zia, General Pervez Musharraf spent his first few years as head of the Pakistan government in Washington's doghouse, initially when Clinton was president, then, after January 20, 2001, when George W. Bush occupied the White House. He too had come to power in a military coup, in October 1999, when he overthrew Prime Minister Nawaz Sharif following Sharif's abortive effort to replace him as army chief of staff with a more pliant general. Musharraf's authoritarian rule and his failure to set a timetable for fresh elections and a return to democracy displeased Washington. The United States was also troubled by his government's effort to expand Pakistan's nuclear arsenal and its policy on Kashmir, where elements based in Pakistan continued to cross the Line of Control and engage in violent activity on the Indian side.

Washington was also highly concerned by Musharraf's continuing support for the Taliban regime in Afghanistan, which Pakistan had helped bring to power in the mid-1990s. With Saudi Arabia and the United Arab Emirates, Pakistan was one of only three countries that recognized the Taliban. Like all leaders of Pakistan, Musharraf considered a friendly Afghanistan that shunned strong ties with India a key foreign policy objective. He believed that Taliban rule in Kabul met this longstanding Pakistani strategic requirement. Although moderate in his own ideological outlook, Musharraf

---

41. Bernard Gwertzman, "Pakistan Agrees to U.S. Aid Plan and F-16 Delivery," *New York Times*, September 16, 1981.

was prepared to accept the extremist Islamic political and social practices of the Taliban that had outraged opinion in the United States and elsewhere. He and his government also accepted the increasingly close ties that were developing between the Afghan regime and al-Qaeda.

The Bush administration continued Clinton's efforts to persuade the Musharraf government to use its influence in Kabul to break up the Taliban–al-Qaeda connection and get the Taliban regime to hand over al-Qaeda leader Osama bin Laden for trial before an international tribunal. President Bush stressed the need for action against al-Qaeda in a letter he sent Musharraf soon after taking office.[42] When Condoleezza Rice, Bush's national security adviser, made the same point to Pakistan foreign minister Abdul Sattar in Washington a few months later, Sattar urged senior U.S. policymakers to engage the Taliban.[43] A further Bush-Musharraf letter in August again failed to move the Pakistanis. On the eve of 9/11 the administration was still considering what to do to change Musharraf's position. It was not ready to confront Islamabad.[44]

Pakistani military analyst Shuja Nawaz has correctly observed that "Afghanistan's tragedies have a way of becoming a boon for Pakistan's dictators."[45] As noted, the Soviet invasion of Afghanistan transformed U.S. relations with Islamabad and made Zia a Reagan administration favorite. 9/11 had a similar impact on the Bush administration's appraisal of Pervez Musharraf.

Events moved much faster and more decisively in 2001 than they had in 1980 and 1981. But many of the elements that had characterized the Pakistan military government's negotiating tactics and style in the Zia period were again evident when Musharraf dealt with American demands in the immediate aftermath of 9/11 and then went on to develop a long-term security and political relationship with Washington.

These included the Pakistanis taking advantage of what they perceived to be America's greater need than their own for the renewed ties. As the Pakistanis saw it, they were doing the Americans a favor by joining the U.S. cause. These perceptions set the stage for renewed use of the guilt trip in their dealings with Washington. And, once again, the demands they put to the American side reflected their continuing concern about a threat from India and their interest in using U.S. assistance to deal with it. To this was

42. Thomas H. Kean, Chair, and Lee H. Hamilton, Vice Chair, *The 9/11 Commission Report: Final Report of the National Commission on Terrorist Attacks upon the United States* (New York: St. Martin's Press, 2004), 207.

43. Ibid., 207; and Abdul Sattar, interview.

44. Kean and Hamilton, *The 9/11 Commission Report*, 207.

45. Nawaz, *Crossed Swords*, 538.

added their fear that the United States would turn to India (and against Pakistan) if Pakistan did not respond positively. The India-centric aspect of Musharraf's approach to the United States was less blatant than Zia's had been. This may have reflected Musharraf's awareness that U.S.-Indian relations had greatly improved after the end of the Cold War. But the military equipment Musharraf sought from Washington—most notably once again F-16 aircraft—was as limited in its usefulness against Islamic terrorists as U.S.-supplied arms had been for Zia in meeting potential Soviet threats.

Although there were important tactical differences between the two general-presidents' negotiating styles, the way Musharraf came to decisions and dealt with Americans also resembled Zia's in many respects. Like Zia, Musharraf handled all significant issues personally. He was careful to consult with his senior uniformed colleagues in the armed forces when he formulated his positions on important matters. Civilian members of his cabinet played a lesser role. The Ministry of Foreign Affairs was even more on the periphery than it had been in the 1981 negotiations. When Musharraf invited his foreign ministers to sit in on meetings, they were seen but rarely heard.

Articulate and outspoken, Musharraf, like Zia, cultivated top American leaders on a personal basis. He quickly won the respect of the president, Vice President Richard Cheney, Secretary of Defense Donald Rumsfeld, and Secretary of State Colin Powell. With both Powell, a retired four-star general, and the secretary's influential deputy Richard Armitage, a tough former combat veteran, he often used the same soldier-to-soldier approach Zia had found effective with his own American military and ex-military contacts. When dealing with immediate issues, he seemed to favor representatives of the Defense Department and CIA. But he was also careful to maintain good relations with the succession of strong career Foreign Service officers who led the embassy in Islamabad during his eight and a half years in power.

The Bush administration moved immediately after the 9/11 attacks to enlist Pakistan in the U.S.-led global war on terrorism and oblige it to provide full support to American efforts to destroy al-Qaeda. Lieutenant General Mahmud Ahmed, the director general of ISI and at the time a Musharraf confidant, was meeting on Capitol Hill with members of Congress when word came of the attacks. Accompanied by the Pakistan ambassador, he met the following day at the State Department with Deputy Secretary Armitage and other senior officials. In his memoir, published in 2006, Musharraf famously quotes Mahmud Ahmed as telling him that Armitage had said, "not only that we [Pakistanis] had to decide whether we were with America or with the terrorists, but that if we chose the terrorists, then we should be prepared to be bombed back to the stone age."[46] It seems unlikely that Armitage actually used those words. What is important is that the Bush administration was determined to be as tough as necessary to bring Pakistan into the American camp.

This was the gist of the discussion top administration security officials held in the White House on September 13. According to *The 9/11 Commission Report*, "The [participants] agreed that the overall message should be that anyone supporting al Qaeda would risk harm. . . . [They] . . . focused on Pakistan and what it could do to turn the Taliban regime against al Qaeda. They concluded that if Pakistan decided not to help the United States, it too [along with the Taliban] would be at risk."

Painfully aware of the U.S. reaction to the 9/11 attacks and the danger it posed for Pakistan, Musharraf held a long series of meetings over the next few days to help him develop a position. By far the most important of these sessions were those with the army corps commanders and other senior military officers. He also met with his cabinet colleagues, the governors of the provinces, prominent civilian political figures, senior editors and newspaper columnists, Muslim religious leaders, and representatives of the business community. He faced two issues. The first was whether he should execute a 180-degree turn in his Afghanistan policy by abandoning the Taliban and throwing in his lot with the Americans should they decide to move against the regime in Kabul that Pakistan had helped bring to power. The second was the degree of cooperation he should give the Americans if he joined their effort.

Wendy Chamberlin, an experienced Foreign Service officer who had served as ambassador to Laos, had arrived earlier in September to assume charge of the U.S. embassy in Islamabad. She had met Musharraf at a private dinner a few days before 9/11 and had been impressed by the vision of a moderate Pakistan opposed to terrorism he spelled out for her. By the time Chamberlin formally presented her ambassadorial credentials to him on September 13, the attacks had created an entirely new situation in U.S.-Pakistan relations.

The one issue that Washington had instructed its new ambassador to take up with Musharraf at what would ordinarily have been a ceremonial occasion was "whether Pakistan was with the United States or against it," nothing more. She did so, and when she did not get a clear reply, asked him to tell her what he needed "to get to yes." When Musharraf continued to waffle, Chamberlin recalls telling him, "It's in both of our interests for you to be

---

46. Musharraf, *In the Line of Fire*, 201.

with us. I know you are with us. You told me of your vision: you want to end terrorism." According to the ambassador, Musharraf told her "we support you unstintingly."[47] That was what she wanted to hear. When the meeting wound up, Chamberlin told waiting reporters what Musharraf had said.[48] She thought that this tactic, though risky, would lock in his agreement.

Musharraf's assurances to Ambassador Chamberlin went beyond the public statement he had made a few hours earlier. In that statement, he declared that "Pakistan had been extending cooperation to international efforts to combat terrorism in the past and will continue to do so. I wish to assure President Bush and the U.S. government our unstinted cooperation in the fight against terrorism." This was not the same thing as telling a U.S. representative in a face-to-face meeting that Pakistan would specifically back American efforts against the Taliban if these proved necessary, the purport of what Musharraf told Chamberlin.

What would be the nature of that promised cooperation? The next day, the administration followed up Musharraf's assurances to Chamberlin and presented a list of seven areas where Pakistan could play a helpful role. These were

- to stop al-Qaeda operatives at its border and end logistical support for bin Laden;
- to give the United States blanket overflight and landing rights for all necessary military and intelligence operations;
- to provide territorial access to U.S. and allied military intelligence and other personnel to conduct operations against al-Qaeda;
- to provide the United States with intelligence information;
- to continue to publicly condemn the terrorist acts;
- to cut off all shipments of fuel to the Taliban and stop recruits from going to Afghanistan;
- to break relations with the Taliban government, if the evidence implicated bin Laden and al-Qaeda and the Taliban continued to harbor them.

Chamberlin stresses that Musharraf did not regard Washington's list as conditions or demands. He considered them suggested modalities for cooperation. He told the ambassador he did not intend to negotiate as a lawyer

---

47. Wendy Chamberlin, interview.

48. According to the usually reliable Islamabad correspondent of the *Hindu*, Chamberlin told the press: "We had a frank discussion of the situation. It was direct. We had a meeting of the minds. Let me point out that I am leaving after my first meeting on the occasion of presentation of credentials on a positive note. The President has made a positive and strong statement. In the course of the meeting, he repeated several times that he is with us."

but to act like a general. He wanted to develop cooperative understandings, not haggle over conditions.

Musharraf continued to take this nonconfrontational approach in the years he dealt with American interlocutors on political issues and the scope and level of military and economic assistance. He never put a price tag on anything, in contrast to Zia in the "peanuts" episode. What he was clearly looking for was American understanding that he was on their side, that he had made a politically difficult decision in accepting a seemingly complete "U-turn" in Pakistan's policy toward Afghanistan in response to Washington's request. He wanted negotiations on the details of the restored bilateral security relationship to take place on the basis of his government's substantial acceptance of its new role in Bush's global war on terrorism. Musharraf was confident that the United States, in its generous way, would be forthcoming in these negotiations. It was an artful use of the guilt-trip technique Pakistan had used with the United States when the two governments had initiated close security ties in the mid-1950s and early 1980s. The American side readily fell in with this more subtle and attractive approach.

In his often self-serving memoir, Musharraf describes at some length how he dealt with these points, and, more generally, how he wrestled with the broader problems 9/11 and the American reaction posed for him and for Pakistan. As elsewhere in the book, which he promoted vigorously during a visit to the United States in 2006, he tried to project himself as a hard-headed soldier who made decisions rationally. This was the persona that Musharraf displayed to impress senior American officials. "I made a dispassionate, military-style analysis of our options, weighing pros and cons. Emotion is all very well in drawing rooms, newspaper editorials, and movies, but it cannot be relied on for decisions like this."[49] The president recalled that he had dismissed the idea of confronting the United States. (Pakistan's military forces would be destroyed, its economic infrastructure decimated, and, disastrously for Pakistani interests in Kashmir, the Americans would turn to the Indians, who had already offered their support.) The ultimate question, he wrote, was whether it was in Pakistan's national interest to commit suicide for the Taliban. Not surprisingly, the answer he says came to him was "a resounding no." But he recalls that he also found positive reasons for supporting the United States: assistance for fighting domestic terrorists, economic advantages, and a central place for Pakistan on the world stage.

Although *The 9/11 Commission Report* reports that Pakistan quickly accepted all seven "demands," this is almost surely an overstatement. Both

---

49. Musharraf, *In the Line of Fire*, 201.

Musharraf and Ambassador Chamberlin demur. In his memoir, Musharraf recalled that he did not agree to provide blanket overflight and landing rights to conduct military and intelligence operations or to use Pakistan naval ports, air bases, and strategic border locations to conduct all necessary operations against the perpetrators of terrorism and those who harbored them. Chamberlin has similar recollections of how Musharraf reacted.[50]

Musharraf also wrote that he then vetted his decision with his cabinet and the military corps commanders. Although some of the corps commanders expressed doubts about Musharraf's proposed answer, he "answered every question until all doubts were removed and everyone was on board." Discussing Musharraf's position, the U.S. embassy in Islamabad reported that he "said the GOP [government of Pakistan] was making substantial concessions in allowing use of its territory and that he would pay a domestic price. His standing in Pakistan was certain to suffer. To counterbalance that he needed to show that Pakistan was benefiting from his decisions."[51] In other words, the price should be right not because Musharraf was demanding it, as Zia had, but because the United States "owed" it to the Pakistanis for what they were undertaking on America's—not their own—behalf.

Meeting again with Ambassador Chamberlin, Musharraf told her that Pakistan would support Washington if it was going to dismantle the Taliban regime but said that Pakistani citizens were his responsibility—that is, that he could not agree to the United States going after Pakistanis who were working with the Taliban. He also pressed some ideas of his own. These probably reflected the views of the corps commanders. They included U.S. undertakings not to overfly Pakistani nuclear sites or place American combat troops on Pakistani soil. Washington had no problems with these points. The president also requested that the United States take Pakistan's side on the Kashmir issue and help resolve the dispute. Chamberlin deflected this, telling Musharraf that the negotiations were not about Kashmir; introducing the issue of U.S. support as a quid pro quo for Pakistani support on the Taliban would not work.

Once basic agreement was reached, Washington moved quickly to take advantage of Musharraf's positive approach. Within a week, a team came out from Washington and met senior Pakistani military officers in an ISI safe house to talk about how the new arrangement would work. They focused on matters such as the U.S. use of Pakistani airspace and intelligence surveillance of Afghanistan. American participants in the meeting were struck by

---

50. For an interesting analysis of Musharraf's reaction, see Nawaz, *Crossed Swords*, 540–42.

51. Quoted in Kean and Hamilton, *The 9/11 Commission Report*, 331.

both sides' focus on accommodating one another's needs. The only thing the Pakistanis asked for was that U.S. aircraft not enter Pakistan airspace from India. (The U.S. side agreed.) According to one American participant in the talks, assistance levels were not even discussed at this point.

On the economic side, things moved just as fast and smoothly. Almost immediately, the United States provided $500 million from a 9/11 supplemental appropriation to the Pakistan Treasury for balance of payments support and started working with international financial institutions to develop further funding.

A high-level U.S. delegation led by Under Secretary of State Alan Larson came to Islamabad soon afterward. Working with Finance Minister Shaukat Aziz, Larson proposed a formula for debt relief that provided a quick response but that did not involve a vote in Congress. This omission relieved the U.S. government of a burden but came as a disappointment to the Pakistanis, who looked on a formal congressional vote as a strengthening of the U.S. commitment to Pakistan.

These discussions were the first building blocks of what became a huge assistance program. From 2002 through 2009, the United States provided Pakistan with some $11 billion in military assistance, of which $7.7 billion was in largely unaccountable "coalition support funds" intended as reimbursement for Pakistani assistance in the war on terrorism. In the same period, Washington allocated over $4.5 billion for economic and development assistance, including food aid.[52]

Although some tough bargaining was involved in working out the details, the two sides came to agreement on the main issues they faced over the Musharraf-Bush years remarkably easily given the size of the funds and the stakes involved. A couple of big-ticket items remained vexing for years. Pakistan's call for F-16s remained on the negotiating table until 2005, when the Bush administration agreed to make the planes available over American public and congressional opposition. Pakistan's interest in duty-free access of Pakistani textile exports to American markets was stoutly opposed by the powerful U.S. domestic textile industry and never met (though the Pakistanis did win a few minor concessions).[53]

Implementing U.S.-Pakistan agreements was generally tougher than reaching them during the Musharraf-Bush era. The very loose conditional-

---

52. K. Alan Kronstadt, "Direct Overt U.S. Aid and Military Reimbursements to Pakistan, FY 2002–2010" (PDF presentation prepared for the Congressional Research Service, Washington, DC, August 3, 2009).

53. This discussion of the economic negotiations draws on the authors' interviews with Patricia Haslach, Andrew Haviland, and Alan Larson.

ity that the United States agreed to in the crisis atmosphere in 2001 became more problematic for it with the passage of time. Much of the original aid program was given in the form of cash or its near equivalent, against a Pakistani pledge to spend more on education and health. U.S. efforts to document the fulfillment of this pledge ran into a confusing paper trail. The rather thin documentation provided for reimbursements under the Coalition Support Funds was sharply questioned in congressional hearings in July 2007. The Pakistanis reacted badly when, in an effort to head off challenges to the funding of the program, the U.S. administration changed the procedures to require much more careful accounting for the various aid streams. And in the anti-American atmosphere prevailing in Pakistan, the Pakistanis discouraged labeling U.S. aid projects with the customary U.S. logos, making it difficult for the United States to take credit for helping the Pakistani people.

On the military side, the U.S. side was angered by what it considered inadequate Pakistani efforts against the Afghan Taliban and their supporters in along the Pakistan-Afghanistan border and against terrorists there and elsewhere in the country. The Musharraf government tried to allay this unhappiness by arresting impressive numbers of high-visibility militants just before prominent Americans visited Pakistan. They were quietly released later.

But despite these differences, the bilateral relationship established in 2001 remained firm. As had happened with both Ayub and Zia, the U.S. leadership looked on Musharraf as the personification of its ties with Pakistan. The relationship was also strong at the reinvigorated military-to-military level, a particularly important link given the key role of the senior leadership of the Pakistan Army even after Musharraf restored constitutional government and installed a cabinet drawn mostly from the political world. It remained so until Musharraf lost power following the February 2008 parliamentary elections.

8

India-Pakistan Negotiations

Heading off India-Pakistan conflict has been the single most important U.S. policy objective in the region since the two countries became independent. The degree of U.S. involvement in India-Pakistan diplomacy has varied greatly over the years. In the early days after partition, the United States was a major international actor in efforts to arrange a peaceful settlement of the dispute between India and Pakistan over Kashmir. Until the outbreak of their 1965 war, a strong consensus in Washington favored an active U.S. diplomatic role either unilaterally, in concert with Britain, or through international bodies. After 1965, the United States backed off. It offered to be helpful if both countries desired it, but did not play a direct role in the off-again, on-again initiatives to define and bring about a permanent settlement. After both countries went tacitly and then explicitly nuclear, U.S. diplomacy on Kashmir and other India-Pakistan issues primarily took the form of crisis management. The United States encouraged both countries to pursue long-term efforts to bring about better relations. But its role was episodic, modest, and very discreet.

This chapter will look at how Pakistanis deal with the United States in the context of India-Pakistan negotiations. It will examine first how the basic U.S.-Pakistan model described in this study functions in a trilateral context, with a special focus on crisis management negotiations since 1990. It will then look at the negotiations that ended Pakistan's incursion into the Kargil area of Indian-administered Kashmir in 1999. These negotiations involved a civilian leader, Prime Minister Nawaz Sharif, dealing face-to-face with the president of the United States in an India-Pakistan context. The crisis ended without a major war, an outcome Washington had worked hard to bring about. But Pakistan's withdrawal from the area was one of the factors leading to the military coup in which the army chief of staff, General Pervez Musharraf, ousted Sharif three months later. The coup underscored once again the high stakes Pakistani leaders face in any India-Pakistan confrontation.

Negotiating with India—and with the United States

Pakistan cannot and does not use the same negotiating tactics with India as it does with the United States. The core geopolitical insecurity that guides its policy and negotiating strategy is built around India, so it applies with even greater force to India-Pakistan negotiations. For the Pakistanis, India is the existential enemy. Any negotiator must above all be vigilant not to fall into the traps a duplicitous foe might set. There is no margin for error.

The structure of Pakistan's governmental authority affects its negotiations with India even more than it does those with the United States. Decisions are centralized. Top political and military leaders approach these negotiations painfully aware that their hold on power, not to speak of their legacy, may be at stake. India-Pakistan negotiations have major political ramifications. Key constituencies, from the army's corps commanders to political and religious networks all over the country, are ready to pounce on a government they believe may be conceding too much to India. This is especially true in Punjab, Pakistan's largest and most politically powerful province.

A military leader's dominant role does not necessarily equate to a harder line. For example, Musharraf on several occasions publicly announced "outside-the-box" positions on a possible Kashmir settlement with India that were much more forthcoming than the traditional Pakistani stance. In October 2004, he stated publicly that he was prepared to move away from Islamabad's demand for the plebiscite called for by the 1948–49 United Nations resolutions, provided India did not insist that the Line of Control become the international border. He went even further in December 2006 when he declared that the line could remain in place but that people should be allowed to move freely across it. Areas on each side of the line would have "self-governance or autonomy."[1] Musharraf made all of his declarations on Kashmir directly to the media in off-the-cuff speeches or interviews. Senior foreign ministry officials were not informed in advance, let alone consulted, about these potentially dramatic changes in Pakistan policy.

---

1. Schaffer, *The Limits of Influence*, 186–187; "Musharraf Calls for Debate on Kashmir Options: Status Quo No Solution," *Dawn*, October 26, 2004, www.dawn.com/2004/10/26/top4.htm. Delphic references in the newspaper article to "change in status" mean, in the Pakistani context, that he was no longer insisting on the plebiscite.

By early 2007, secret back-channel negotiations conducted on the Pakistani side under the direct supervision of the president appeared on the verge of a breakthrough, at least on the main principles of a settlement. But domestic challenges that threatened his regime and growing violence in Pakistan's western borderlands increasingly distracted Musharraf, and he was obliged to abandon his initiative. He fell from power before he could resume it.[2]

In launching his initiatives publicly with no advance preparation, Musharraf was acting in accord with his background as a military officer. He was convinced that he alone rather than the civilian leadership had the standing to make decisions on Pakistan's national security. He was also taking advantage of his ability—unique to military leaders at the pinnacle of Pakistan's government—to change policy by simply announcing a change. Choosing a more flexible line toward India as the way to do this is unusual, but given the hierarchical nature of the military and Musharraf's combined military and governmental power, it was within the established rules of the Pakistani political game.

The rules for civilian leaders are very different. In October 2008, two months after succeeding Musharraf as president, Asif Zardari said in a press interview that India was "not a threat" to Pakistan. Three days later, his official spokesman reinterpreted his remarks to downplay this positive change in attitude. It is noteworthy, too, that the new civilian president did not pick up where Musharraf had left off in negotiating with the Indians—either through the established back channel (which soon lapsed) or any other point of contact.[3]

Suspicion of India, policy inertia, and political and bureaucratic caution combine to make civilian officials extremely hesitant to modify the accepted ways of doing things unless higher authority clearly instructs them otherwise. In his study of India-Pakistan negotiations, Dennis Kux described MFA officials as pillars of the status quo and stalwart opponents of change, particularly when it came to policy toward India. Their faithfulness to traditional positions gives great stability and predictability (and, alas, a kind of inevitability) to bilateral negotiations.[4] In 2005, India and Pakistan finally agreed on the modalities for opening bus travel between their respective

2. Schaffer, *The Limits of Influence*, 190; Steve Coll, "The Back Channel: India and Pakistan's Secret Kashmir Talks," *New Yorker*, March 2, 2009, www.newyorker.comreporting/2009/03/02/0904021a_fact_coll.

3. Barbara Plett, "India Not a Threat to Pakistan," *BBC News*, http://news.bbc.co.uk/2/hi/south_asia/7653687.stm; "Latest News," *Dawn*, October 6, 2008, www.dawn.com/2008/10/06/rss.htm.

4. Dennis Kux, *India-Pakistan Negotiations: Is the Past Still Prologue?* (Washington, DC: United States Institute of Peace Press, 2006), 21–22.

parts of Kashmir, but only after the problem of documentation had been the subject of desultory negotiations for nearly two years. Both countries' foreign and home ministries had been involved; none of these naturally cautious organizations was disposed to break any new ground, and agreement was reached only when the national leaders on both sides made clear that they wanted results.

The remaining major factor in Pakistan's negotiating style, the cultural dimension, operates quite differently in negotiations with India than in those with the United States. The sense of grievance observed in Pakistan-U.S. dealings is even stronger here. It carries the weight of over sixty years of Pakistani frustration over India's perceived readiness to use its power to damage Pakistani interests. The loose resemblance to an "elder brother" relationship that can come into negotiations with the United States is absent in dealings with India; indeed, such a notion would be offensive to Pakistanis. The Pakistani negotiator will above all defend Pakistan's sovereign *equality* with India. The dependence, however distasteful, and the sense of obligation that Pakistani leaders and negotiators seek to create when dealing with the United States are totally absent from the India relationship (though Pakistanis will tell their *American* interlocutors that as the larger power, India should make concessions). At the same time, the cultural affinities between the two societies have a kind of leavening effect that shows up, for example, when cricket teams travel between these two cricket-fanatic countries. Whenever a major people-to-people event takes place, travelers return with emotional tales of having been received like visiting family by ordinary people in the other country. This nostalgia, and even affection, coexists with a still raw bitterness.

In dealing with the United States on India-Pakistan issues, Pakistani negotiators follow the basic model described earlier in this study. Pakistan's first goal, indeed, has usually been simply to get Washington involved, in the belief that U.S. intervention would neutralize India's greater size and power and produce a more favorable result. In particular, Pakistan has sought to engage the United States on Kashmir. Pakistanis often argue that the United States owes it to Pakistan to provide the same level of high-level involvement in peacemaking on Kashmir as it does to negotiations between Israel and the Palestinians. Sometimes the message comes in highly visible form. In the spring of 2000, a few months after the resolution of the Kargil crisis and Musharraf's accession to power, the authors visited Islamabad, which was then preparing for the much-heralded visit of President Clinton a few days later. Each of the many pedestrian overpasses on the twenty-minute drive from the airport to town was festooned with a banner reading "Kashmir: Nuclear Flashpoint" or some similar message designed to persuade the American president in a typically unsubtle way that he needed to intervene and resolve Kashmir.

The assumption that U.S. intervention would help Pakistan obtain a Kashmir settlement on favorable terms has become increasingly questionable. Since the late 1990s, Washington's primary goal in South Asia has been stability, a policy that in practice favors India as the status quo power. Pakistani security analysts quietly acknowledge this. They also worry about the impact of a more serious positive relationship between Washington and New Delhi. Nonetheless, bringing in the United States continues to have a powerful attraction, and Pakistani diplomats and political leaders almost reflexively press for more active American diplomacy. Part of the attraction may lie in the fact that India has for decades resisted any third-party involvement in Kashmir or in other India-Pakistan issues. So a decision by the United States to get involved is seen in Islamabad as a satisfying procedural victory for Pakistan and a setback for India. Pakistanis accordingly welcomed early reports that the Obama administration's special envoy for Afghanistan and Pakistan, Richard Holbrooke, would have a mandate to deal with India-Pakistan issues. The reports turned out to be premature. When Washington announced that he would not, there was an outcry in the Pakistan media, which saw an Indian hand in the decision. As with so many other examples in this study, U.S. engagement in India-Pakistan diplomacy brings out Pakistan's fundamental ambivalence about the United States: it wants a powerful patron but believes the United States cannot be relied on when things get tough.

At the Table

Pakistan's plea for a more active U.S. role is advanced uncritically, apparently with little thought about how it will actually affect the outcome. By contrast, once the actual negotiations get started, Pakistan's institutionalized suspicion remains as strong as ever, and it spills over beyond India to the American negotiators as well. Pakistani leaders and negotiators want the United States on their side, but they have rarely been willing to change their positions in response to U.S. advice, and they do not seek this counsel.

The last time the United States was directly and deeply involved in facilitating negotiations between India and Pakistan designed to solve the Kashmir issue was in 1962–63. In the wake of the improvement in U.S.-Indian relations resulting from U.S. support for India during its 1962 border war with China, the Kennedy administration saw an opportunity to create a lasting India-Pakistan reconciliation. Under strong U.S. (and British) pressure, New Delhi and Islamabad eventually agreed—with considerable misgivings—to conduct bilateral negotiations. They approached the talks with what quickly proved to be starkly different ideas of the terms of a satisfactory outcome.

The process was atypical in that the initiative for American engagement came from Washington, but Pakistani resistance to the ideas for a settlement that the United States promoted was in keeping with the usual pattern. The talks went through six rounds of meetings between ministerial-level interlocutors from India and Pakistan. American diplomats hovered outside the negotiating rooms, in the vivid words of U.S. ambassador to India John Kenneth Galbraith, "like the ghost of Banquo." Before the talks had even begun, both the Indian and Pakistani governments took public actions that they must have known were likely to imperil the negotiation and disconcert its American sponsors. Prime Minister Jawaharlal Nehru stated in the India parliament that changing the governing arrangements in Kashmir would be bad for the Kashmiris. His counterpart in Islamabad, President Ayub Khan, announced that Pakistan and China had reached an agreement on the line dividing the parts of Kashmir that they controlled, an area India claimed along with the rest of the state. When bilateral negotiations stalled, Washington introduced a proposal to bifurcate the Valley of Kashmir, the area at the heart of the dispute. The idea was instantly rejected by both New Delhi and Islamabad, as were other American suggestions. Neither country was willing to deviate in any significant way from its opening position, whatever pressures or inducements the United States brought to bear. As the talks sputtered to an ignominious conclusion, Galbraith commented with his usual acerbity that "we succeeded in bringing the Indians and Pakistanis into new opposition to ourselves. Nothing else was accomplished."[5]

Crisis Management

Since the early 1990s, the principal form of U.S. involvement in India-Pakistan diplomacy has been crisis management. On three occasions, tamping down a war scare became a major focus for U.S. diplomatic activity for several months. During the 1990 spring maneuver season when the Kashmir

---

5. John Kenneth Galbraith, *Ambassador's Journal: A Personal Account of the Kennedy Years* (Boston: Houghton-Mifflin, 1969), 564; Schaffer, *The Limits of Influence*, 77–89.

issue, dormant for the better part of two decades, had just again come to a boil, military movements by the two countries raised alarms about the possibility of war by miscalculation. In 1999, Pakistan sent troops across the Line of Control dividing the Indian- and Pakistani-administered parts of Kashmir at Kargil, in the high Himalayas, leading to a localized war. And in December 2001, an attack on the Indian parliament by militants operating from Pakistan led to an extended and extensive confrontation between the two armies along the international border and the Line of Control. Energetic U.S. diplomacy was important in heading off any serious fighting in the 1990 and 2001–02 crises. In the 1999 one over Kargil it eventually succeeded in ending an already bloody battle.

In all three cases, Washington got involved because it believed there was an unacceptable risk that a tense situation could lead to war, and that this could escalate to nuclear conflict. (Although neither India nor Pakistan had proven nuclear weapons before their 1998 tests, it was widely accepted well before then that they could acquire them quickly once a political decision was reached to do so.) U.S. crisis management diplomacy, with its focus on a race against time, was usually well received and sometimes even sought by India as well as Pakistan. This contrasted with India's consistently negative reaction to broader American and other international efforts to facilitate peace negotiations. On each occasion, the United States was more concerned about escalation than either Pakistan or India. The U.S. government became highly energized and focused intently on the immediate objective of ending the risk of a major conflict. But even before Washington considered that the primary threat of war had passed the Pakistanis' primary motivation in accepting U.S. involvement had shifted: they wanted to force the Kashmir issue itself to the top of the international agenda. Indeed, in the case of Kargil, "internationalization" of the dispute seems to have been a major Pakistani goal from the start.

In all three cases, the U.S. crisis management effort culminated in direct high-level intervention by Washington-based officials. In 1990, a team led by Deputy National Security Adviser Robert Gates went to Islamabad and New Delhi to deliver a sober message about the importance of avoiding war, along with an offer of U.S. support for India-Pakistan confidence-building measures. The Kargil crisis nine years later was resolved when President Clinton met with Pakistan's prime minister in Washington. And in the 2001–02 confrontation, Deputy Secretary of State Richard Armitage traveled to the region to extract the key agreement from Musharraf.

Each time, the shape of the resolution was discernible but not yet fully agreed before the high-level intervention took place. The U.S. involvement provided the context for one or both countries to back down from the confrontation. This takes nothing away from the skill of the high-level negotiators. Choreography and face-saving are critical to crisis management, and in their absence crises can worsen even if the outlines of a settlement are coming into view.

In 1990, the initial U.S. diplomatic effort, and the part that arguably did most to diminish the risk of war, was carried out by the U.S. ambassadors in Islamabad and New Delhi, Robert Oakley and William Clark, acting on their own initiative. The Pakistan government approached Oakley with great concern about intelligence reports of threatening Indian military movements. When Clark learned of this from Oakley, he sent a defense attaché to the area where the movements were said to be taking place. The attaché's reassuring report was then passed to the Pakistanis. Over a period of several weeks, the two embassies worked effectively to assess and ultimately debunk alarmist reports that both governments were receiving from their intelligence services. The speed and credibility of the ambassadors' rumor vetting tamped down the real concerns in Pakistan that India was contemplating a major attack.

The most difficult part of the 1990 negotiations with Pakistan came during the high-level phase, the Gates mission, and it illustrates some of the effects of divided and uncertain authority between civilians and the military. Oakley and Clark's rumor-control effort had involved only the army, but Gates and his team wanted to talk with the full "troika" of Pakistani decision makers. Besides General Mirza Aslam Beg, the army chief, this group included President Ghulam Ishaq Khan and Prime Minister Benazir Bhutto. Ishaq was a powerful figure with close relations with the army and had been the country's most senior civil servant before he became president on the death of Zia ul-Haq. Bhutto had only recently taken office.

Bhutto was out of the country.[6] Gates did meet Beg and Ghulam Ishaq. Unlike the usual pattern for high-ranking visitors from Washington, the meeting with the latter was tense and confrontational, much more so than the subsequent discussions the U.S. team had in New Delhi. Pakistani officials looking back on this episode suggest that Ghulam Ishaq believed

---

6. Gates offered to meet Bhutto in the Middle East, where she was planning to stop. Scheduling rapidly turned into a comedy of errors, and Bhutto and Gates never met. The reasons for this were not clear. Perhaps she did not want to meet Gates without having her key advisers close at hand, or the army chief and president, not trusting her, may have contrived to make an already complicated logistical situation impossible.

Gates sought to disable Pakistan's nuclear program. They argue that his nationalism, prickly personality, and perhaps apprehension over what the army would do next—always a concern of Pakistan's civilian leaders—led him to react with a harshness that guests in Pakistan almost never see. If this is in fact the case, the Gates mission's meeting with Ghulam Ishaq, and possibly its nonmeeting with Bhutto too, further illustrate the pressures that civilian officials face when dealing with major national security issues.[7]

Indian and Pakistani officials have argued that there was no nuclear danger in the 1991 crisis.[8] But the U.S. perception that there was a nuclear risk intensified the motivation of the U.S. officials involved. Aware of this, India and Pakistan concluded that they could manipulate U.S. nuclear concerns for their own purposes. One Pakistani security analyst and retired military officer has argued that India and Pakistan, since acquiring de facto nuclear capability, have both in practice become dependent on the United States to step in and persuade them to step back from crises, a phenomenon he refers to as "the independence-dependence paradox."[9] But the potential for manipulation goes beyond the expectation that the United States will step in as firefighter. Both India and Pakistan use crises of this sort to reinforce their position in the region in broader ways. In the three instances discussed here, Pakistan was trying to garner international attention to Kashmir, both for its own sake and also, in the case of civilian-led governments, in an effort to show the country and the army that it was faithfully advancing the Kashmir cause. India saw the crises as ways to demonstrate to Washington Pakistan's irresponsibility and its sponsorship of terrorist and insurgent groups.

This terrorist issue, rather than nuclear conflict, was the primary theme in the 2001–02 crisis. After the attack on the Indian parliament, Pakistan responded predictably: initially by denying responsibility, then by saying there was "no evidence" of the involvement of the Pakistan-based Lashkar-e-Taiba (LeT), as India alleged. Pakistan had formally banned LeT three months earlier, after 9/11, but had done little to prevent the terrorist organization from operating freely in Pakistan under a new name. India made the equally

---

7. This account of the 1991 crisis draws on the authors' own recollections (Teresita Schaffer was deputy assistant secretary of state for South Asia at the time) and on their interviews with Tanvir Ahmed Khan and Shahryar Khan; see also P. R. Chari, Pervaiz Iqbal Cheema, and Stephen P. Cohen, *Four Crises and a Peace Process: American Engagement in South Asia* (Washington, D.C.: Brookings Institution Press, 2007), 94–112.

8. See Chari, Cheema, and Cohen, *Four Crises and a Peace Process*, 80–118. Teresita Schaffer, however, recalls being asked by an Indian embassy official about rumors that Pakistan was readying its nuclear assets for deployment.

9. Feroz Hassan Khan, "The Independence-Dependence Paradox: Stability Dilemmas in South," *Arms Control Today*, October 2003, www.armscontrol.org/print/1381.

predictable demand for extradition from Pakistan of those accused of a string of terrorist actions against India, notably the founder of LeT, who had led the hijacking of an Indian airliner to Afghanistan in 1999.

The U.S. decision to put LeT and one other prominent Pakistan-based group on its list of foreign terrorist organizations in December 2001 made it clear that Washington saw Pakistan as responsible, in the sense that the problem arose from illegal activity on Pakistani soil. With Secretary of State Colin Powell in the lead, the Bush administration mounted a major effort to persuade Musharraf to end his government's relationship with the militants. In January 2002, a month after the attack on the Indian parliament, Musharraf made a speech to a gathering of clerics putting forward a vision of Islamic moderation. It included the statement that "no organization will be allowed to perpetuate terrorism behind the Kashmiri cause." This was followed by the arrest of several senior members of LeT and other key militant organizations. It appeared to Washington that Pakistan was making a major change of direction. Within a short time, however, the militant leaders had been released, and the initiative looked cosmetic. Wanting to believe that things had turned around, the United States continued for a time to see the good news rather than the bad. It was not the last time it would do so.

It was the second part of the 2001–2 crisis, a May 2002 attack on a housing facility in Kashmir for dependents of Indian military personnel stationed in the state, which led to Deputy Secretary of State Armitage's crucial mission to India and Pakistan the following month. Well before that time India had decided on coercive diplomacy. It massed its troops on the international border and the Line of Control in Kashmir opposite Pakistani forces, who had been obliged to mobilize as well. Washington's top leadership was already deeply engaged in the crisis. Musharraf had received telephone calls from President Bush as well as Powell.[10]

What Armitage negotiated with Musharraf was an understanding between Pakistan and the United States that Pakistan would not allow territory controlled by Pakistan to be used for terrorism, and that he would do his utmost to end infiltration into territory controlled by India.[11] It is significant that the agreement was with the United States: Armitage was

---

10. After Musharraf had pledged to "fight to the last drop of our blood" in a public speech, Secretary of State Colin Powell telephoned him and asked to talk "general to general." His message was clear: "You know and I know that you can't possibly use nuclear weapons. . . . So stop scaring everyone." Cited in Polly Nayak and Michael Krepon, *U.S. Crisis Management in South Asia's Twin Peaks Crisis* (Washington, DC: Henry L. Stimson Center, September 2006).

11. "U.S. Seeks Reassurance from Musharraf," Voice of America, June 25, 2002, www.voanews.com/english/archive/2002-06/a-2002-06-25-6-US.cfm?moddate=2002-06-25.

not creating an India-Pakistan agreement. In relaying Musharraf's pledge to the Indians, Armitage noted that he did not believe Musharraf's government was capable of completely eliminating infiltration, but was confident the president would honor his pledge of best efforts. The Indian government chose to accept this understanding. After testing it for a few months, during which infiltration went down significantly, India took the pledge as a basis for ending the mobilization, which it had already concluded was becoming too costly and no longer productive.

Given the highly public character of India's mobilization, the United States felt it was essential to put Musharraf's undertaking into the public domain. The Indians reportedly urged him to do so. Armitage had discussed this with Musharraf, but the latter was nonetheless apparently taken aback when his promise was made public. The nature of the promise too was a victim of a classic U.S.-Pakistan clash of interpretations: Armitage had undertaken to press India to resume talks with Pakistan, a pledge that to American ears sounded like standard platitudes but that Musharraf had seen as a way of using the crisis to get back to the Kashmir problem.[12]

In this instance, India was more successful than Pakistan in using U.S. concerns about an India-Pakistan war to create a diplomatic outcome to its liking. Pakistan's efforts to shed responsibility failed, and this episode was a rude awakening for Musharraf, who had until that point assumed that Pakistan's cooperation against Afghanistan would lead the United States to turn a blind eye to Pakistan's role in problems with India. Once again, the different purposes the United States and Pakistan brought to their close relationship had led to a fundamental misunderstanding.

In all these negotiations, Pakistan understandably saw its own interests as being much more directly at stake than those of the United States. Yet again, Pakistan was looking for friendship and support without feeling an obligation to accept American advice that would challenge its policy. As before, and since, it then came away disillusioned about America's role in South Asia and confirmed in its view that it cannot rely on Washington.

As American diplomats have repeatedly found, a striking feature of triangular diplomacy is how similarly many of the Indian and Pakistani actors behave when dealing with one another. In both countries, change in policy has to come from the top (which in both cases includes the military, but in India's case keeps them subordinate to political authority). In both govern-

---

12. The discussion of the 2001–2 crisis draws on Nayak and Krepon, *U.S. Crisis Management in South Asia's Twin Peaks Crisis*, and on the authors' interviews with Wendy Chamberlin and Richard Armitage.

ments, even fairly senior officials are discouraged from being creative. Indian and Pakistani civilian officials belong to the international world of diplomatic elites and share broadly similar local cultures. Both government systems approach bilateral negotiations with great reluctance to change long standing policies, even when these are evidently no longer tenable. And although Pakistan in principle wants the United States involved and India does not, in practice both are disinclined to allow Washington much influence over their negotiating stance. For Islamabad and New Delhi, the United States serves at times as a facilitator, but more often its involvement in India-Pakistan relations provides a convenient excuse for backing away from a dangerous crisis.[13]

U.S.-Pakistan Negotiations in the 1999 Kargil War

Of the three key crises in which the United States played an active diplomatic role, only the Kargil episode included intense fighting and wound up in the hands of the top national leaders in both Pakistan and the United States. A closer look at the Kargil drama illustrates both the dynamics of U.S. involvement in India-Pakistan diplomacy and the different pressures Pakistani civilian leaders face compared to their military counterparts.

In May 1999, the Indian army became aware that Pakistan had surreptitiously seized commanding heights on the Indian side of the Line of Control that overlooked Kargil, a small town on the strategically vital highway linking the Kashmir Valley to areas to the north crucial to India's military position in the state. The Pakistanis had moved forward during the forbidding winter months, when the two armies normally withdrew their forces to lower, warmer ground. The incursion caught the Indians unaware.

India reacted vigorously and the two sides were soon involved in open combat. The Pakistanis speciously claimed that they had given no military or financial support to the intruders, whom they described as indigenous Kashmiri mujahideen freedom fighters. In fact, Pakistan had infiltrated its own troops, in particular the Northern Light Infantry; the role of the mujahideen was at most minimal. The Indians declared their determination to drive out the intruders and refused to negotiate on any terms other than complete Pakistani withdrawal.

---

13. Unless otherwise sourced, the discussion of U.S. involvement in India-Pakistan diplomacy draws on the authors' recollections and their interviews with Riaz Khokhar, Bruce Riedel, Col. (ret.) David Smith, Col. (ret.) Jack Gill, and former Indian foreign secretary Salman Haider.

In moving its troops across the Line of Control, Islamabad apparently aimed once again to return the Kashmir issue to world attention and lead the international community to become involved in efforts to bring about a settlement on terms favorable to Pakistan. Some analysts have argued that the Pakistan army saw the operation as a suitable retaliation for India's 1984 action in moving troops onto the Siachen Glacier, a particularly forbidding part of the old Kashmir state where the Line of Control had never been fully defined. At the very least, the Pakistanis calculated that the operation might move the Line of Control to Pakistan's advantage in a "fait accompli" strategy designed to take advantage of surprise before the Indians could organize an effective defense or counterattack. They hoped that their nuclear tests the preceding year would prevent India from responding forcefully. They did not intend to turn the Kargil operation into a major political crisis.

The origins of Pakistan's intrusion remain a matter of dispute. As Peter Lavoy points out in the seminal 2009 study of the Kargil crisis that he edited, Pakistani accounts quickly became intertwined with the civil-military dispute between supporters of Prime Minister Sharif and those of General Musharraf, who as noted overthrew Sharif three months after the adventure had definitively failed.[14] The Kargil operation had evidently been masterminded by Musharraf and approved by Sharif. In his 2006 autobiography, Musharraf proudly but misleadingly acknowledged his own role.[15] The most plausible explanation of Sharif's behavior is that he went along with the operation believing that Pakistan could deny authorship. But what the prime minister knew and when he knew it remain the subject of much self-interested and self-exculpatory debate in political and military circles in Pakistan.

From the outset of the Kargil confrontation, Washington worried that the fighting could spin out of control and lead to a fourth India-Pakistan war. It soon concluded that Pakistan was to blame. The State Department made clear to Pakistan ambassador Riaz Khokhar that Pakistan must withdraw its forces immediately. Khokhar, one of Pakistan's top diplomats, recalls

---

14. Peter R. Lavoy, "Introduction: The Importance of the Kargil Conflict," in *Asymmetric Warfare in South Asia*, ed. Peter R. Lavoy (Cambridge: Cambridge University Press, 2009), 5.

15. Musharraf, *In the Line of Fire*, 87–98. Musharraf wrote that the Kargil operation was "only the latest in a series of moves and countermoves at a tactical level by India and Pakistan along the Line of Control in the inaccessible, snowbound Northern Areas [of Kashmir]." He held that it was "the Kashmiri freedom fighting" mujahideen who had occupied the Kargil heights, a concoction that still remains the official Pakistani interpretation (though many Pakistanis, including military and civilian officials, acknowledge that it is false). He suggested that the Pakistan army's moves, which he said were coordinated with the mujahideen, were designed only to fill the gaps in Pakistan's defensive position on the Line of Control in anticipation of an attack by superior Indian forces.

that he had not been accurately informed by the Ministry of Foreign Affairs about the nature of the intrusion. Only the mujahideen had been involved, he was told; the Pakistan government had nothing to do with it. Khokhar *was* able to find out on his own from senior military contacts in Islamabad what was actually going on. But acting on instructions, he presented the official Pakistani position to his State Department interlocutors. He recalls that they were friendly but firm, telling him that they recognized the difficulties he faced as an ambassador, that is, he had to follow instructions. Khokhar says he quickly concluded that the Kargil enterprise was a bad idea and that Pakistan forces should withdraw.[16]

As fighting intensified, Washington stepped up its diplomatic offensive. President Clinton sent personal messages and made phone calls to Sharif and Indian prime minister Atal Behari Vajpayee. Talking to Sharif, the president bluntly rejected his contention that only the Kashmiri separatists were involved. General Anthony Zinni, head of U.S. Central Command, came to Islamabad to underscore this message in conversations with Sharif and Musharraf. Ambassador William Milam, who participated in both of Zinni's main meetings, recalls that in the long session with General Musharraf it appeared from the chief of staff's body language that although he was the author of the Kargil strategy he now wished to withdraw.

By late June, after six weeks of fighting, Nawaz Sharif recognized that Kargil had become a fiasco for Pakistan. He had been rebuffed by the Chinese when he flew to Beijing to seek their support. Back-channel efforts to arrange for him to stop in New Delhi on his way back and to sign an agreement to withdraw from Kargil and resume the peace process he and Vajpayee had initiated earlier in the year had collapsed. Washington continued to insist that Pakistan withdraw behind the Line of Control and threatened to hold up an International Monetary Fund loan that Pakistan sorely needed. The Indian military were slowly but relentlessly pushing the Pakistani troops back toward the Line of Control. It was also clear to the Pakistanis that their claim that Kashmiri freedom fighters had undertaken the incursion had failed. This had become evident much earlier to at least one senior Pakistani official. He recalls going to the Defense Committee of the cabinet a week after the incursion became known to tell its members that "no one is accepting this [Kashmiri freedom fighter] story; it is a botched operation."[17]

16. Riaz Khokhar, interview.

17. Authors' interview with a retired Pakistani official.

Back in Islamabad after his unsuccessful visit to Beijing and his failed effort to meet Vajpayee in New Delhi, Nawaz edged toward a decision to pull back. He sought counsel from General Musharraf. The army chief offered none. He expressed confidence in the situation on the ground in Kargil and said he was satisfied that with so many of their troops tied up in the battle the Indians could not attack Pakistan elsewhere. Musharraf's bottom line was that the issue was a political one and that the prime minister, not the military, had the responsibility to make a decision on withdrawal. Given the Pakistani military's historic insistence that it play the leading role in issues involving national security, this acquiescent attitude suggests that Musharraf recognized the perils of Pakistan's position but wished to shift the blame for defeat to the civilian leadership.

In desperation Sharif phoned Clinton and appealed to him to pull Pakistan's chestnuts out of the fire. He wanted the president to stop the fighting and set the stage for an American-brokered Kashmir settlement. He evidently believed, as most Pakistanis always had, that an intervention by Washington would favor them. At the very least, an announced willingness on America's part to become involved would provide Sharif cover for a failed operation even if it did not lead to a resolution of the conflict on terms favorable to Pakistan. But Clinton said he would intervene only if Pakistan agreed to withdraw.

Anxious to find a way out, Sharif again phoned the president and asked to see him face to face. Clinton firmly stuck to his guns; he would become involved only if the Pakistanis pulled back. Faced with this rebuff, Sharif told the president that he was ready to come immediately to Washington to seek U.S. help. As Bruce Riedel, a member of the National Security Council staff closely involved in the negotiations, relates, "The President repeated his caution—come only if you are ready to withdraw, I can't help if you are not ready to pull back. [Clinton] urged Sharif to consider carefully the wisdom of a trip to Washington under these constraints."[18] Sharif did not tell Washington he accepted Clinton's conditions. He merely told the president that he was coming to Washington and would be there the next day.[19]

Riedel and Deputy Secretary of State Strobe Talbott, who had become the United States' point man for South Asia, provide almost identical ac-

18. Bruce Riedel, *American Diplomacy and the 1999 Kargil Summit at Blair House* (Philadelphia: University of Pennsylvania Center for the Advanced Study of India, 2002), 6.

19. In his memoir, General Zinni maintains that at his final meeting with Sharif in Islamabad, the prime minister agreed to order a withdrawal of Pakistani forces and requested the general to set up a meeting for him with Clinton. See Tom Clancy with General (ret.) Tony Zinni and Tony Koltz, *Battle Ready* (New York: G. P. Putnam's Sons, 2004), 347. Other American officials who played a role in the Kargil crisis disagree with this interpretation. In their view, which the authors share, Sharif agreed to withdraw only when he met Clinton in Washington on July 4.

counts of the dramatic Fourth of July meeting between Clinton and the self-invited Sharif at Blair House, the VIP presidential guest quarters across Pennsylvania Avenue from the White House.[20]

Clinton was absolutely firm in rejecting Sharif's reiteration of the long-time Pakistan plea that the United States intervene directly and press India to commit to resolve the larger Kashmir issue within a specific time frame. The president sternly insisted that the Pakistan army and its Kashmiri-insurgent allies withdraw completely and promptly behind the Line of Control. Only then could the United States help Pakistan. Such a full withdrawal without preconditions would give Washington leverage with India.

The president was prepared to support a resumption of the India-Pakistan peace process and asserted that the United States would work hard to help advance their bilateral dialogue. When Sharif contrasted the robust effort the United States had undertaken to bring about a Mideast settlement with its much less activist approach on Kashmir, the president made the obvious retort that unlike the situation in South Asia all the parties to the Arab-Israeli dispute wanted America to play a role. He warned Sharif in strong language of the danger of accidental nuclear war if India concluded that it had to cross the Line of Control because of Pakistan's actions. Clinton's fears on this score had been heightened by reports he had received just before the meeting that the Pakistani military was preparing nuclear-armed missiles for possible use in a war against India. (India and Pakistan had both successfully tested nuclear weapons a year earlier.) It became evident to the American side that Sharif did not know everything his armed forces were doing and did not have complete control over their activities.

Sharif, for his part, was obviously worried about the consequences the Kargil operation would have for his own political standing. He had brought his wife and children to Washington with him. This led some of the American negotiators to conclude that he feared he could not safely return to Pakistan if he came away from Blair House empty-handed. As the meeting went on and his arguments were rejected, the prime minister became increasingly distressed. He eventually told the president that he desperately wanted to find a solution that would offer some cover. Unless he had something to point to, he claimed, fundamentalists, or the army egged on by fundamentalists, would overthrow him.

---

20. For Riedel's description of the face-to-face negotiations, see *American Diplomacy*, 9–14. Talbott's appears in his *Engaging India*, 165–69. The summary of their recollections that follows is drawn from Schaffer, *The Limits of Influence*, 161–65.

At the conclusion of the conference, Sharif accepted an American draft press release that said that he had "agreed to take concrete and immediate steps for the restoration of the Line of Control." The draft statement called for a cease-fire, but only after the Pakistanis had withdrawn. The prime minister accepted these terms but asked for one addition, a sentence that would say "the President would take personal interest to encourage an expeditious resumption and intensification of the bilateral [India-Pakistan] efforts once the sanctity of the Line of Control had been restored." Clinton agreed, and the conference ended.

The Fourth of July negotiations were probably the most extraordinary ever conducted between leaders of the United States and Pakistan. The talks were prompted by a sense of desperation on the part of Nawaz Sharif, who needed some kind of face-saving device to save him from the consequences of the failed Kargil adventure. His negotiating position was exceedingly weak, as his coming to Washington uninvited underscored.

Despite these unusual circumstances, the negotiations reflected several broad negotiating tactics Pakistanis have often used with Americans. Sharif, who had met the president on a number of earlier occasions, sought to deal with him on a personal basis, first through phone calls, then in insisting on a Washington visit. In the course of the five-hour discussions, he twice asked that Clinton meet with him alone, a request that the president turned down. (The American side feared that unless one of their negotiating team was present Sharif might distort whatever he and Clinton had privately agreed to.) Like so many other Pakistani negotiators, the prime minister spelled out at length for his American interlocutors India's bad record on the Kashmir issue, implicitly contrasting it with Pakistan's. Thus in his view India, not Pakistan, was ultimately to blame for Kargil, and Washington needed to intervene in a way helpful to Islamabad.

Sharif argued that it was America's responsibility as a great power to bring about a Kashmir settlement and suggested that Washington was again at fault for not pushing for one. He contrasted the sustained efforts the United States had made to help move the Arab-Israeli dispute to closure and its feeble intervention on the Kashmir issue, another example of Pakistan's use of the guilt trip. Yet another was his claim that unless Clinton offered him some cover, he might well be overthrown. Thus if fundamentalism or martial law swept away Pakistan's democratic institutions (such as they were under Sharif), the United States would have itself to blame. Sharif's stated concern about a military coup, along with Musharraf's refusal to become involved in what the general termed a political matter, explain one unusual feature of this negotiation: the absence of army representation on the traveling delegation. But otherwise, the pattern was a familiar one.

The negotiations inadvertently also illustrated another pattern: poor communications between civilians and the military inside the Pakistan government. The prevailing view in the army was that Sharif should not have dashed off to Washington in such a weak position. Senior military officers also believed that the Americans had insisted on Sharif meeting Clinton one-on-one, seeing this as a way to isolate the prime minister, whereas the American negotiators' recollection was that it was Sharif who requested such a meeting, which in the event never took place. Finally, the army view was that the allegation of nuclear preparations was an American invention designed to pressure a nervous prime minister into agreeing to an unfavorable settlement.[21]

In any event, Sharif's tactics did not work. Well aware of the facts on the ground in Kargil, Clinton was not swayed by the prime minister's arguments. Although the president accepted the Pakistani proposal that he publicly agree to take a personal interest in the resolution of India-Pakistan disputes, his undertaking was only a face-saving device that Sharif could use at home to claim that his lightning visit to Washington had achieved some success.

The other stark difference between this example of summit negotiations by a civilian leader and those with military leaders that were examined in the last chapter is the civilian leader's vulnerability. The military leaders exuded confidence—sometimes justified, sometimes not. Sharif's fears for his political future were readily visible. His overthrow just three months later, in a military coup that he had sought American help to avert, demonstrated that these concerns were not groundless. It also ended whatever prospect there had been for Clinton's becoming more closely involved in efforts to resolve India-Pakistan differences.

In any event, such an intercession was unlikely to have been to Pakistan's advantage. As mentioned earlier, following the Indian and Pakistani nuclear weapons tests in May 1998, Washington had come to regard stability as its main interest in South Asia. It became less concerned than it had been about the equities of a Kashmir settlement. The use of violence to change the status quo had become an unacceptable option in nuclear-armed South Asia. This explains the joint statement's reference to the "sanctity" of the Line of Control, a newly coined term. India, as the status quo power, would be the beneficiary of these changed circumstances unless it agreed to give up Kashmir territory in a negotiated settlement, a decision no Indian leader could

---

21. Brigadier (ret.) Feroz Hassan Khan, correspondence with authors, October 2009.

take without committing political suicide. But the Pakistanis' acceptance of that phrase was another demonstration of Sharif's desperation.

The president made this revised U.S. approach clear when he briefly visited Pakistan in March 2000, after Sharif's ouster. "International sympathy, support, and intervention cannot be won by provoking a bigger, bloodier conflict," Clinton warned his Pakistani TV audience at that time. "This era does not reward people who struggle in vain to redraw borders in blood."[22]

Clinton's words remain valid today. Washington will offer no encouragement to Pakistani revanchist policies in Kashmir. Any modest role it plays in helping New Delhi and Islamabad reach a settlement will include recognition that the territorial arrangements in the state must be left substantially unchanged. Washington's acceptance of the growing importance of India in helping the United States achieve its global policy objectives will only strengthen this resolve.

---

22. President Clinton, in a televised speech, Pakistan Television, March 25, 2000, www.nti.org/e_research/official_docs/pres/32500pres.pdf.

9

Negotiating with Pakistan: Lessons for Americans

The United States and Pakistan can claim some important successes in their negotiations over the years. For both, the three major negotiations described in chapter 7 represented high points, when the two countries built long-term relationships in response to external events. The same episodes included some of the low points as well. For the United States, the Carter administration's inability to reach any understanding with Pakistan in the immediate aftermath of the Soviet invasion of Afghanistan was both a negotiating and a policy failure. For both countries, the two "divorces" that followed the first two close U.S.-Pakistan collaborations represented failures of policy. They also demonstrated the most important weakness of both sides' negotiating approach. This was that the collaborative relationship that resulted from these negotiations was built on a willingness of both sides to disregard the ways their strategic objectives diverged. When the divergence became too glaring the relationship collapsed.

Smaller-scale negotiations present a mixed record. The United States won some successes, such as the withdrawal of Pakistani troops from Kargil. It also suffered some failures: its effort to dissuade Pakistan from testing a nuclear device is an important example. Pakistan, too, enjoyed some victories, including persuading Washington to reimburse it for undelivered F-16 aircraft. Success for one side often brought benefits to the other as well: Pakistan's withdrawal from Kargil ended an engagement that had become embarrassing for the country and the army, for example, and its obtaining reimbursements for the F-16 payments removed an irritant that had also troubled the United States. Success in some cases turned out to be ephemeral. Pakistan's agreement to end infiltration into Indian-controlled territory in 2002 is a good example.

Success and failure are not simply a function of negotiating technique. The basic policy drivers and geopolitical concerns of both sides were probably the single greatest predictor of whether an important negotiation would end in success—for one or both sides—or failure. Negotiating style still matters, however, especially since so many of the negotiations between the United States and Pakistan aim at defining our national terms of engagement, or reengagement. The style used in negotiations affects the way the countries continue to deal with each other after formal negotiations have concluded. U.S. negotiators cannot expect (and should not try) to counter all the characteristics of Pakistan's prevailing negotiating style, but understanding them is an essential start.

This study's analysis has focused on the three main sources of Pakistan's approach to negotiations with Americans: its geopolitical position, its culture, and the structure of authority within its government. Looked at in the larger global context, Pakistan fits into a category that U.S. officials encounter in other countries as well: asymmetrical negotiations. These are characterized not only by disparity of power between the negotiating partners—a fairly common situation for U.S. negotiators—but also by the weaker power's inclination to use its weakness as a negotiating asset. This has been part of the diplomatic tool kit of Egyptian negotiators seeking to maximize the value of their annual aid package, for example. The Egyptians intimate that a reduction in funding could damage their country's fragile economy and lead to political developments potentially harmful to U.S. regional interests. During the early years of U.S. textile negotiations with Bangladesh, the same calculus led the Bangladeshis to rely, often unrealistically, on their country's poverty as the argument that would make the U.S. grant generous quotas. This "weakness as strength" tactic has a rough analogue in the use of dependency relationships (*amae*) by Japanese officials. In general, it is likely to show up, in ways that fit the particular culture concerned, in U.S. negotiations with countries that depend on Washington for important security needs (and are important for American security goals) and whose cultural environment includes a hierarchical society and a rich network of social obligations.[1]

In considering how to negotiate most effectively with Pakistan, U.S. negotiators need to examine three groups of issues. First are questions of cul-

---

1. William B. Quandt, "Egypt: A Strong Sense of National Identity," and Nathaniel B. Thayer and Stephen E. Weiss, "Japan: The Changing Logic of a Former Minor Power," in *National Negotiating Styles*, ed. Hans Binnendijk (Washington, DC: Center for the Study of Foreign Affairs, U.S. Department of State, 1987), 105–25 and 45–75, respectively; Teresita Schaffer's recollections from her time as the State Department's country director for Egypt, 1987–89; and both authors' recollections from their service in Bangladesh, 1984–87.

tural style. Second are issues arising from the disparity in national power and the difference in the structure of the two governments. Third, and by far the most important, are issues arising from the diverging, at times quite contradictory objectives that have so often afflicted U.S.-Pakistan relations. Here, U.S. negotiators face a challenge of both policy and negotiating style: to what extent do the United States' and Pakistan's different national objectives limit the relationship the two countries can sustain? Put another way, can two countries whose tactical goals overlap but whose strategic priorities diverge significantly negotiate a reliable basis for cooperation?

The discussion here is geared primarily to officials, but the cultural advice applies with equal force to those representing businesses, universities, or nongovernmental organizations. Especially at a time of rampant anti-Americanism, private Americans need to be conscious of the way Pakistanis look on the U.S. government as well as more generally on the United States and its citizens.

At the Cultural Junction

Texas Congressman Charlie Wilson was the single most important congressional figure in securing generous funding for the U.S.-Pakistan collaboration in Afghanistan in the 1980s. His negotiations took place within the U.S. government and Congress, not with Pakistan, but he was a major player in U.S.-Pakistan relations for the better part of a decade, received like royalty by President Zia ul-Haq, and looked on by many Pakistanis as their not-so-secret weapon in Washington. Wilson was the kind of larger-than-life figure of whom American movies and stereotypes are made. His hard-drinking, profane persona was hardly calculated to appeal to someone like the sober Zia, and his propensity for showing up in Pakistan with glamorous American women on his arm (and in his hotel room) pushed every negative Pakistani cultural button.[2] He was lionized in Pakistan, however, because he delivered the resources Pakistan wanted and the U.S.-Pakistan relationship needed. One suspects that some of the seemingly straitlaced army officers he dealt with may have privately enjoyed and envied his womanizing bad-boy image.

Wilson would not be a good role model for U.S. negotiators, but he is a useful reminder that one can flamboyantly flout many cultural sensitivities and still have a powerful impact. An important question for U.S. negotiators

---

2. George Crile's *Charlie Wilson's War* (New York: Grove, 2003) and the movie of the same name made from it give countless examples. See, for example, 101–29. The authors recall preparing for any number of Wilson's visits to Islamabad that fit this description.

is when to tailor their behavior to Pakistan's sensitivities, and when and how to stick to a more American style and values.

Despite his colorful lifestyle, Wilson honored the first rule of cultural effectiveness in Pakistan: he built personal relationships. U.S. negotiators, especially those visiting Pakistan for the first time, would do well to add a few days to their visit, and to allow extra time for their initial meetings with key interlocutors, perhaps one and a half or two hours rather than the standard one hour. This would improve the prospects for the key parties to get to know each other as people, to discover what nonofficial interests they may have in common, and to find ways of communicating that go beyond both sides' approved talking points. Especially for those who expect to have important business with Pakistanis in the future, keeping up with old friends is equally important. It does not guarantee negotiating success, but it provides some of the social lubrication that helps negotiators find common ground.

Building a relationship should not, however, mean making one person synonymous with U.S.-Pakistan relations. Senior U.S. officials need to create a personal connection with a broad range of Pakistan's important players, civilian and military, government and opposition. The U.S. ambassador has a particular responsibility here, one that recent ambassadors have worked hard to discharge. This is always tricky in a suspicious and polarized atmosphere like Pakistan's. The army is an essential part of this mix, but, as noted in chapter 4, it is important to avoid having senior contacts with the army undercut civilian authority. Washington-based officials also need to diversify their contacts enough to immunize them against the charge of picking "our guy" and snubbing others. U.S. officials who have one obvious counterpart, such as the chairman of the Joint Chiefs of Staff, need to ensure that their sources of information are diverse enough to avoid getting locked into their opposite number's view of the world. Personal connections across the political and bureaucratic spectrum are probably the key hedge against one of the major pitfalls of negotiating with Pakistan: the risk of being tripped up by officials who are politically weak, unable to wield the authority they theoretically have, or otherwise ill placed to deliver a reliable government of Pakistan commitment.

Personal relations create expectations. As illustrated in greater detail in chapter 3, the frank talk that Americans consider a normal consequence of friendship is not viewed the same way in Pakistan. But a relationship of some candor with Pakistani officials or political leaders can provide the context for recalibrating expectations, allowing Americans to "act like Americans" and to speak bluntly with less risk of causing offense. It also provides a setting in which an American official can put his or her position in the context of the American sense of honor. Pakistanis are accustomed to thinking of honor as a peculiarly Pakistani sensitivity; recalling that Americans too take honor seriously can be important.

A strong personal bond was almost certainly a major factor in Deputy Secretary of State Richard Armitage's ability to secure an undertaking from President Musharraf to shut down infiltration into India during the crisis that followed the attack on India's parliament building in 2001. Armitage argues strongly that Musharraf valued his frank talk.[3] Looking at the pattern of U.S.-Pakistan relations, it becomes clear that Musharraf did so because of his personal bond with Armitage, and because of the mutual respect between the two men.

As is often the case, some kinds of frankness are easier to swallow than others. Words that attack national pride or honor will wound regardless of the personal relationship. For Pakistanis they may indeed wound more deeply coming from someone they had considered a friend. Negotiators need to convey respect at both the national and personal level. Senior Pakistani military officers, unaccustomed as they are to criticism within their domestic setting, are especially sensitive to criticism from foreign friends.

As already noted, frankness and honesty can run aground on the strategic deception that is considered normal and unobjectionable in Pakistani statecraft. U.S. negotiators should expect that inconvenient truths will be kept from them. Often, this will take place under a veil of ambiguity, in the hope that the U.S. side will hear what it wants to hear and not listen too closely. This generally occurs because divergent U.S. and Pakistani objectives are coming to the fore. The problem this poses has more to do with policy than with style.

American negotiators in Washington generally face a "hospitality gap." The U.S. government is more restrictive with official entertainment than its Pakistani counterpart, and the work involved in entertaining at home is more burdensome for American than for Pakistani officials. But ramping up the level of hospitality is worth a lot. An invitation home, a personal culinary specialty, some other individual touch—these are things that stand out for Pakistani visitors to Washington. At a minimum, those who receive Pakistanis in the office need to offer tea or coffee regardless of whether the U.S. government provides it.

Much of the relationship building that is so critical to U.S.-Pakistan negotiations starts with the U.S. ambassador and the staff of the U.S. mission

---

3. Richard Armitage, interview.

in Pakistan. This job is almost impossible to do if staff cycle in and out of Pakistan for tours of duty lasting only a year, something that has become commonplace as a result of the danger to U.S. officials in Pakistan and the restrictions they face on bringing their families with them. The United States pays the price, however, in fewer and shallower personal relationships, and in greatly diminished cultural awareness. U.S. policy and negotiations will suffer greatly unless a way is found to have the key U.S. officials at the embassy and consulates in Pakistan serve the formerly traditional three-year tours.

Cultural differences also distort the way a negotiator's message is received. U.S. officials usually consider a legal argument as a trump card, and one based on prohibitions in U.S. law is the strongest case they can make. In dealing with a Pakistani audience, this frequently comes across as an all-purpose dodge to prevent the United States from honoring its broader commitment to Pakistan. One Pakistani general with long experience in dealing with Washington commented that "the lawyers are always in the room, and the lawyers always say no."

One painful example occurred in the 1991 Persian Gulf War. The Pressler Amendment ban on military supply to Pakistan was still in force, and Pakistan's civilian prime minister, Nawaz Sharif, had just agreed to join the U.S.-led coalition confronting Iraq, despite considerable controversy and the open opposition of his army chief. The United States wanted to supply the Pakistani troops engaged in this common endeavor with the equipment they would need. After much agonizing, Washington eventually concluded that the Pakistanis could use U.S. equipment in the Gulf, but that they would have to leave it behind when they went home. This legal hairsplitting struck Pakistanis as insulting, and undercut the "rule-of-law" argument U.S. officials like to make.[4] One will have more impact in Pakistan by making a policy argument with the law serving to underscore a position that has some inherent logic to it in terms of the U.S.-Pakistan relationship. As the example of the Gulf War demonstrates, sometimes that simply is not possible.

Two subjects can cut off communication if handled wrong. The first is an invidious comparison between Pakistan and India, which may easily come across as unacceptable favoritism no matter how carefully it is phrased. The second is Islam. The view that the United States does not understand Islam and is hostile to Muslims is widely shared. Questions work better than statements. Unless one is dealing with a representative of an Islamic religious party, it is sometimes easier to introduce a sensitive subject related to Pakistan's Islamic character by starting from the views of Pakistan's founder,

---

4.   Teresita Schaffer's recollections from her time as deputy assistant secretary of state.

Mohammed Ali Jinnah, or of more contemporary political leaders who want Pakistan to remain, or become, a modern, moderate Muslim nation.

History looks different from the other side of the cultural junction. Pakistan's narrative, as seen in the preceding chapters, stresses a threatening India and an unreliable United States. The American perspective instead highlights Pakistan's unwillingness to respect the limits the United States had put on its ability to help Pakistan. This underscores the importance for negotiators of studying the record of past negotiations with Pakistan. Attempting to persuade Pakistani counterparts to accept the U.S. view of history is generally useless, but negotiators need to avoid being blindsided when the Pakistanis put forward their version. Personal relationships may be the negotiator's only hope for moving a conversation out of the well-worn groove of mutual recriminations.

One frequent—and sensitive—issue is how to deal with Pakistani statements that are widely accepted (or at least widely used) but that the U.S. side considers either irrational or blatantly untrue. Forewarned is forearmed: a negotiator working with Pakistan needs to be well briefed on what to expect, and to be prepared for certain Pakistani arguments that in the United States' view are completely wrong. Listening with respect to one's Pakistani counterpart is a must. It is important to signal that one finds a particular line of reasoning untrue or illogical, without being diverted into a pointless "battle of the narratives" that will convince no one and may make things worse. Rather than simply concur, or smile and nod, in an effort to move quickly beyond the walk through Pakistan's view of the historical role of the United States, American officials would be better advised to acknowledge Pakistan's concerns, but note that they see that role very differently. The United States has provided enormous assistance to Pakistan over the years. The Pressler Amendment, seen in Pakistan as a grave injustice, was enacted with Pakistan's support in order to continue the third-largest assistance program in the world. The message should be that both countries have important interests at stake, and that the United States and Pakistan are trying to pursue jointly those that coincide.

More fundamentally, U.S. officials should not expect their arguments to persuade Pakistan to change its basic threat perceptions. But those who are working with Pakistan over an extended period would do well to invest the time and effort to encourage their counterparts to reflect on the importance of challenges outside the standard, India-centric view. The attacks by the Pakistani Taliban and the military operations in northwestern Pakistan in 2008 and 2009 have had an impact on government and military thinking.

Some Pakistani military and civilian leaders also recognize that Pakistan's economic performance has major security implications.

The issue of different historical narratives has particular relevance to press relations and public diplomacy at a time of record anti-Americanism. Pakistan's feisty media, especially the electronic media, routinely play "gotcha" when interviewing Americans. The style is not so much asking difficult questions as asking questions with attitude. The most effective approach combines respect and frankness. When Secretary of State Hillary Clinton visited Pakistan in October 2009, she had a grueling schedule of public and media appearances, which she fulfilled despite a major bombing that occurred on the eve of her visit. She met with audiences that were eager to vent their suspicion of the United States. She addressed their queries in measured tones, but without giving ground. She did not turn the anti-American mood around single-handedly, but she did earn widespread respect for grace and guts. [5]

As part of a long-term strategy of changing people's views of the United States, this was a good beginning, but it requires further strengthening. Many critics, both Americans and Pakistanis who recognize the importance of robust U.S.-Pakistan ties, have complained that the United States derives surprisingly little popular appreciation for its huge assistance programs. One problem often cited is the near invisibility of U.S. economic aid. Critics argue, with good reason, that Washington needs to fund programs and projects that catch the popular Pakistani imagination if it wants to have American assistance to ordinary Pakistanis strengthen U.S.-Pakistan relations. By the same token, Pakistanis need to be able to identify U.S.-funded projects as coming from the United States. It is worth recalling the huge wave of appreciation in Pakistan for the dramatic and highly visible effort by the U.S. military to provide relief to people in Pakistan-administered Kashmir following the disastrous earthquake that struck that remote mountainous region in October 2005.[6]

Dealing with deliberate lies is difficult. Especially when one is speaking with political leaders or top officials, accusing one's interlocutor of lying is unlikely to get anywhere. If the top levels of the United States government are being lied to, someone closer to the Pakistani officials involved—often the best candidate will be the U.S. ambassador—may need to quietly remind the responsible Pakistani officials that in the American cultural context, this

---

5. See, for example, Alex Rodriguez, "Clinton's Pakistan Visit Reveals Widespread Distrust of the United States," *Los Angeles Times*, November 1, 2009, http://articles.latimes.com/2009/nov/01/world/fg-clinton-pakistan1.

6. The positive impact of similar U.S. relief efforts during the massive floods that inundated Pakistan in the summer of 2010 was less effective in relieving anti-American sentiment, which was fueled at the time by the negative Pakistani reaction to a spike in U.S. military intrusions into Pakistani territory.

behavior can seriously impair the bond they are trying to establish with the American leadership.

When U.S. negotiators believe they are being lied to, they should ask themselves "why?" The lie may mean that Pakistan has no intention of following through, because it is unwilling or unable to deal with the issue in the forthright manner Americans profess to want. In such cases, "getting at the truth" is likely to be an exercise in frustration and futility, and finding the truth is usually not the primary U.S. objective. The task in these circumstances is to find a "work-around"—an alternative route to the negotiator's goal, or an alternative pressure point.

In other cases, Pakistani officials might lie to achieve a more specific objective—protecting an intelligence asset, for example, or defending a security concern they believe the United States might threaten. The February 2010 arrest of a senior Afghan Taliban personality known as Mullah Baradar in a joint U.S.-Pakistani intelligence operation, for example, was billed as a major turnaround in Pakistan's policy toward the Afghan Taliban. A less-noticed detail in the news was the statement that Baradar "ran" the Quetta Shura, a group of senior Afghan Taliban who worked out of the capital of Pakistan's Balochistan Province.[7] For about two years before the arrest, Pakistani military spokesmen had denied that there was any such group, and had indicated that they had no intelligence on which to base an arrest because the United States had failed to supply them with the necessary information. U.S. officials who know their counterparts are stonewalling should carry on based on their understanding of the facts. Sometimes, as in this example, a public event intervenes and blows the cover story. In other cases, the U.S. negotiator needs to figure out, once again, how to respond to the unstated objective a Pakistani counterpart is pursuing. Ultimately, this, rather than the dissembling, is the important issue.

Authority and Structure

One of the first rules of negotiating is to know where authority lies in the country represented across the table. The principal problem this poses for U.S. negotiators dealing with Pakistan is how to handle civil-military relations. As noted, the military is an essential player in Pakistan, and it has more often than not been the single most important force on the issues that drive U.S.-Pakistan relations. That has certainly been the case since 9/11.

---

7. Mark Mazetti and Dexter Filkins, "Secret Joint Raid Captures Taliban's Top Commander," *New York Times*, February 16, 2010, www.nytimes.com/2010/02/16/world/asia/16intel.html.

The government was headed by a general until 2008. Even after the restoration of civilian government, however, the focal point of U.S.-Pakistan relations remained policy toward Afghanistan, and, closely related to this, Pakistan's handling of the militant threat along the Afghan border and elsewhere. In these matters, the army dominates, and within the army, ISI.

The challenge for the U.S. negotiator is to develop rapport with the army leadership without inadvertently reinforcing the army's role in the country's politics and government at the expense of civilian leadership. Americans are drawn to the army's can-do manner and are easily impressed by army officers' crisp, professional style. For a U.S. official, the most efficient and most natural way to negotiate is to focus on the person or institution most likely to deliver the goods—or to prevent their delivery. There is a fine line between accepting the army's vital role and undercutting the sometimes shaky and possibly less effective elements of civilian government. The United States needs to be on the right side of that line.

The strategic dialogue talks held in Washington in March 2010 illustrate how tricky this process can be. The talks themselves took place between senior civil-military delegations headed by both countries' foreign ministers. They were set to begin March 24. In the wake of the arrest of a number of Afghan Taliban figures in Pakistan in the preceding month, expectations were at an all-time high. The bigger news story, however, occurred in the three days before the formal talks began. Pakistan's army chief, General Ashfaq Kayani, arrived March 21, and by the time the "strategic dialogue" started he had already met separately with General David Petraeus, then the regional commander whose area of responsibility included Pakistan; the chairman of the Joint Chiefs of Staff, Admiral Mike Mullen; and Secretary of Defense Robert Gates. Kayani had put forward the issues most important to the army.[8] The political message was clear: the army, while formally supporting the civilians, was reasserting its own primacy in the informal process by which the Pakistan government runs.

The army also dominated the U.S. press play before and after the meeting, not only through major stories about Kayani's standing in Pakistan and his meetings in the United States but also through prominent op-ed pieces in which senior American commentators testified to Pakistan's new dedication to the defeat of the Taliban. At least one of these reflected effective Pakistani

---

8.   Karen de Young and Karin Brulliard, "In U.S.-Pakistan Meetings, a Chance to Move Past Mutual 'Trust Deficit,'" *Washington Post*, March 24, 2010, www.washingtonpost.com/wp-dyn/content/article/2010/03/23/AR2010032304147.

outreach to the American journalistic establishment.[9] A few weeks later, journalists reporting from Pakistan presented a much more complex view of Pakistan's strategy toward Afghanistan and its arrest of Afghan Taliban personalities, including the observation that Pakistan had freed several Afghan Taliban it had previously arrested. By then, however, the strategic dialogue was over, its success duly recorded in both capitals. The U.S. team clearly got one of the hoped-for benefits out of the dialogue: a much-needed antidote to the atmosphere of suspicion from which U.S.-Pakistan ties had suffered. But Pakistan managed to set the story line, and to create an atmosphere that played up the sense of obligation Pakistan—and specifically the army—was trying to create.

This episode also illustrates the challenge U.S. government negotiators face in managing their own side. As already noted, Pakistani officials have a clear perception of where their friends are, and where the greatest dangers lie. In these circumstances, they can use normal bureaucratic and legislative-executive rivalry within the United States to undercut U.S. objectives. And they can, as seen in this case, play on the military-to-military tie to make contrary views from other parts of the U.S. government look small-minded. The remedy, which government insiders will recognize as hard to implement, is to pay particular attention to internal discipline, and to invest considerable time and effort in ensuring that the different parts of the government speak from the same script.

Many Pakistanis—like many other non-Americans—understand poorly the U.S. separation of powers between executive and legislative, and this can lead to epic misunderstandings. A striking example was the uproar that attended the passage of the Kerry-Lugar bill in October 2009. The legislation was designed to triple U.S. economic assistance to Pakistan to $1.5 billion a year over a five-year period, as a demonstration of long-term U.S. interest in Pakistan and as a vehicle for supporting civilian authority. Both the U.S. administration and the Pakistan government worked hard to secure passage.

As it made its way through Congress, however, the Washington legislative process took over. Members of Congress concerned about Pakistan added not only general statements of U.S. sympathy with the difficulties Pakistan was facing and the sacrifices it incurred in fighting insurgents connected with the Afghan Taliban but also a formidable list of conditions for which

---

9. See, for example, Michael O'Hanlon, "Pakistan's War of Choice," *New York Times*, March 24, 2010, www.nytimes.com/2010/03/24/opinion/24ohanlon.html, and Arnaud de Borchgrave, "Commentary: Pakistan Army: Back on Top," United Press International, March 29, 2010, www.upi.com/Top_News/Analysis/2010/03/29/Commentary-Pakistan-army-Back-on-top/UPI-90891269866386/.

the United States had to certify Pakistan's performance. Despite administration efforts to eliminate specific references to India and reduce the hectoring tone in the bill, the final product included an imposing number of recurring reports the U.S. government would be obliged to file with Congress. These included assessments of Pakistan's antiterrorism accomplishments and detailed accounts of the degree to which Pakistan's civilian government was exercising control of the military.

The army spokesman issued a statement terming the conditions "unacceptable," and the Pakistani political world and media erupted in outrage on cue. Both U.S. and Pakistani officials were taken by surprise, including Pakistan's very active ambassador in Washington, who had been deeply involved in the congressional negotiations. This kind of legislative sharp-pencil work had been used with little or no controversy in the past. Even the much maligned Pressler Amendment had enjoyed the support of General Zia ul-Haq's government as a means of continuing a major aid program, and there was no significant opposition in Pakistan to its original passage. But in 2009, the normal workings of Washington ran headlong into Pakistan's sense of sovereignty in an atmosphere of reflexive anti-Americanism. The civilian focus of the aid and especially some of the detailed conditions having to do with civilian control of the military touched a raw nerve in the Pakistan Army. The Pakistan government initially moved to tamp down the uproar by proposing a parliamentary resolution rejecting the U.S. conditions. The bottom line was that an economic aid package intended as a major emblem of U.S. support and a signal that Washington's interest in Pakistan went well beyond its military role—and initially received in that light by the Pakistan government—had suddenly become a monument to misunderstanding between the two political systems, and a problem requiring a new set of negotiations.[10]

Weakness and Leverage

One of the major things the U.S. negotiator can offer Pakistan is its power—as "carrot" or as "stick." Using that power in the negotiating setting is tricky. The history of U.S.-Pakistan relations is full of examples of threats, explicit or implicit, that simply led Pakistanis to try to obscure their problematic behavior, as in the case of their nuclear weapons program. But a compelling

---

10. Irfan Gauhar, "PM Takes Politicians on Board over U.S. Aid," *Daily Times*, October 12, 2009, www.dailytimes.com.pk/default.asp?page=2009\10\12\story_12-10-2009_pg1_8. See also Hasan-Askari Rizvi, "Analysis: Kerry-Lugar and the Domestic Debate," *Daily Times*, October 11, 2009. For text of the bill, see "Text of S-1707: Enhanced Partnership with Pakistan Act of 2009," www.govtrack.us/congress/billtext.xpd?bill=s111-1707.

crisis may speak for itself and drive the negotiating process forward. The clearest example came in the immediate aftermath of 9/11. The crumbling Twin Towers of the World Trade Center conveyed in ways no negotiator's brief could have that the United States had been attacked and that a country's response to any request for help would identify it as friend or adversary. At the time, this galvanized a favorable Pakistani response and an astonishingly smooth negotiating process.

When the immediate crisis had passed, Pakistan's leaders bristled at their recollection of the insistent U.S. demands. President Musharraf described Deputy Secretary of State Armitage's meeting with his intelligence chief, Lieutenant General Mahmud Ahmed, as "rude."[11] In response to a different kind of demonstration of U.S. power, the conditions contained in the 2009 U.S. aid legislation for Pakistan, one of Pakistan's best-known political analysts, Hasan-Askari Rizvi, used the same word.[12] The day after 9/11, the United States got what it needed from Pakistan in spite of this verbal heavy artillery. Under more normal circumstances, the results will be better if one gives a bit more space to the Pakistani government's and negotiator's dignity.

At other times, of course, Pakistan has used its weaknesses as a strategic asset in its negotiations with the United States—a tactic some have referred to as "having the lower hand" or "coercive deficiency."[13] After 9/11, when the United States leaned on Pakistan to step up the pace of arresting al-Qaeda leaders, the Pakistani leadership let it be known that too much U.S. pressure could upset the fragile equilibrium in a strategically important country. The argument led U.S. negotiators and policymakers to soften their tone and live with a troubling and ambiguous set of Pakistani relationships with insurgents in Afghanistan.

In response to the argument that the stability of Pakistan is at risk, the United States usually tries to provide technical and financial assistance to help strengthen institutions and expand the economy, and military aid that will bolster security and cement U.S. ties with the army. However, while aid can be an important negotiating asset, the institutional weaknesses in Pakistan that generations of American governments have hoped to address cannot be fixed quickly, and arguably cannot be fixed by foreigners in any case. Economic and institutional support, in other words, are necessary in the long term, but insufficient and ineffective in the time horizon that U.S. policymakers are often trying to respond to. Military assistance is valuable

---

11. Musharraf, *In the Line of Fire*, 201.

12. Rizvi, "Analysis: Kerry-Lugar and the Domestic Debate."

13. We are indebted to John Limbert and William Zartman for these wonderfully evocative phrases.

to the army, but American unwillingness to take Pakistan's side in the rivalry with India exerts a stronger pull on both official and popular sentiment.

The aid-oriented approach needs to be supplemented by a close look at two standard tools from the negotiator's kit: alternatives and leverage. The United States has approached its biggest negotiations with Pakistan as if it had no alternatives, and as if economic assistance and military supply provided major leverage—leverage that the United States was most reluctant to use, however. Once the terms of the relationship were set, the United States appeared to have achieved its principal objectives and built its policy around the promised support from Pakistan. Thus, for example, the basing patterns and supply lines established to support the U.S. presence in Afghanistan after 9/11 overwhelmingly ran through Pakistan. Not until years later, when the gap between Pakistani and U.S. objectives became more obvious and the bilateral relationship more contentious, was any serious effort made to diversify supply lines by identifying alternatives to Pakistan. An earlier effort to do so could have positioned the United States better to deal with the problems that developed. Roger Fisher's concept of the Best Alternative to a Negotiated Agreement (BATNA) applies here, not as the way of measuring whether a negotiated agreement is adequate but as a guide to expanding U.S. options if the agreement runs into difficulties while being implemented.[14]

Using U.S. assistance as leverage can founder on the twin rocks of Pakistan's "lower-hand" strategy and congressionally mandated conditions applied to both military and economic assistance. The U.S. government has always been reluctant to cut off aid. Congressionally required conditions more often than not trigger strenuous efforts by the executive branch to justify the continuation of aid. The classic example came in 1990, when President George H. W. Bush decided that he could no longer certify that Pakistan did not possess a nuclear explosive device. His administration made an unsuccessful last-ditch effort to persuade the Congress to pass legislation temporarily waiving the required aid cutoff in order to buy time for Pakistan to undo what it had done and become eligible for assistance once again.[15] In the end aid was cut off. The U.S. government had publicly tried and failed to add some flexibility to the legislation in order to make room for negotiation. In the end, it had neither carrot nor stick.

---

14. Roger Fisher and William Ury, *Getting to Yes: Negotiating Agreement without Giving In* (New York: Penguin, 1983).

15. Teresita Schaffer, as deputy assistant secretary of state responsible for South Asia, was one of the officials who unsuccessfully presented the George H. W. Bush administration's request to the relevant congressional committees in late September 1990.

Clearly, economic and military assistance are important to Pakistan, and they are part of what the United States brings to the negotiating table. Using economic assistance to leverage economic policy changes is part of the mutually accepted bargaining language. However, especially when a negotiation that is broader in scope than economic policy has moved into the implementation phase, the U.S. negotiator needs to deploy other kinds of leverage.

The clearest examples are all blunt instruments, not to be used lightly, with potentially powerful effects but also major possible unintended consequences. Public, high-level expressions of skepticism about Pakistan's ability to deliver on its undertakings can have a bracing effect, as was the case after Secretary Clinton's testimony before the House Foreign Affairs Committee in April 2009. Her remarks were unusually pointed: "Not only do the Pakistani government officials, but the Pakistani people and the Pakistani diaspora . . . need to speak out forcefully against a policy that is ceding more and more territory to the insurgents, to the Taliban, to al-Qaeda, to the allies that are in this terrorist syndicate."[16] This statement may have helped inspire the Pakistan government's efforts to build a domestic consensus in favor of taking on the Pakistani Taliban in the Swat Valley. It may also have suggested that unless Pakistan "shapes up," the United States would reexamine its options, thus reinforcing Pakistan's skepticism about U.S. staying power, with potentially harmful effects. In similar fashion, raising the possibility that U.S. policy toward Kashmir might move closer to the Indian position could be a salutary reminder that the U.S. relationship cannot be taken for granted—or a dangerous reinforcement of the Pakistani narrative of U.S. inconstancy.

Besides developing additional alternatives and sources of leverage for the United States, the negotiator needs to reflect on how Pakistan sees its own alternatives and leverage. Since 9/11, and on previous occasions as well, Pakistan has based its approach to the United States on two assumptions: that Pakistan is vulnerable, and that the United States needs Pakistan more than the other way around. Pakistan's potential alternatives to a strong relationship with the United States are primarily China and its longtime Arab friends, Saudi Arabia and the United Arab Emirates. None of these countries, and indeed no combination, can fully replace the blend of military support, economic assistance, and access to the international power structure that Pakistan wants from the United States. But they can provide some of these elements: military supply from China, funding from the Persian Gulf.

---

16. Cited in Elise Labott, "Clinton: Pakistan in Danger," CNN, www.cnn.com/2009/POLITICS/04/22/clinton.pakistan/index.html.

These friends, moreover, have certain advantages compared to the United States: they are relatively uncritical and are willing to go much farther than the United States toward supporting Pakistan in its rivalry with India. China has also provided critical assistance to the Pakistani nuclear program.

While the United States has no problem per se with Pakistan's close ties with all these countries, Pakistan could take these links in directions that pose serious policy problems for the United States. The activities of Pakistan's nuclear scientist A.Q. Khan in Iran, Libya, and North Korea are a case in point. Twice the United States opted not to take action against Pakistan after learning about his nuclear transfers, despite the major damage they did to vital U.S. interests. Khan's actions were not part of a larger strategy of negotiation with the United States, but Pakistan used its strategic importance and potential vulnerability to neutralize the U.S. ability to respond.

This is not an issue of negotiating style but of policy. The United States needs to consider under what circumstances it is willing to put its relationship with Pakistan on the line because of the dangers Pakistan's actions pose for broader U.S. interests. That brings us to the most fundamental challenge for the U.S. negotiator: the gap between Pakistani and U.S. objectives.

Dealing with Divergent Objectives

U.S.-Pakistan negotiations, as noted above, are an example of asymmetrical diplomacy in the way they reflect the relative power of the two partners. There is also a more troublesome asymmetry between the two countries' objectives. During their periods of most intense collaboration, Pakistan and the United States have decided to disregard significant differences in their strategic goals and priorities. The previous chapters discuss at length the objectives on which the United States and Pakistan have differed over the years, principally U.S. unwillingness to take Pakistan's side in its rivalry with India, the two countries' different priorities in Afghanistan, and Pakistanis' unwillingness to be bound by major U.S. goals that run counter to their perception of Pakistan's security interests (for example, U.S. objections to their nuclear program). In managing the relationship, both countries identified and cultivated areas of tactical agreement as well as more limited areas of strategic convergence. But the consequences of building a strategically important relationship on such a contested foundation affect the way U.S. negotiators go about their job and constrain the type of relationship they may be able to maintain with Pakistan in the future.

For the negotiator, there are two principal lessons. The first is to be conscious of what one is negotiating. Sometimes the real and stated purposes of a negotiation are the same. But often, a seemingly technical negotiation is a stand-in for the larger relationship, a road test of whether the United States has overcome the presumption of infidelity, a demonstration of whether the relationship is to be an enduring friendship or a series of specific bargains. The United States does not have to accept this heavy symbolism, nor should its negotiators buy into the "guilt trip" that often lies behind it. But they need to understand what larger issues may be in play and if possible find alternative means of dealing with them.

A classic example came during the post-9/11 negotiations between Under Secretary of State Alan Larson and Finance Minister Shaukat Aziz. The Pakistanis, from Musharraf on down, had been pressing for debt relief. Larson recalled Secretary of State Colin Powell saying the issue was "imprinted on his forehead." In the minds of the Pakistanis, this meant not just financial relief but the political symbolism of a vote in Congress. The State Department had devised a way to stretch out Pakistan's debt payments without having the funding "score" against the U.S. budget deficit. Larson was able to persuade Aziz, and through him Musharraf, that this would solve the financial problem and that the U.S. government's skill in thinking up this solution was evidence of its desire to help Pakistan.

The problem was solved—but, it turned out, only temporarily. Within a year or two, Larson recalled, Pakistan was once again pressing for debt cancellation, and for a vote in Congress. This particular vote in Congress never came. The one Pakistani economic request that the United States did not meet, expansion of market access for Pakistani textiles, would also have required a vote in Congress, one that Washington hands will recognize as among the most difficult cases to make on Capitol Hill. In this case, Pakistan was negotiating not just financial flows but the nature of their relationship. The immediate financial issue was elegantly resolved by "reprofiling" Pakistan's debt. The relationship question remained on the table, coming up periodically when the Pakistanis saw an opportunity to press for the "gold standard" of congressional endorsement.[17]

The second principal lesson is that the negotiator needs to recognize the mental reservations that lurk in the grand bargains between Pakistan and the United States, both past bargains and those that might be struck in the future. The differences between the two countries' strategic objectives are

---

17. This section draws on authors' interviews with Richard Armitage, Alan Larson, Abida Hussein, and Shahryar Khan.

not going to disappear. Even making very optimistic assumptions about the future course of India-Pakistan relations, Pakistan will still have a deeply ingrained sense of insecurity and the United States will not want to make its foreign policy dependent on Pakistan's relations with its neighbors to the degree that would make Pakistan comfortable. So the negotiator needs to recognize that in addition to launching a long-term relationship, the United States and Pakistan will need to manage significant differences in objectives. They should do this with their eyes open.

In the final analysis, the persistent gap between U.S. and Pakistani objectives raises fundamental questions about the kind of relationship the two countries can sustain. Both profess to want a deep and serious friendship that will stand the test of time and is more than a series of "transactions." Both, at the same time, have strong reasons for resisting each other's hopes for more complete policy alignment. The tensions that arise periodically over the intrusiveness of congressionally imposed conditions on U.S. aid or over Pakistan's disregard of American sensitivities regarding its nuclear program illustrate how each side routinely overestimates its ability to change the other's behavior and underestimates its ability to complicate relations.

Rather than assume that a long-term relationship is out of reach, U.S. policymakers and negotiators should accept that some important areas will remain outside the ambit of the larger U.S.-Pakistan understanding. Negotiators should be explicit about the specific issues that are most important to the United States, even if that raises the specter of the "transactional relationship" that Pakistani commentators use as a derogatory term. They should be careful about making or implying sweeping promises they are unlikely to be able to fulfill. Ambassador Wendy Chamberlin's blunt refusal to accept Musharraf's call for U.S. involvement in the Kashmir issue, which he requested as an American quid pro quo for Pakistan's support in the wake of 9/11, is a good example of when to say no. Presidential letters to Pakistani leaders in the 1960s hinting at U.S. support for Pakistan in its rivalry with India fed Pakistani hopes, and in the end only made the letdown more bitter. In other words, aiming for a broad relationship is appropriate, but it is wise to be specific about the most important implicit "transactions" it needs to embody. In practice, the Pakistanis will be equally specific—as they have been in the past, for example, with their focus on debt relief and F-16s.

Much of the story of U.S.-Pakistan negotiations emphasizes the vulnerability and volatility of the relationship between these two fractious allies. But at the same time there is a remarkable resilience to the U.S.-Pakistan connection. The issues that have led the United States to seek closer ties with

Pakistan in the past are major geopolitical problems: Pakistan's proximity to Afghanistan and the ill-governed and volatile countries of Central Asia, its nuclear-armed rivalry with and irredentist designs against India, its significant position in the world of political Islam at a time when extremist Islamic forces see the United States as the center of their global struggle. Pakistan's own internal stresses make it vulnerable to crises. In the future, these factors will continue to make Pakistan important for U.S. interests. Pakistan is the second largest Muslim-majority country in the world after Indonesia, and the Pakistan-based leadership of some of the world's major international extremist organizations will remain a major U.S. preoccupation for a long time. These factors have often led Pakistani leaders to assume they were indispensable to Washington.

But the United States is also, in other ways, indispensable to Pakistan. Despite the resentment of U.S. infidelity that colors Pakistanis' view of the United States, Pakistan's policymakers have always wanted a strong relationship with Washington. The United States has historically been able to ride out periods of heightened anti-Americanism and to overcome policy missteps that might have reaped a bitter harvest, because its power and resources were uniquely valuable to the Pakistani leadership. In 1991, only months after the United States cut off aid to Pakistan because of its nuclear program, the Pakistan government offered to help the United States establish connections with the newly independent countries of Central Asia, arguing that its Islamic bond with these Muslim countries might be helpful to Washington. The U.S. administration politely declined the offer, but the message was clear: Pakistan, at a low point in its relations with the United States, was looking for new ways to revive the tie with Washington.

This suggests that the United States is to some extent protected against the consequences of negotiating or policy missteps by the intrinsic importance for Pakistan of having a strong relationship with Washington. Any Pakistan government will seek to keep open its military supply lines with all its major suppliers, and the United States is the best source of state-of-the-art equipment. When India tested a nuclear device, Pakistan's civilian leaders followed suit—but only after agonizing about the consequences for its relations with the Americans. The United States has repeatedly personalized its policy toward Pakistan, most obviously during the long periods of military rule, but also during the 1990s, when elected civilian leaders took turns at the helm. But the successor governments were always quick to establish themselves with Washington. The speed with which the Pakistani government elected in 2008 began cultivating the United States, despite the bad taste in its mouth as a result of the seven-year romance between the Bush administration and Musharraf, illustrates the phenomenon.

It would be a mistake, however, to assume that Pakistani leaders will always see ties with Washington as an essential foundation for their security. On the roller-coaster ride of U.S.-Pakistan relations, with every swoop upward, the memory of the last downturn is a little sharper, and skepticism of U.S. intentions a bit harsher. The revived U.S. relationship with India since 2000, from Pakistan's perspective, can be tactically useful, but many Pakistanis regard it as strategically dangerous and are watching for and dreading the moment when the United States definitively throws in its lot with India.

Reviving troubled relations is getting more difficult. The uproar over the Kerry-Lugar bill is not the first time congressional "meddling," as Islamabad sees it, has caused offense in Pakistan. But this episode suggests that it is becoming more challenging to ride out popular discontent. The fact that the Pakistan government was caught off guard by the vehemence of the reaction in the army and the press is noteworthy. The two previous "divorces" between the United States and Pakistan came at the United States' initiative—not unprovoked and certainly not unforeseen, but at U.S. instigation nonetheless. If Pakistan continues on the democratic path, a resentful public opinion, one all too ready to believe dark stories of U.S. hostility to Islam in general and Pakistan in particular, may place greater limits on what the United States and Pakistan can do together. One cannot exclude the possibility that a future Pakistan government, military or civilian, might in effect dare the United States to walk out again. And if a future government of Pakistan had a fundamentally different character, such as one in which Islamic extremist organizations had a significant leading role, the resilience would be badly strained, and the task of managing differences in both policy and negotiating style starkly complicated.

The United States and Pakistan can still work together in support of the objectives they share, though these may need to be more carefully defined than in the past. There will still be plenty of negotiating to do and many more limited objectives on which the two countries can find common ground. But the limitations on U.S.-Pakistan relations are likely to become more visible. The most important lesson for U.S. policymakers and negotiators is to recognize both the potential and the limits of Pakistan as a U.S. partner.

Index

About the Authors

Howard B. and **Teresita C. Schaffer** both had careers of over three decades in the U.S. Foreign Service. Recognized as the State Department's principal experts on South Asia, they both served as deputy assistant secretary of state for South Asia.

He is senior counselor at the Institute for the Study of Diplomacy at Georgetown University, where he teaches courses on diplomatic process and South Asia. Before retiring from the U.S. Foreign Service, he served as U.S. ambassador to Bangladesh and as political counselor in both New Delhi and Islamabad. His earlier assignments were to Kuala Lumpur and Seoul. His publications include *Chester Bowles: New Dealer in the Cold War, Ellsworth Bunker: Global Troubleshooter, Vietnam Hawk,* and *The Limits of Influence: America's Role in Kashmir,* which won the American Academy of Diplomacy's 2009 Douglas Dillon Award for the best book on the practice of U.S. diplomacy. He speaks Urdu, Hindi, and French, and is a graduate of Harvard College.

She served as U.S. ambassador to Sri Lanka and as economic officer in Islamabad. Other diplomatic posts included Tel Aviv and New Delhi. She directed the South Asia Program at the Center for Strategic and International Studies from 1998–2010. Her publications include *Pakistan's Future and U.S. Policy Options, Kashmir: The Economics of Peace Building,* and *India and the U.S. in the 21st Century: Reinventing Partnership.* She has taught at Georgetown University and American University. She speaks French, Swedish, German, Italian, Hebrew, Hindi, and Urdu and has studied Bangla and Sinhala. She is a graduate of Bryn Mawr College.

About the Cross-Cultural Negotiation Series

In the early 1990s the United States Institute of Peace initiated a series of both conceptual and country-specific assessments on the theme of cross-cultural negotiating (CCN) behavior. In addition to the most recent volume in the series, *How Pakistan Negotiates with the United States: Riding the Roller Coaster,* previous volumes have explored American, Iranian, Chinese, Russian, North Korean, Japanese, French, German, and Israeli and Palestinian negotiating behavior. The basic assumptions that underlie the studies in the CCN series are that negotiating is the usual, if not always the preferred, technique of international problem solving, and that greater understanding of the dynamics of negotiating, greater appreciation of the cultural and institutional influences of a counterpart's behavior, and greater self-awareness will help make specific negotiating encounters more productive. This objective of making negotiations more fruitful—and thus preventing, reducing, or eliminating the use of violence to settle political disputes—conforms with the Institute's congressional mandate to promote the peaceful management and resolution of international conflicts.

- *American Negotiating Behavior: Wheeler-Dealers, Legal Eagles, Bullies, and Preachers* by Richard H. Solomon and Nigel Quinney
- *Negotiating with Iran: Wrestling the Ghosts of History* by John W. Limbert
- *India-Pakistan Negotiations: Is Past Still Prologue?* by Dennis Kux
- *Case Studies in Japanese Negotiating Behavior* by Michael Blaker, Paul Giarra, and Ezra Vogel
- *How Israelis and Palestinians Negotiate: A Cross-Cultural Analysis of the Oslo Peace Process* by Tamara Cofman Wittes, editor
- *French Negotiating Behavior: Dealing with La Grande Nation* by Charles Cogan

- *How Germans Negotiate: Logical Goals, Practical Solutions* by W. R. Smyser
- *Chinese Negotiating Behavior: Pursuing Interests through 'Old Friends'* by Richard H. Solomon
- *Negotiating on the Edge: North Korean Negotiating Behavior* by Scott Snyder
- *Russian Negotiating Behavior: Continuity and Transition* by Jerrold L. Schecter
- *Arts of Power: Statecraft and Diplomacy* by Chas. W. Freeman, Jr.
- *Culture and Conflict Resolution* by Kevin Avruch
- *Negotiating Across Cultures: International Communication in an Interdependent World* by Raymond Cohen

United States
Institute of Peace Press

Since its inception, the United States Institute of Peace Press has published over 150 books on the prevention, management, and peaceful resolution of international conflicts, among them such venerable titles as Raymond Cohen's *Negotiating Across Cultures*; *Herding Cats* and *Leashing the Dogs of War* by Chester A. Crocker, Fen Osler Hampson, and Pamela Aall; I. William Zartman's *Peacemaking and International Conflict*; and *American Negotiating Behavior*, by Richard H. Solomon and Nigel Quinney. All our books arise from research and fieldwork sponsored by the Institute's many programs. In keeping with the best traditions of scholarly publishing, each volume undergoes both thorough internal review and blind peer review by external subject experts to ensure that the research, scholarship, and conclusions are balanced, relevant, and sound. As the Institute prepares to move to its new headquarters on the National Mall in Washington, D.C., the Press is committed to extending the reach of the Institute's work by continuing to publish significant and sustainable works for practitioners, scholars, diplomats, and students.

VALERIE NORVILLE
DIRECTOR

Board of Directors